D1617188

HELLFIRE
and
LIGHTNING RODS

ECOLOGY AND JUSTICE

An Orbis Series on Global Ecology

The Orbis Series *Ecology and Justice* publishes books that religiously and theologically integrate concerns for our imperilled Earth as an interconnected life system with concerns for just and sustainable social and economic systems that benefit the entire human community.

Books in the Series seek ways to:
- free human beings, animals, and the Earth as-a-whole from exploitative bondage
- understand and develop visions of life on Earth that increase sensitivity to ecological issues in an integrative manner
- deepen appreciation and expand dialogue on the theological and spiritual ramifications of the cosmological depths at the heart of life
- promote inclusive, participative strategies that enhance the struggle of the Earth's voiceless poor for justice.

Viewing the present moment as a challenge to responsible creativity, the Series seeks authors who speak to ecojustice concerns and who bring into dialogue and debate a range of Christian, secular, world religions, scientific, and new paradigms of thought.

Also in the Series

John B. Cobb, Jr., *Sustainability: Economics, Ecology, and Justice*
Charles Pinches and Jay B. McDaniel, editors, *Good News for Animals?*

ECOLOGY AND JUSTICE SERIES

HELLFIRE
and
LIGHTNING RODS

Liberating Science, Technology, and Religion

Frederick Ferré

ORBIS ✸ BOOKS

Maryknoll, New York 10545

The Catholic Foreign Mission Society of America (Maryknoll) recruits and trains people for overseas missionary service. Through Orbis Books, Maryknoll aims to foster the international dialogue that is essential to mission. The books published, however, reflect the opinions of their authors and are not the official position of the society.

Library of Congress Cataloging-in-Publication Data

Ferré, Frederick.
    Hellfire and lightning rods : liberating science, technology, and religion / Frederick Ferré.
        p.   cm. — (Ecology and justice)
    Includes bibliographical references and index.
    ISBN 0-88344-856-4
    1. Human ecology—Religious aspects—Christianity.   2. Religion and science—1946-   3. Technology—Religious aspects—Christianity.
4. Science—Philogophy.   5. Religion—Philosophy.   6. Postmodernism—Religious aspects—Christianity.   I. Title.   II. Series.
BT695.5.F47   1993
215—dc20   92-39488
                                                                    CIP

For my mother
Katharine Pond Ferré
with love and admiration

Contents

PART FIVE
ORGANICISM IN RELIGION

Preface

When is a book's "proper" time? Is it when its thoughts are first conceived? When parts of it are first made public? Or when its message as a whole is likely to communicate and perhaps make a difference?

This book is oriented to the future, but it rests on a significant past, out of which I have drawn themes to orchestrate what I hope is a clear, contemporary call to reforms in science, technology, religion, and modern cultural history. This is an immense domain, as I am keenly aware. "Angels," some colleagues kindly remind me, "fear to tread" in such immensities. I agree; but though I may be the proverbial fool for trying, I have at least not "rushed in." On the contrary, my thoughts on these matters have evolved through more than four decades of philosophical reflection.

At the start of the 1950s my undergraduate studies were in history, leading to my first graduate degree, which was in philosophy of history and concentrated on the agents of historical change, especially as these may relate to religious conviction. Later my doctoral studies, and my first publications, dug more deeply into the logic of such religious convictions in general, in particular in domains of logic and language where religious and scientific discourse counter or reinforce one another.

This led, from the early 1960s, to a long preoccupation with philosophy of science itself, especially with its logic of explanation and its background assumptions involving theories of reality, knowledge, and value. From science it was a short step to technology, after it dawned on me in the middle 1960s that the same assumptions behind science were issuing, through science-led technology, in practical consequences—many of them highly alarming for human society and the natural environment alike.

Since the late 1960s I have been teaching courses, doing research, writing, and lecturing publicly on what for me is the most critical of all critical points for thought and practice: the point of intersection where environmental policy, technology, science, and basic social values—including religion, ethics, aesthetics, and economics—come together and mutually influence one another.

That is the general intellectual autobiography from which the book emerges. Every chapter in it, previously published or not, has its own corresponding story within that framework. Every chapter has been extensively revised and brought up to date.

The earliest is chapter 5, "Explanation in Science and Theology," which was prepared in 1970 for the Science-Theology Discussion Group. This small group, which met semiannually at Union Theological Seminary in New York City, was made up of philosophers, theologians, and scientists who loved to talk and argue. William Pollard, Harold Schilling, John Compton, Ian Barbour, Daniel Day Williams, Roger Shinn, and the other regular members of the group contributed to my views more than they could have imagined as my thoughts were beaten into shape by their friendly resistance and encouragement.

Next came the invitation to deliver a week-long series of philosophy lectures at Chautauqua, New York, in the summer of 1974. I wrote the early versions of what are now chapters 1, 11, 12, 13, 14, and 15 for presentation in that rightly honored outdoor setting. They were delivered to an immensely responsive audience just as President Richard Nixon was in the final throes of his departure from the White House. It seemed then that the moment was ripe for my message. But when in 1976 I published a revised and expanded version of my lectures as *Shaping the Future: Resources for the Post-Modern World*, it soon became clear that Chautauqua crowds are not reliable predictors for the reading public at large. That book, unique among my works, was a crashing disappointment. The manuscript might as well have dropped from the airplane over Kansas as my publisher transferred headquarters in that period from New York to San Francisco. Perhaps the publisher really did lose track of it, since I never saw a single advertisement on its behalf or read a single review. But I now think that this silence is better understood another way: The American public was not then ready to hear any deeply disturbing message about economic limits or far-reaching reforms. Instead, in that period it was preparing to embrace Ronald Reagan for two presidential terms as its happy-go-lucky, "morning in America," high priest of consumerism. There are many reasons — not least among them the egregiously visible consequences of the Reagan "philosophy" — to believe that many minds are now more open to challenge and change.

The first drafts of chapters 7 and 9 were written in 1978. The present chapter 7, "Religious World Modeling and Postmodern Science," was first prepared for presentation (and lively discussion) at the Divinity School of the University of Chicago during my year in residence at the University of Chicago as fellow of the National Humanities Institute. Chapter 9, "Myths and Hope for Global Society," was also written in Chicago and appeared in *The Georgia Review*, an interdisciplinary journal I admired for its high literary quality long before I contemplated a move to the University of Georgia.

In 1980 I published chapter 8, "Limits, Myths, and Morals," also in *The Georgia Review*. This was a paper composed toward the end of the 1970s for presentation to the faculty and students of Dickinson College in what amounted to a farewell address at the end of eighteen fruitful and important years on that faculty. Also in 1980 I wrote and presented an early version of chapter 10, "What's Holding Us Back?" to an important symposium on Technology, Science, and Religion, sponsored by the Department of Religion at the University of Virginia. I was glad to have reactions from fellow-speakers Stephen Toulmin, Charles Hartshorne, and Joseph Kockelmans on that occasion. That material has not been previously published.

Chapter 6 was drafted in 1981, just after my move to the University of Georgia. The essay, "Organizing Images and Scientific Ideals," was first presented for discussion at a morning group of the Society for Values in Higher Education, meeting on the campus of Vassar College. Also in 1981 I presented the substance of chapter 16, "Toward Postmodern Faith," as keynote address for the Society of Christian Philosophers, meeting at Eastern Kentucky University.

Chapter 3 is a composite of two papers, both previously unpublished. The latter three sections were initially presented as "An Incarnational Approach to Technology" in 1986 at the New York Colloquium on Philosophy and Technology, held at Polytechnic University, Brooklyn, New York. The first two sections of the chapter were written two years later and presented in October 1988 under the title, "Technology as Mirror and Lens for Humanity," at the World Congress of Philosophy, Brighton, England. Also in 1988 I composed the first draft of what is now chapter 4, "Technological Faith and Christian Doubt," and presented it as keynote address for the annual meeting of the Society of Christian Philosophers, meeting at Wofford College, Spartanburg, South Carolina.

Finally, in 1990, just twenty years after the first material in the book was composed, I wrote what is now chapter 2, "Hellfire and Lightning Rods." This was presented as keynote address for the First Annual Interdisciplinary Conference, "Science, Technology, & Religious Ideas," sponsored by the Institute for Liberal Studies, Kentucky State University, Frankfort, Kentucky. Though printed for private circulation by Kentucky State University, the title essay of this book has not previously been published for a general public.

Now that the past has been recognized, I want to add an appreciative word about the present publishers. This volume was energetically recruited for Orbis Books by one of my favorite colleagues, Jay McDaniel, professor of religion and philosophy and director of the Marshal T. Steel Center at Hendrix College, Conway, Arkansas. McDaniel, later with the capable assistance of William R. Burrows, my editor at Orbis Books, convinced me that the product of two decades of my wrestling with science, technology, and religion would be worth revising, reshaping, and reordering for fresh circumstances and new audiences. Both stressed the importance of the vital intellectual community of the global South, to which Orbis Books has developed significant access. I found their arguments compelling. I neither want nor intend to give up addressing the people of the global North, where I live. But I am eager to add readers in the global South and to convince them that science and technology are not beyond thoughtful reforms that could help the cause of a just and sustainable world. Reform will not be easy. But it is not beyond hope.

As I write these words, the Earth Summit, so called, is under way in Rio. Radio, television, the print media — all are full of abrasive information that grates on the conscience of many here in the North. We hear about the shameful foot dragging of the present American administration, and we are ashamed; we are exposed (some for the first time) to increasingly clear and assertive counter-positions from the global South. It is a historic moment of consciousness-raising that may portend permanent change. Squarely on the world's agenda from now on will be the realization that we must engage in profound critique of the assumptions undergirding our daily lives. It will, I think, be impossible for populations, North and South, to avoid radical rethinking of technology and what at root it rests on: basic knowledge and basic values, i.e., science and religion. The day for this book will then have arrived. If so, we need to make sure that our thinking is as *clear* and *responsible* as it is *penetrating* and *radical*. I hope that my words in what follows will help.

I have myself been helped by friends and colleagues. Besides William Burrows, my editor, who has done yeoman labor in reading and criticizing a manuscript that originally was twice as large as what I cut to the size of this present book, I want to thank colleagues George Allan (Dickinson College), Ian Barbour (Carleton College), Betty Jean Craige (University of Georgia), Victoria Davion (University of Georgia), and David Ray Griffin (Claremont School of Theology). These good friends have each offered me welcome ideas for cutting, rearranging, amplifying, qualifying, and shoring up my arguments. I am most indebted to them, though none can share the blame for defects that still remain.

Finally, my editorial assistants, Lora McDonald-Lanier and Mona Freer, have shown energy beyond the call of duty at the various stages of manuscript preparation. Lora was with me during the early months, when my papers had to be classified, sorted, and scanned — and then rescued from the howling indignities inserted by imperfections in my optical reading software. Mona has been with me on all manuscript matters since, from picking up the software tangle Lora had to leave behind when she moved from Georgia, through preliminary readings of the uncut 750-page manuscript, through helpful discussions of alternative organizational schemes, to final trimming, proofreading, and index-making tasks that, we both hope, will make the book easier to read and use. To both these helper-partner-colleagues I raise my hat in gratitude beyond the reach of words.

Acknowledgments

I wish to thank the following publishers for permission to reprint and revise material previously published in this book:

American Journal of Theology and Philosophy for "Faith for the Future," vol. 4, no. 1, January 1983, pp. 3–13, reprinted here with grateful acknowledgment.

Contemporary Philosophy for "Myths and Hope for Global Society," vol. XII, no. 9, May 1989, pp. 9–15.

Faith and Philosophy: Journal of the Society of Christian Philosophers for "Technological Faith and Christian Doubt," vol. 8, no. 2, April 1991, pp. 214–224. Reprinted with the permission of the editors.

"Organizing Images and Scientific Ideals: Dual Sources for Contemporary Religious World Models" first appeared in *Metaphor and Religion: Theolinguistics* 2, edited by J. P. van Noppen, 1983, pp. 71–90.

Prentice-Hall, Inc., for "Explanation in Science and Theology," which appeared in *Earth Might Be Fair: Reflections on Ethics, Religion, and Ecology*, edited by Ian G. Barbour, 1972, pp. 14–33. Reprinted by permission of Prentice-Hall, Inc., Englewood Cliffs, New Jersey.

State University of New York Press for "Religious World Modeling and Postmodern Science," from *The Reenchantment of Science: Postmodern Proposals*, edited by David Griffin, 1988, pp. 87–97 and "Toward a Postmodern Science and Technology," in *Spirituality and Society: Postmodern Visions*, edited by David Griffin, 1988, pp. 133–141. Reprinted by permission of the State University of New York Press. Copyrights held by the State University of New York Press.

The Georgia Review for "Limits, Myths, and Morals," in vol. XXXIV, no. 3, Fall 1980, pp. 481–494. Reprinted here with grateful acknowledgment.

1.

Introduction

The Ending of the Modern World

The most important fact about our current historical situation is hard to accept: that the modern world of the industrial Northern Hemisphere is in its last days (or already largely ended) and that we, its inhabitants, are — ready or not, like it or not — entering a turbulent period of transition to a very different world of postmodernity.

This fact, accepted or not, is occasioning deep spiritual distress in the global North, unfocused and shallow though it may presently be. Convulsive shifts are occurring deep in the bedrock of our cultural assumptions. Hitherto mainly unquestioned expectations of continuous growth, hitherto mainly unchallenged virtues of technical expertise, hitherto mainly unexamined images of the future as endless variations on the familiar themes of modernity itself — all have come under scrutiny and have been found wanting.

Much of the current distress felt by those living in the global North during this transition springs from sheer bewilderment in the face of collapsing certitudes; much arises from fear of the crumbling of material affluence, on which life's meaning has been too firmly anchored. The urgent need is for philosophic perspective broad enough and for religious resources strong enough to cope with change on an order of magnitude that occurs seldom in human history.

Civilizations, we know, do sometimes come to an end. The world of classical Greece, the world of imperial Rome, the medieval world, have all flourished and declined and been replaced. The modern world, we must remember, is no less mortal. When changes go deep enough there is good point in speaking of worlds coming to an end and new worlds being born. Ours is one such time in history, and our destiny is to live at the crossroads leading to whatever postmodern world the present may produce.

1

THE HISTORICAL BACKGROUND OF OUR CRISIS

The modern world began in the seventeenth century, rising, with the appearance of modern science, out of the very different worlds of Renaissance humanism and, before that, medieval civilization. Modernity blossomed in the eighteenth century with the industrial revolution; it gathered momentum and geographical extent by conquest and by imitation in the nineteenth century; it came to its climax in the twentieth century, though shaken by two great internal wars—involving newly modernized Japan as well as earlier modernized European powers. The collapse of the Soviet Union leaves the United States of America, the European Community, and Japan as the principal heirs of modernity.

This modern world is ending now. Its very climax in the twentieth century reveals the impossibility of its indefinite continuation. Why?

First, we must keep in mind that the earth is no longer, and never will be again, naively bountiful, after three hundred years of avid exploitation by the ever-expansive appetites of the modern world. Much of the easily mined copper and other essentials for high technology, most of the easily extracted oil and other energy sources required for recognizably modern living—these have been used up already in the centuries-long process of building the world we now inhabit.

Thus, second, in the coming century if humanity should have the good fortune and the good sense to learn how to avoid major war, this provides all the more reason—if we are at such a great transition point in the human story on this planet—to foresee the inevitable end of the modern world. Such anticipations arise not merely because the end of warfare would pose such a vivid contrast to the warring history of modernity, though it would certainly do so, but more importantly because the escape from the end by war would allow the modern world to work out to their natural limits some of the dynamics that have been essential to modernity itself from its beginning. I refer, of course, to the impossible curves of exponential growth that have characterized the modern world and only now, at the climax and near the end, show themselves so startlingly as nemesis.

One such curve is population. A characteristic of modernity, from its early origins in Europe to its current impact on developing nations in what is loosely called the South, has been the reduction of the death rate and the bounding upwards of population. The agricultural revolution of early modern times, then the industrial revolution, now the "Green Revolution," have tended to support the steady increase of populations. But people do not grow merely additively, by arithmetic progression; they grow, as Malthus saw long ago, by multiplication or geometrically. Like money in a bank at compound interest, where money that is earned (and left) itself starts earning, so people who are born (and live) themselves produce more people. At first the growth appears well under control, but a characteristic of geometric growth is the suddenness with which the growth curve rises toward the end. Anything growing at a geometric rate has its own characteristic doubling time (a bank account growing at 7 percent compounded interest, for example, doubles approximately every ten years), and anything that doubles regularly has this surprising exponential upshoot characteristic. The authors of *The Limits to Growth* illustrate it well:

> There is an old Persian legend about a clever courtier who presented a beautiful chessboard to his king and requested that the king give him in return 1 grain of rice for the first square on the board, 2 grains for the second square, 4 grains for the third and so forth. The king readily agreed and ordered rice to be brought from his stores. The fourth square of the chessboard required eight grains, the tenth square took 512 grains, the fifteenth required 16,384, and the twenty-first square gave the courtier more than a million grains of rice. By the fortieth square a million million rice grains had to be brought from the storerooms. The king's entire rice supply was exhausted long before he reached the sixty-fourth square.[1]

I attempted to follow this story on my electric desk calculator, but my machine, which can display up to 99,999,999, overloaded after only twenty-six doublings! Exponential increase begins with deceptive innocence, but inevitably it zooms out of sight.

We are now at the alarming end of this characteristic mathematical curve with regard to world population. The prospects of disastrously overloading the world system — analogous to the sudden overloading of my calculator — are suddenly very vivid.[2] A few more doublings, only, and social collapse on a scale unprecedented in the whole of human history awaits large portions of humanity. Since the rate of doubling in some areas has itself been increasing, people alive today will witness the cataclysmic consequences in famine, chaos, and plague that will surely sweep the world unless something is done immediately to halt the process of exponential population increase.

There are those who doubt that the population problems of the developing nations need necessarily threaten the fully modernized areas of the world. The "let them starve" theory purports to trade on realism despite its moral callousness. It is true that most fully modernized nations seem to have overcome the worst aspects of population growth through voluntary restraints on reproduction rates. It is false, however, to imagine these momentarily fortunate nations as secure in their own "lifeboats."[3] The proliferation of nuclear capability among modernizing nations shows how problems of war may someday be linked to problems of population, as nations driven sufficiently desperate by starvation force attention to their need. The balance of terror holds little restraint for governments that could be facing as many millions of deaths from famine and plague as from war. We are truly the inhabitants of one world.

Population dynamics alone could guarantee the end, then, of the modern world as we have known it. But other essential features of our world show precisely the same fatal exponential characteristics and will therefore inevitably overload the finite planetary system no matter how bountiful our planet or how clever our technological devices. The reason is clear: namely, that exponential growth inevitably bumps against *any* limit, however distant or generous, since the doubling process itself is inherently open-ended. One might debate just how distant and generous the earth's limits are in various dimensions that are characteristic of our modern world:[4] the dimension of the nonrenewable natural resources we need to manufacture our goods and to power our industries; the dimension of the earth's capacity to absorb the pollution generated by our modern way of life; the dimension of the earth's capacity to produce more food for more people without finally poisoning the soil and ecosphere beyond recovery. One might debate these and other limits on matters of detailed estimates of how soon our characteristically modern exponential curves meet their implacable end, but that there are limits—that the earth is finite and not infinite—this is not open to reasonable doubt. Thus since the modern world's demands for energy, for foodstuffs, and for manufactured goods, as well as the modern world's output of people and pollution, are all firmly on exponential curves, the modern world—if it escapes ending by war—will not escape ending.

Either the ending will be involuntary and tragic—through the dooms of starvation and disease or through widespread pollution catastrophe or through economic collapse due to exhaustion of nonrenewable resources—or the ending will be voluntary and, as I have said earlier, merely horrendously difficult. The difficulty will be in parting with characteristics that have been the familiar defining marks of the modern world: progressivism will need to be given up for stability; growth will need to give way to steady-state or even shrinking expectations; exploitation of nature will need to be replaced by balancing with nature.

The old order of the past three centuries is ending. The new, postmodern world has not emerged. Therefore these are times of great transition in which all our resources, spiritual and intellectual no less than material, need full deployment to meet the challenges of our present and our future.

There is no point in trying to *predict* what the successor age with its characteristic consciousness will be like. Events will play too great a part in shaping it. What would human consciousness be like in a postmodern age brought about by endless warfare over natural resources or local ethnic hatreds? How would it be like (or different from) human consciousness set within a desperately overcrowded world or one set in a period of planetary ecological collapse? How would these "doom models" compare with human consciousness in a postmodern world that has renounced the dynamics of material growth and the obsession with consumption—successfully managing both its social conflicts and its relations with the natural environment? No one can say for sure what the next age will be like, except that it will be different in basic ways from the modern, and that the characteristic human consciousness of the postmodern world will be correspondingly different from the dominant consciousness—how we value, perceive, feel, and believe—that we mainly share today.

Still, while it is futile to predict future consciousness, it is not unreasonable to hope to influence current consciousness. And since this is a time of transition in which emerging values, perceptions, feelings, and beliefs will have much to do with shaping current decisions giving rise to the future events that will in turn reciprocally influence future consciousness, we stand at a point of potentially significant leverage.

THE CONCEPTUAL BACKGROUND OF OUR CRISIS

A useful task of an introduction like this is to lay out some of the conceptual tools needed in what follows. I shall try to avoid most technicalities, but settling on certain common concepts will be useful before we proceed further.[5]

In the first place I am convinced that if we are to deal with the deepest foundations of great historical movements we had better take a careful look at religion, broadly defined. Any conception of religion that limits our view to the recognized institutionalized religions—Christianity, Judaism, Islam, and the rest—will leave out of account religious phenomena of the utmost historical importance. The recognized religions (ideally) function for their adherents as all religions do—providing a focus for worship, a vision of reality, a basis in shared values and perceptions for community, and a sense of personal significance—indeed, they provide what we must recognize as paradigm cases of what it means to perform fundamental religious functions. But these functions have also been performed by other spiritually powerful agencies—for example Communism in certain circumstances, or Nazism for many under Hitler, or nationalism or ethnic identity for many today—which thereby become the real functional religions for their adherents, even though those adherents may continue to give lip service to one of the institutional religions in their society.

Religious leaders of the more traditional variety have been quick to recognize the threats posed by their "unofficial" rivals, and in this recognition they have acknowledged in fact—whether or not they have withheld the honorific label of "religion" from their rival—the religious potency of many apparently secular phenomena. This potency—the fundamental potency of any functioning religion—is at the level of primary values. Religion is first of all a matter of "worthship." Religion is basically a way of valuing—or, better, of being grasped by a sense of worth that transcends all other seeming worths and comprehends every true worth. Religion is our most intensive and comprehensive way of valuing.[6]

But valuing is itself fundamental to every aspect of our life. What we find intensely worthy, as in the act of worship, pervades our *feelings*, of course. But valuing is not limited to the domain of feeling alone. *Perception* itself has been shown to be intimately tied to primary, often preconscious valuation. I shall return to develop this point; at the moment it should suffice merely to recall that perception is always selective, based on an implicit judgment of importance. The organism lives — sees and hears as well as feels — by its basic values. *Belief*, too, at the dynamic interface of perception, emotion, and action, is also profoundly relevant to our life as valuers; and, obviously, what we *do*, how we behave, is public expression of our functioning value structures.

Therefore if religion is at heart a value phenomenon, it carries with it inevitably the whole self in all its aspects — feeling, perceiving, thinking, and acting. And indeed we find that all religions reach into, and organize, life at all these levels. There are characteristic attitudes and *feelings* associated with every religion; each religion guides its adherents to see the world in its characteristic way; thought, *beliefs* (often, though not always, logically systematized "doctrine") play a part in all religions; and characteristic *behavior,* ritually and/or ethically supported, is universally present as well.

One virtue of approaching religion from a broad functional perspective and identifying its root as "worthship" is the freedom it gives from the common intellectualistic error of identifying religion with doctrine. Some intellectual content is always present, as we have seen, since persons are conscious, thinking beings. But religion is not first of all a way of thinking, much less of formal theologizing; religion is first of all a way of responding to intimations of worth — responding totally, humanly, not excluding ideas therefore, but not first of all responding by systematic doctrine. Systematic doctrine comes later, if it comes at all. And systematic doctrine — logical theology — when it is associated with a religious tradition as, for example, in Christianity, is in the service of those more basic intimations of worth that constitute the religious consciousness. Later I shall deal more fully with the importance of these theological functions. But here the central point to recognize is that on the ideational side of religion the basic intimations are to be found expressed not in theology but in the value-drenched stories and images associated with relatively unformalized thought. Such images, vivid pictures, stories, tales, etc., together constitute a shifting, potent worldview (not necessarily logically consistent but mythopoetically coherent) that expresses and reinforces the values of the devoted community. This is the mythic matrix from which the full religious phenomenon — combining feeling, perception, belief, and action — arises, and to which all aspects of the religious phenomenon return for reinforcement and renewal.

By *myth* of course, I intend no suggestion of falsity. Popular usage of this sort is shallow. Rather I define *myth* (or *mythos*) in terms of its depth functions: of representing paradigms for fundamental values and of proffering answers to fundamental uncertainties. Treating *mythos* in this fashion opens the way to appreciative study and discriminating criticism that is prevented by literalist assumptions. An important way into the understanding of any basic historical phenomenon will consequently be through its mythic matrix, if we can find it.

The practical importance of identifying the mythic matrix is considerable if our interest is in observing how societies form their fundamental characters and shape their basic policies of action. R. M. MacIver put it well:

> By *myths* we mean the value-impregnated beliefs and notions that men hold, that they live by or live for. Every society is held together by a myth-system, a complex of dominating thought-forms that determines and sustains all its activities. All social relations, the very texture of human society, are myth-born and myth sustained. . . . When we speak here of myth we imply nothing concerning the grounds of belief, so far as belief claims to interpret reality. We use the word in an entirely neutral sense.[7]

From central values, from the functioning religion of a culture, behavior naturally follows, as we have seen; and collective behavior patterns, coupled with common fundamental goals and common fundamental ways of perceiving the world, constitute for better or for worse civilizations like the classical Greek or the medieval, the Hindu or the modern world, whose spiritual roots we shall soon be attempting to trace and whose spiritual successor we shall then be attempting to envision.

What is the mythic matrix of the modern world? What are the images that for roughly three centuries have expressed and reinforced the characteristic values of modern consciousness? If we can begin to find our way into these questions, we will be in a position to explore their implications more fully in the following chapters. We will then also be able to consider alternative mythic frameworks, more suitable to our world of common threats but multiple worldviews. Still later I shall propose what I call "Multi-mythic Organicism" as a way of drawing the power of many myths together to address our shared dangers. But first we need a clearer view of the origins of the modern *mythos* in whose grip the developed North still finds itself struggling.

Earlier I noted that the origins of the modern world in the seventeenth century were simultaneous with the origins of modern science. This was no mere coincidence. Typical scientific practices and early methodological decisions suggested (and were generated by) images of how things basically are and ought to be. These images together constituted the potent mythic matrix that gave rise, when systematized, to the metaphysic of scientism. The scientistic worldview, eventually accepted in gross form as the common sense of modernity, has structured the consciousness of the modern world. Since human consciousness is always deeply laden with value intimations, the spiritual virtues and vices implicit in scientific practice have become the spiritual virtues and vices of the modern world.

In this way modern science, besides being a secular set of particular practices designed to provide specific answers to limited questions, became the generator of a religious movement that vanquished one civilization, the medieval, and gave birth to a new world in its own image. The crisis of the passing away in our time of this modern world so generated is, therefore, the crisis posed by modern science being extended beyond inquiry to theophany, the crisis of scientism as mythic matrix for our lives. The nub of the search for a livable postmodern world is the task of finding a worthy successor for scientistic consciousness without abandoning the genuine virtues of science itself.

Thus stands my thesis, simply stated. Telling the story more fully gets more complicated.

First, it should not be supposed that the worldview of modern science owed nothing to the *mythos* of biblical consciousness in which the former gestated through centuries of noteworthy premodern scientific practice. I cannot here discuss that long preparation, though it is a most impressive story being told with ever-increasing respect by contemporary historians of science. Even without the details, however, modern science could hardly be imagined—and in historical fact, of course, never did arise—apart from an incubation in a prior *mythos* which the biblical picture of the world supplied. That biblical picture shows God, the rational creator, omnipotently ruling the universe in every minute detail.

Think of the possible alternatives. One might picture a visible universe full of mere happenings with no significant order or merely illusory order. Such a picture of the natural order is what is reflected in Hindu consciousness of *maya,* the tricky (*magic* comes from the same root), half-real, unstable surface of appearances. Such consciousness could support no investment of effort in scientific observation or meticulous search for underlying laws. Such a way of perceiving the world would never lead one to notice nature as predictable, manipulable—or, indeed, *worth* trying to predict or manipulate.

Another picture of the universe might depict God as creator and omnipotent ruler over nature but omit from the picture (and thus from the matrix of supreme values) the rationality of God—the divine steadiness, faithfulness, regularity. Such an image might represent God's rule over nature as arbitrary or, from the human viewpoint, capricious. And, indeed, the Islamic consciousness of Allah comes close to depicting such a character. God's sovereignty, for Islam, must permit radical unpredictability; God's inscrutable will is near the center of Islamic veneration. In such a matrix of religious imagery, despite its proven capacity to generate high culture and splendid scholarship, the prerequisites for sustained empirical science were not present.

To take a third example, we can easily imagine a *mythos* in which the ultimate powers, though rational, are not in full control over nature. Perhaps they are in conflict with another contrary power, as in the Zoroastrian vision of the universe; perhaps, as in forms of Gnosticism and neo-Platonism, there are inherent limits in what can be done with the recalcitrant and imperfect material world. In any of these cases the basis for scientific work, which as Alfred North Whitehead puts it, "instinctively holds that all things great and small are conceivable as exemplifications of general principles which reign throughout the natural order,"[8] simply is absent.

The biblical *mythos,* however, uniquely provided the combination of values that could support the birth of modern science. Christian Europe alone developed what Whitehead describes as "the inexpugnable belief that every detailed occurrence can be correlated with its antecedents in a perfectly definite manner, exemplifying general principles."[9] And this value-laden belief has profound consequences for practice. "Without this belief," Whitehead goes on, "the incredible labours of scientists would be without hope. It is this instinctive conviction, vividly poised before the imagination, which is the motive power of research — that there is a secret, a secret which can be unveiled."[10] The possibility of this conviction rests on the kind of God whose basic character emerges from (a) reverently accepting biblical stories and (b) deeply valuing Greek rationality, as Christians began to do at a very early point. Whitehead again expresses the argument succinctly.

> When we compare this tone of thought in Europe with the attitude of other civilizations when left to themselves, there seems but one source for its origin. It must come from the medieval insistence on the rationality of God, conceived as with the personal energy of Jehovah and with the rationality of a Greek philosopher. Every detail was supervised and ordered: the search into nature could only result in the vindication of the faith in rationality. Remember that I am not talking of the explicit beliefs of a few individuals. What I mean is the impress on the European mind arising from the unquestioned faith of centuries. By this I mean the instinctive tone of thought and not a mere creed of words.[11]

The "impress" that Whitehead speaks of was essential for the birth of modern scientific practice; but, as we know, these practices, once born, reinforced new images of reality inconsistent with the old biblical picture, which new images then gradually replaced the old as the effective "instinctive tone of thought" — what I have been calling the mythic matrix — in Europe and then, largely, in the rest of the world.

The story of the triumph of modern consciousness is old and often told. It involves calling off the roster of the spiritual heroes of our culture: Galileo, Newton, Darwin, Freud, Einstein — and the multitude of the faithful servants of objective truth, unnamed hosts of witnesses to the spiritual power of the modern vision finally ascendant.

In the beginning the struggle between alternative visions of reality, with their profound value implications, was clear and dramatic. Galileo, the Copernican visionary, confronted the established representatives of Christian *mythos* with a dramatic intensity that continues to ring down the ages. On reading Galileo it becomes evident that two "world systems" (as he called them) are indeed in rivalry. Two grand images of reality, not just two theories of astronomy or different views about dynamics, are locked in deadly combat. The diplomatic maneuvering, the legal niceties, the attempts at compromise that surrounded that controversy seem strangely irrelevant once this is seen. There can be no compromise when the center of the sacred—the mythic matrix—is at stake. For Galileo, a whole new set of values was represented by the picture of the universe he saw and advocated—Earth no longer seen as sundered absolutely and qualitatively from the heavens, but now itself as much a "heavenly body" (note the value implications!) as Jupiter or the moon; the laws of motion written in the precise and universal language of mathematics instead of the vague anthropocentric abstractions of the Aristotelian schoolmen; and the authority of unfettered reasoning and empirical observation affirmed over the massive weight of tradition or institutional coercion.

Tradition and coercion seemed to win that time, of course. But the victory was costly and transient. Galileo's vision could not be confined by house arrest, and the saga of scientific imagery gradually shaping modern consciousness is well known to all. Again and again biblical pictures of the world were forced from the field in unseemly disarray after initial struggle. Newton vanquished lingering opposition in astronomy or physics with the towering genius of his mechanical world-picture. Darwin confounded believers in the special creation of humanity with his overwhelmingly compelling vision of vastly expanded time frames and the purposeless mechanism of natural selection. Freud tore away the sanctuary of the human psyche, replacing the image of God in ourselves with a disturbingly different image. Einstein turned our universe into a strange, unfamiliar place of warping space-time fields and of matter made from energy.

By the midtwentieth century the triumph of the scientistic worldview was at a climax. Voices of dissent were occasionally heard, of course, but modernity had never been so nearly unanimous. The magic wand of scientific technology had transformed the world: it provided more bread than ever before in history; it established round-the-clock circuses on television; it healed the sick; it restored hearing to the deaf; it reached the moon; it explained the thunder; and it was giving promise of life abundant for all— eliminating the curse of Adam—on and on into the indefinitely progressive future.

Little wonder, then, that the authority of modern scientistic consciousness was overwhelming, even among the uneducated who have never been known for sophisticated scientific thinking but who accept their functioning religious imagery from whatever priests seem best in touch with the Powers That Be. The authority of the laboratory coat—even when worn by an actor and seen merely in image on a television tube—has been well exploited by those who seek profit from the faithfulness of the multitudes.

Not merely the multitudes, however, but the intelligentsia were mainly won by the scientistic worldview in the midtwentieth century. In philosophy the dominant Anglo-American movement was either logical positivism, which made itself explicitly into the handmaiden of scientific practice, or forms of analysis (spun off from logical positivism) retaining characteristic preference for clarity, precision, and for dividing problems into their minimum parts. Even in Christian theology itself, to make this victory of modern consciousness complete, the progressive young theologians of midcentury were rejoicing in the secular city (Cox) and were announcing religionless Christianity (Bonhoeffer), Christ without myth (Ogden), the secular meaning of the Gospel (van Buren), and, of course, the death of God (Hamilton, Altizer).

The triumph was nearly complete. The tide of modern consciousness had engulfed us all. Most of us are still largely modern, for that matter, in what Whitehead call the "instinctive tone of our thought," and feel the high values in genuine science with deep poignancy. There is much that is noble in the strivings after clarity and objective truth, precision, and warranted fact. Must the scientific enterprise itself be tarred with the excesses of modern civilization?

THE MODERN *MYTHOS* AND OUR ALIEN UNIVERSE

My position, briefly, is (1) science was the most potent agency that formed the consciousness of the distinctively modern North; (2) there are fatal flaws in this modern world that make its ending certain; (3) these flaws are directly traceable to flaws in modern consciousness; thus (4) "scientism," or science functioning beyond its secular limits as mythic matrix of this obsolescent culture, has itself been proven significantly flawed.

First, is scientific practice capable of being extended to generate a spiritual vision? I shall argue that this is indeed the case and that what I shall call the "scientistic" vision is at the root of much that is characteristic of modern culture.

Any fundamental religious phenomenon, as I shall show in this book, is organized by deeply felt values issuing in characteristic behavior that is considered linked to the "sacred" or ultimately worthy. Sometimes it is difficult or impossible to distinguish whether the linkage is a ritual or an ethical one. Abstaining from meat on Fridays, when this was required of Roman Catholics, seems a pretty clear case of a ritual linkage, while abstaining from adultery, for example, seems a pretty obvious case of ethical linkage. But the categories have a way of merging under some circumstances. Many strict Catholics felt moral compunctions about meatless Fridays—and is it not an ethical failing to violate one's duty of obedience to legitimate ecclesiastical discipline? One old monk, I am told, felt so deeply about the prohibition that the first Friday it was lifted (by legitimate ecclesiastical authority) he refused to eat the celebration steaks served by the monastery cooks: "The Holy Father can go to hell if he wishes," he moaned, "but I'll not eat meat on Friday." Such "scrupulosity," as Catholic moral theologians call it, even where no ethical point seems at issue, is a good sign that we have entered a religious context, where valuing is intense and zealotry is always only a step away from zeal.

Likewise indicative of religious dynamics at work are those cases where what looks like ethical injunctions function like ritual ones. Refraining from adultery, normally, is an ethical policy with much ethical point. But under some circumstances, where the ethical point is lost, the prohibition, if regarded, serves instead as a ritual. To take an extreme example from a science fiction story I read long ago, the plot entailed that the entire population of the world had somehow been wiped out except for two adult human beings, a man and a woman. The human race would perish unless they had children who could begin to replenish the world. But, alas, the couple were not married and there were no clergy left alive to tie the sanctifying knot. The man was willing to risk it, but the woman took the Seventh Commandment absolutely. The world ended, as I recall, with a whimper.

It is not easy to draw a line, then, when sacred values are at stake, between behavior relevant to such values linked by ethical or by ritual sanctions. Let us say that ritual action is action relevant to sacred values that is performed for its own sake or as a symbol of the ultimately worthy. Let us say that religiously sanctioned ethical action is action relevant to sacred values that is performed for the furtherance of some religiously valued end or good. Then I believe we can see that scientific practice involves both sacred ritual and religiously sanctioned ethics.

A *ritual* of science would involve a way of doing things the propriety of which is deeply felt to touch on the ultimately worthy that is valued for its own sake, regardless of whether good is gained or lost thereby. One such sacred ritual, present since Descartes' famous founding of modern thought in methodological doubt, is deliberate suspense of judgment in the absence of sufficient evidence. Scientific thinkers must not believe anything to any degree more strongly than the objective evidence warrants, even if it means failing to believe something that is in fact true and missing, to that extent, the good end of maximizing the stock of true beliefs. The bad-in-itself, avoided by this sacred ritual, is credulity, the state of consciousness most disvalued by the scientific community. The good-in-itself, symbolized by and implicit in this central ritual, is critical objectivity.

The most famous defense of such ritual scrupulosity, despite the possible loss of truth, was made by W. K. Clifford in the nineteenth century when he wrote: "If I let myself believe anything on insufficient evidence, there may be no great harm done by the mere belief; it may be true after all, or

I may never have occasion to exhibit it in outward acts. But I cannot help doing this great wrong towards Man, that I make myself credulous."[12]

Most of us now, I am sure, share Clifford's disapproval of credulity. We admire critical objectivity as an intrinsically valuable state of consciousness. We are, after all, dwellers in the latter days of the modern world, sharing most of the values that science-generated objective consciousness has victoriously instilled throughout our culture. But we should at least notice that Clifford's argument, though we may instinctively nod when we hear it, supports a mode of behavior that other types of consciousness might not find self-evidently valuable at all. Belief without objective evidence—belief, that is, by subjective hunch, by poetic suggestion, by authority of shaman, by sheer delight in what is believed, by fear of disbelief, by social solidarity, by moral duty, by love or loyalty or the like—such believing is an ever-present human possibility that under different value priorities might be affirmed as far better than critically objective suspense of judgment. What, it might be asked, is so absolute about objective consciousness *as such* that it merits losing the potential values of believing beyond or without evidence? What is so sacred about ritual avoidance of credulity that it makes modern scientistic consciousness prefer to lose friendship or beauty or even truth itself, perhaps, rather than to profane objectivity?

These, if uttered, would be basic rival religious challenges to basic science-generated religious values. We should not expect a ready answer, since the highest value can never—in principle—be justified. As highest, it is the ground of all justification. To attempt to justify it by some other value would be to make the other value higher; it can only be justified by itself, which means that it is beyond the context of justification. Thus we must view scientific ritual avoidance of credulity as touching upon a functioning religious ultimate, symbolizing and incarnating the intensely valued objective: critical consciousness itself.

I have started at the top, as it were, of the ritual hierarchy in scientific practice. But even minor practices reflect the centrality of sanctified objective consciousness. There is, for example, a ritual way of writing up experimental reports that strikes me as portentous, for all its familiarity. The ritual is to write everything in the passive voice, with all references to the experimenter eliminated, if possible, but if not, at least transformed into the third person. All first person remarks or actions are systematically eliminated. Instead of: "Then I put the test tube into the Bunsen burner while glancing at the clock," we are taught to write: "Next, the test tube was introduced into the flame and the time noted." Men and women don't see or hear or smell things; on this ritual "observations are made." People don't put things on scales or place rulers against things: "measurements are performed." The ritual of scientific writing style systematically impersonalizes. Why? Is there any practical or ethical point to such a formal practice? I suspect that neither clarity nor precision would need to be sacrificed in a laboratory report that used first-person active language;[13] but the mood, the tone, the subliminal feel would be very different. And so would the symbolism, which now works to cultivate a consciousness in which the peculiarities of individual subjectivities count not at all. The persons who do or see or measure don't matter; what matters, as symbolized and reinforced by the ritual language, are the objective events, the recorded observations, the performed measurements. It is negligible that some particular person did this or that; it is important only that this or that happened under carefully defined circumstances. The ritual writing style of science, though a minor symbol, no doubt points to the sacred value matrix of objective consciousness and participates in it as well.

Ritual, as I said earlier, is not clearly distinguishable from ethics when both rise from the same ultimate value center, but I have attempted to give instances that seem to me mainly drawn from the ritual side of science as a functioning religious phenomenon. Now let me comment on science-generated consciousness as profoundly under moral authority as well. Some persistently confuse the ideal of *objectivity* in scientific practice with moral *neutrality*. They are quite different. The ideal of objectivity of science is the ground of powerful moral commitments. As Israel Scheffler writes in *Science and Subjectivity* (a passionate polemic in defense of objective consciousness): "A major aspect of significance has been the moral import of science: its dynamic articulation of the impulse to responsible belief, and its suggestion of the hope of an increased rationality and responsibility in all realms of conduct and thought."[14]

This moral import, Scheffler argues, is particularly expressed in the demand of objective consciousness for belief based on controls independent of any person's wishes. He opens his book with the sentence: "A fundamental feature of science is its ideal of objectivity, an ideal that subjects all scientific statements to the test of independent and impartial criteria, recognizing no authority of persons in the realm of cognition."[15] Like Saint Paul's depiction of God, objective consciousness is "no respecter of persons" (Rom. 2:11). Our duties are to obey no final authority but critical reason. This valuation is not merely intensive but also comprehensive. Objective consciousness is not only to be the highest authority in explicitly scientific contexts but in all domains. This Scheffler refers to as "the underlying moral impulse of positivism,"[16] and goes on to spell out the positivist unity of science doctrine as follows: "to affirm the responsibilities of assertion no matter what the subject matter, to grant no holidays from such responsibilities for the humanities, politics, or the social sciences in particular, despite their strong capacities for arousing emotion and stimulating partisanship."[17]

Consequently a comprehensive morality of impartiality, self-control, personal accountability, and democratic antiauthoritarianism rises out of objective consciousness. We recognize this morality, I think, as worthy of respect. It invokes high values. They are values we rightly wish we could attain for ourselves and our society.

Jacob Bronowski yet further develops his list of the values springing from the quest for objective truth. In *Science and Human Values* he identifies moral traits that are essential for the very existence of science. The objective quest requires respect for *independence*, he notes, because where there is responsible belief one must think one's own thoughts and judge evidence for oneself. Further there must be a high place for *originality*, if novel truths are to emerge. Independence and originality will result in dissent, of course, which means that a morality rising from objective consciousness will need to value *freedom of expression, tolerance*, and mutual *respect*. All the virtues of modern liberal democracy, in fact, are implicit in the practice of science; the vices we still see around us, Bronowski urges, are cultural holdovers from premodern credulous ages and institutions.[18]

I hope by now that I have succeeded in my first aim of this chapter: namely, in replacing what Scheffler calls the "myth" of the "cold, aloof scientist"[19] with some sense — however sketchy — of the vibrant valuational power implicit in scientific enterprises. What seems cold to others is passionate self-discipline in the service of sacred clarity; what seems aloof is dedication to impersonal standards by which objectivity is maintained. Objective truth is the end; objective reason is the means. End and means cohere and reinforce one another — vision and practice, ritual and morality — into a unity that makes objective consciousness the motivating center of a major functioning religious phenomenon.

By asserting that it is a functioning religious phenomenon, of course, I do not mean to suggest that the modern world actually lives fully by or through the ideals of objectivity. No more did medieval people live fully by or through the ideals of Christianity. But as Christianity — fully exemplified only in a few saints, supported by priests and ecclesiastical institutions, and generally accepted at the instinctive level as authoritative by the bulk of medieval society — put what Whitehead call its "impress" on the thought, feelings, perceptions, and characteristic institutions of Christendom, so likewise objective consciousness — fully exemplified only in a few scientific heroes, supported by working researchers and their institutions, and generally accepted at the instinctive level as authoritative by the bulk of modern people — has put its "impress" on the thought, feelings, perceptions, and characteristic institutions of modernity, wherever in its progressive expansion the modern world has taken root.

It is appropriate, now, to trace the impact of scientism on our cultural history — that is, watch how this phenomenon has manifested its most basic traits in the institutions, policies, and character of the modern world — just as historians trace the impact of Christianity on medieval Christendom. Here I shall select three basic traits of scientific practice for attention: connecting each to the value-laden images of reality that extend scientific practice into a mythic vision; illustrating each from the work of Galileo, as "saint" and "martyr"; and tracing each to consequences in the modern world around us that show the valuational limits of scientism's objective consciousness.

First, an essential trait of objective consciousness, as we have seen, is its requirement that *belief be strictly tied to objective evidence*. No merely private whim, hunch, or feeling is to be allowed standing in the court of objective reason. Without such a requirement it is impossible to conceive of modern science as we have known it.

Galileo grasped this point unerringly. What counts as objective evidence is what can be tested by public methods of weighing, timing, measuring. These characteristics of things can be quantified, checked, and rechecked by anyone, regardless of mood or other private, subjective considerations. More generally, any merely subjective aspects of experience must be irrelevant to the steady progress toward objective truth. What is merely personal or private is unconfirmable, unmeasurable, and secondary for scientific purposes. What will be primary for purposes of providing objective evidence will be aspects of reality that can be checked on by others (that is, "public" aspects of things) and that allow precise, quantitative measurement.

Galileo consequently introduced (and Descartes greatly elaborated) a vital distinction required by objective consciousness between the *primary* qualities of things and their *secondary* qualities. The primary qualities of, say, a billiard ball will be its weight or massiveness, its shape or figure, its motion (including both quantity of time and quantity of distance covered); the secondary qualities will consist, among others, in the shade of color we perceive or the quality of the sound we hear when one ball strikes another or the texture as we feel it on our palms. These latter are all qualitative not quantitative. They are not public and confirmable. What quality of color you see is private to your subjective awareness. Perhaps you are color-blind. Perhaps the quality you privately experience and call "green" is in fact the quality I privately experience and call "red." How could we ever know? What difference would it make?

Moreover, all such qualities seem to be produced by my subjective interaction with the objective world. If a tree falls in the forest and no one is there to hear, so the most famous philosophical puzzle of the modern world runs, is there any sound? The obvious answer, given Galileo's distinction, is that in the sense of "sound" in which *primary* features are understood— the interactions of material bodies with shape and weight, the setting into measurable motion of particles dancing as sound waves pass—there *is* sound; but in the sense of "sound" in which the *quality* of the crackling branches is meant, there obviously is only silence. For the totally deaf (and for the world itself) there are no sounds, only vibrations. The physical vibrations, as primary qualities, are consequently the objectively real features of the universe; qualities of tone are merely subjective.

The real world, the objectively true world, consequently, is made up of what can exist apart from the private irrelevancies of subjectivity. Just as there is no *pain* "out there" in the objective fire, but only "in here" as part of my awareness if I let my body get too close, so by the same token there is no *warmth* in the sense that I feel its comforting glow. What there "really" is, in what we subjectively call heat, is more or less rapid movement (measurable) of tiny molecules (with mass and length and shape). Color, as we of the modern world all believe, is "really" only electromagnetic vibrations, and different hues are "really" only different frequencies on a spectrum of energetic wave phenomena that extends well above and well below the narrow range called visible light, where human subjectivity alone supplies the many-hued rainbow.

This is a compelling image, and one that rises directly and essentially from objective methods. It is familiar. It enters into our authoritative vision of the universe. What is real and basic is the measurable, the material. What is suspect and relative is the qualitative, the private, the merely mental. Thus, at last, if the *sound* of the tree in the forest and the *colors* of the rainbow must be credited to the human mind, not to the objective world, so much more must the *values* we experience along with them — the thrilling dissonance of the crash or the subtle beauty of the rainbow. If the tree-in-the-forest problem is the modern world's most famous and characteristic metaphysical dogma, the most characteristic aesthetic cliché comes out of the same consciousness: "Beauty is in the eye of the beholder." And so, of course, must all values be in a world devoid of quality. Whitehead sadly sums it up: "Nature is a dull affair, soundless, scentless, colourless; merely the hurrying of material, endlessly, meaninglessly."[20]

Protests against this vision of the world, including Whitehead's protest, have been heard. Various lines of criticism have been taken. Whitehead, for instance, argues that it is simply unbelievable. He marshals evidence from poetic insight to show that the basic, concrete data of human experience are overwhelmingly in opposition. Then he concludes that between concrete data of experience and mere theory, one must side with the data and conclude that the theory is wrong. I agree with Whitehead in principle: Theoretical abstraction must give way to concrete experience. But I wonder whether Whitehead takes seriously enough the fact I have been stressing here: that for the modern consciousness this is no mere theory to be used or discarded at will, but instead, this has become a value-laden vision of reality — a way of feeling and relating to the universe. We shall require not merely a different theory — though new theory will be needed — but a change of consciousness itself in order to experience the world another way.

Another major critic of recent decades has been Lewis Mumford, whose attack has been from the standpoint of morality. The "crime of Galileo," he urged, was to alienate humanity from the fullness of our own experience as well as from our universe. It was not so much merely to break with the authority of the Church but, worse, to break down respect for personality. As Mumford writes:

By his exclusive preoccupation with quantity Galileo had, in affect, *disqualified* the real world of experience; and he had thus driven man out of living nature into a cosmic desert, even more peremptorily than Jehovah had driven Adam and Eve out of the Garden of Eden. But in Galileo's case the punishment for eating the apple of the tree of knowledge lay in the nature of knowledge itself, for that tasteless, dessicated fruit was incapable of sustaining or reproducing life. . . .

From the seventeenth century on, the technological world, which prided itself on reducing or extruding the human personality, progressively replaced both nature and human culture and claimed indeed a higher status for itself, as the concrete working-model of scientific truth. "In 1893," Loren Eiseley reminds us, "Robert Monro in an opening address before the British Association for the Advancement of Science remarked sententiously . . . 'imagination, conceptions, idealizations, the moral faculties . . . may be compared to parasites that live at the expense of their neighbors.' " To have pointed the way to this devaluation of the personality, and its eventual exile, was the real crime of Galileo.²¹

To Whitehead's epistemological warning and Mumford's passionate moral protest, I would like to add a word on the practical, social consequences of this aspect of scientistic *mythos*. It has, through its world-picture with its implicit values, reinforced the supreme importance of the "hard-headed" in modern institutions and policies. What really counts is the countable — the measurable, the tangible, the material. The objective consciousness of the modern world can count money, size, output, speed. "More," "bigger," "faster" become transcendent and unexaminable values drawn from fundamental functioning religious imagery and supportive of tendencies toward greed, conflict, and war. Likewise, modern consciousness puts its faith in its hardware — to preserve it from military destruction and ecological collapse. To challenge this instinctive faith in the "technological fix" is to challenge something very deep in our souls. Most of us cannot even imagine another way. In the same way we find it hard to take values other than measurable material values with any great degree of seriousness. The pervasive *ugliness* of the modern world wherever it has spread — from Jersey City to Japan — is one of its most obvious features. It is slightly unfair to compare a medieval cathedral with a modern oil refinery, but not entirely so. These are typical institutions of their respective civilizations and they well represent where the basic values have been invested. Aesthetic considerations in our modern world are arbitrarily split off from the rest of life and are supposed to be left for the women (and effete poets, environmentalists, or other such weaklings), while the "real world" pursues real interests: that is, economic ones. Wherever material, quantifiable, "real" values (jobs, production, income) are threatened by merely subjective, qualitative concerns, the people tend to recoil and their politicians with them.

Conflict, obsessive material consumption, adulation of growth, and pervasive ugliness are not the only social consequences of the modern *mythos*.

In addition, the objective world without intrinsic values becomes mere resource pit and dumping ground. There are no values in the objective world to slow us down. Pollution is in the eye of the beholder. And so it is, painfully! And so it will be, increasingly, until it becomes—as we must hope it is not already—too late to turn back from ecological collapse. One consequence of objective consciousness, then, is *alienation from quality in the universe* with all that this portends for human life.

The supreme value of objectivity requires public evidence, as we have seen, but second, it demands *rigorous clarity* as well. The muddling of things together that can be seen dispassionately apart is the enemy of scientific reason. Scientific practice leads to *analysis* of its subject matter, therefore, and best of all to mathematical analysis with its power and precision. Galileo, again, led the way:

> Philosophy is written in this grand book, the universe, which stands continually open to our gaze. But the book cannot be understood unless one first learns to comprehend the language and read the letters in which it is composed. It is written in the language of mathematics, and its characters are triangles, circles, and other geometric figures, without which it is humanly impossible to understand a single word of it; without them, one wanders about in a dark labyrinth.[22]

To understand the whole, divide the problem, Descartes urged modern thinkers, and analyze it in terms of the mathematics of its smallest components. The objective truth will become clear when these elements are distinctly known, together with the quantifiable laws of their combination.

The stress of early modern scientific practice on clarity through analysis gives us more than a method to follow, it also gives us a vivid image of how things fundamentally are: things are aggregates of tiny parts which have laws of their own, by virtue of which the larger wholes are constructed. The more basic reality is the tiny part, "obviously," and the derivative reality is the compound everyday object, the resultant of many parts working according to their laws.

The cell is more basic than the whole living body in this worldview; the molecule is more basic than the living cell; the atoms of the molecule are more basic than the molecule; and the subatomic particles—electrons, protons, and all the other swarm—are more basic than the atom. They are the "ultimately real." But of course they are not living. Thus nonlife is more ultimate than life, and physics is the fundamental science in every sense: it deals with the fundamental particles of which everything is derived, and it is in principle fundamental to all the sciences which, one by one, reduce to physics. Sociology reduces to individual psychology; psychology reduces to brain physiology and general biology; biology reduces to molecular chemistry; and chemistry in its turn reduces to the subject matter of physics.

This familiar imagery of reductionism coheres well with the objective world-picture of quantifiable material in motion and refines it still further. The most important of the material realities are the smallest particles. All else is derivative and secondary. And therefore the kinds of properties that fundamental particles have are basic to the universe. That rules out life as having any basic status, of course, and further locks mind, an ephemeral third-order by-product of the physical universe, firmly into its subjective limbo. Perhaps subjectivity isn't even there at all, muse some extreme reductionists.

Reductive analysis, though implicit in objective consciousness, contains seeds of its own destruction. I do not refer, merely, to the obvious awkwardness of a living being devoting intense efforts of thought in attempting to show that he or she is neither living nor thinking. That would be a tactic successful only against those few who hold that derivative realities are not real at all but are mere illusions. Most reductive analysts do not take this extreme position, though admittedly they then have the difficult task of explaining where phenomena like life and subjectivity — apparently ungrounded in the basic realities of the universe — can possibly come from. I will not press the fact, either, that reduction is not an accomplished scientific achievement, but only a program believed to be possible in the assumed progressive future of objective consciousness. There have been remarkable relational successes. The science of thermodynamics has been intimately linked to that of statistical mechanics; and molecular biology is currently showing new relationships between genetic stability and molecular chemistry. Such relationships should, after all, be expected in a unified world. Relationship, however, is not at all the same as identity.[23]

What is fatal about reductionist analysis is its claim to be exhaustive and complete in its vision. This is impossible in principle, as Michael Polanyi stresses.[24] Before we begin to analyze an interesting whole, he points out, we must first be able to recognize the whole as interesting. Any consciousness operating by analysis alone could never recognize the difference between the atoms of the frog and of the fly and of the air and water surrounding them. We must — logically must — move *from* holistic awareness of significant unities, *then* to the detailed parts that find their meaning and importance in the wholes within which they function, if we are to understand the universe as it is. Unless we get the *Gestalt* of things first, the process of analysis would never give us unities again.

To this logical point I would like to add another practical dimension that arises when analysis claims exclusive adequacy for consciousness. The ecosphere within which we dwell is a delicately woven web of life. To be understood — more urgently, to be saved from collapse — this vulnerable and immensely complex network must be approached holistically, contrary to the habits of modern analytical consciousness. The consequences of our failures to think and perceive our world in multivalent rather than analytically monovalent ways are already painfully apparent. Barry Commoner repeatedly points these out in *The Closing Circle* and names the proper culprit. Regarding the complex holistic chemistry of air pollution, for example, he writes:

> In order to describe the course of a particular chemical reaction, it is necessary to study it in isolation, separate from other processes that might change the reaction under study. However if, for the sake of such an analysis, a few ingredients are isolated from the mixture of polluted air, this artificial change destroys precisely the complex of chemical reaction that needs to be understood. This is the ultimate theoretical limitation.[25]

An ultimate theoretical limitation? Yes, at least as long as scientistic consciousness remains intent on analysis as the only possible sort of responsible thought. Genuine science may be leaving the typically modern scientistic *mythos* behind, of course, since exclusive emphasis on analysis and reduction is being replaced by holistic systems approaches in certain frontier sciences, notably in ecology itself. I shall have more to say about the possibility of postmodern forms of science later in this book; but here it is important to recognize the continuing pervasiveness of reductive analysis and professional overspecialization as dangerous legacies from the modern *mythos*. The danger, as Commoner shows, is in continuing to relate to our environment through technologies (and policies) that themselves arise from reductive-analytical modes of consciousness.

> In sum, we can trace the origin of the environmental crisis through the following sequence. Environmental degradation largely results from the introduction of new industrial and agricultural technologies. These technologies are ecologically faulty because they are designed to solve singular, separate problems and fail to take account of the inevitable "side effects" that arise because, in nature, no part is isolated from the whole ecological fabric. In turn, the fragmented design of technology reflects its scientific foundation, for science is divided into disciplines that are largely governed by the notion that complex systems can be understood only if they are first broken into their separate component parts. This reductionist bias has also tended to shield basic science from a concern for real-life problems, such as environmental degradation.[26]

The modern world, then, has alienated itself dangerously from the natural environment on which all, ultimately, depend for life. This has been done enthusiastically through the very successes of modern technology, the practical offspring of modern science. We are alienated not merely because we deny intrinsic value to the real world, not merely because we are obsessed with material growth and heedless of the ugliness we spread. We are alienated — and in imminent danger of terrible retribution for our self-alienation—because we have not thought or felt or perceived holistically but rather have torn into the delicate web of life with tubular vision, reductionist assumptions, and exclusively analytical logic. Our tools of objective consciousness have been powerful, but their very effectiveness, ironically, is leading remorselessly to the undoing of the modern world.

Finally I shall note a third scientific practice extended dangerously into religious vision. Objectivity is no respecter of persons, as we have seen. On one level this stands for fearless independence in the face of intimidating authority; on another level, we discover, this stands for deep-seated disregard for personality and its subjective traits. In the latter sense, the methodological decisions of modern science may be seen as fueling a consistent attack *against humanistic visions of the universe.*

Galileo explicitly battled anthropocentrism when he argued for the Copernican displacement of the earth from the center of the astronomical picture; he also battled anthropomorphism when he fought Aristotelian dynamics with its baggage of "final causes." The stone does not fall to the earth because it is "seeking" its own proper place, Galileo argued; and it does not accelerate as it falls "in order" to hurry home to Mother. The stone moves as it does according to fixed mathematical laws. There are no purposes in nature in the modern imagery of things. There are forces and particles and regularities of happening, but never purposes. As Jacques Monod, the noted French molecular biologist, put it: "The cornerstone of the scientific method is the postulate that nature is objective. In other words, systematic denial that 'true' knowledge can be got at by interpreting phenomena in terms of final causes—that is to say, of 'purpose.' "[27]

Galileo was right about the stone, was he not? Can there then be serious objection to the systematic elimination of purpose or subjective interiority from the objective universe by modern consciousness? Yes, indeed there can. Assuming Galileo to be correct about the stone's fall, must the animal and vegetable world also be taken as barren of inwardness or intentions? If we are "objective" in Monod's sense, the question cannot even be seriously raised. Scientistic assumptions rule out the possibility in advance. But from within such a set of assumptions, cultured into a common sense, a consciousness, and a way of life, terrible consequences may follow. One consequence is callous abuse of the natural environment, abetted by dismissing any thought of the intrinsic dignity of nonhuman nature and (anthropocentrically!) reducing all thought of purposes in the universe to human purpose. Another consequence is similarly callous abuse of men and women, as well, once they are effectively depersonalized by the habits and values of the objectivistic *mythos.* Torture and mass death, especially when further distanced by impersonal technology, are acts which we recognize, all too painfully, as marks of the modern (and, alas, much of the modernizing) world.

The high spiritual vision grown out of modern science has led to this. The spiritual flaws in objective consciousness have given rise to materialism,

overconsumption, obsessive growth, ugliness, ecological crisis, anthropocentric insensitivity to nature, and contempt for human dignity. We stand
before an alien universe created, ironically, by the best and most characteristic of our own modern heritage. In the words of Jacques Monod, apos-
tle of the objective consciousness yet sensitive to the spiritual costs, the
debit side, of modernity:

> But there is this too: just as an initial "choice" in the biological evo-
> lution of a species can be binding upon its entire future, so the choice
> of scientific *practice*, an unconscious choice in the beginning, has
> launched the evolution of culture on a one-way path; onto a track
> which nineteenth century scientism saw leading infallibly upward to
> an empyrean noon hour for mankind, whereas what we see opening
> before us today is an abyss of darkness.[28]

Many devotees of the modern *mythos* do not yet fear this darkness. For
them faith in the artificial light of scientific technology is held to be enough
to satisfy any spiritual need. This essentially religious response to technical
skill, its consequences and shortcomings, poses a core problem to be exam-
ined from many angles throughout the remainder of this book.

PART 1

TECHNOLOGY AND RELIGION

2.

Hellfire and Lightning Rods

I begin with a true story about the experience of a fourteen-year-old immigrant from Sweden, living in Minnesota on a farm in 1922. He was at an impressionable stage of early adolescence, the deeply religious son of an extremely conservative Swedish Baptist preacher. The boy had immigrated all alone to America the year before and was now busily learning English, doing farm work to cover his room and board, studying at a local academy by day, and attending frequent Swedish religious services in the evenings.

One evening in a sermon a subject that had been simmering in that religious farming community came to a boil. The preacher had seen the shiny spikes of faithlessness spreading from farmhouse to farmhouse, from barn to hayloft and silo. "Enough!" he shouted: The use of lightning rods to attempt to deflect the wrath of God was sheerest sin. The boy listened with fascination as the preacher demonstrated that attempts to shield lives and property from lightning in this world would be requited with fire — everlasting fire — in the next. Thunderbolts were God's to hurl, not man's to deflect. The fires of hell, deep under the earth on which the congregation now sat and quaked, were even then being stoked for those who insisted on rising in rebellion against God's will by installing newfangled lightning rods. Amen.

My father, Nels Ferré — for it was he who was the adolescent Swedish boy listening to the sermon and discussing it earnestly for months thereafter — had at that time no doubts about hellfire. His father had preached on it often enough. But something did not ring quite true even then. Could God's will be truly foiled by a steel rod and a grounding wire? Was it really wrong to try to protect family and livestock from the storms that swept in from the prairies with such seemingly undiscriminating force? Was God really directing the thunderbolts? Should he believe that the God Jesus called our "Father in heaven" really would punish farmers for taking whatever meager technological precautions might be available?

In due course the young Nels entered Boston University and continued

27

to learn and to question. In physics he learned what generates electricity in the turbulent, supercharged atmosphere of the interior of thunder cells, and he learned about the impersonal conditions that influence lightning strokes on their jagged paths of least resistance to the discharge of electrical potentials. In geology he learned theories about the interior of the earth, none of which included chambers in which Satan might eternally be torturing sinners. He was in a dilemma. The ideas of science were too logically structured, too tightly tied to vast domains of tangible evidence, for him to discard or ignore them, but these ideas were not compatible with the religious ideas of his father or of the Minnesota farm community. He could not abandon his heartfelt religious faith — indeed, in time he himself became a clergyman and a prominent theologian — but he was required by intellectual honesty to resolve his dilemma by modifying his religious ideas in the light of the findings of science.

THE LEARNING PAINS OF CHRISTENDOM

In this story we have a good parable for what happened more generally in response to science within our modern Western civilization. We all know the epic drama, but it is worth review, since it is the starting point for all of us. Once upon a time, the most sophisticated and responsible thinkers of their age had religious ideas that were very much like those of my father before he went to college. Those religious ideas included an image of Earth being at the center of the physical universe, Earth being surrounded by the visible heavenly bodies (which were thought to be made of material entirely different from the vulgar stuff of Earth); these bodies themselves were pictured as embraced by heaven itself, the dwelling of angels, God, and the redeemed, above the highest and most ethereal spheres. Below the crust on which we live was hell. This universe was believed to be not very old. The best calculations were that 4,004 years before the birth of Christ, God had created all this out of nothing in six magnificent days, during which the ancestors of all human beings, Adam and Eve, were brought directly and specially into being and given dominion over all the rest of creation.

Then, gradually, Christendom went to college. One of the earliest "professors" was Nicolaus Copernicus, whom Martin Luther called "the fool" (*der Narr*) for wanting to turn everything upside down, to displace Earth from its center of attention. But if Copernicus could be dismissed as a daffy old eccentric, the really radical challenger of religious ideas was his disciple, Galileo, who added empirical proof, aided by technological instrumentation in the form of his newfangled telescope. Through it, the moon could be seen as having mountains that cast shadows, suggesting that heavenly bodies were made up of matter — dirt and rocks — as vulgar as the stuff we sit on here. Likewise, Jupiter could be seen as another planet with its own moons, which fit with Copernicus' theory; Venus could be seen to have phases, just like our moon—all of which fit the new theory too well to be dismissed, as Luther had recommended. The new ideas were fought, of course. The battle surged back and forth. But in the end the vast majority of religious people found, as my father did in college, that their religious ideas could survive and even improve from rethinking in view of the solid findings of science.

This explains why, in the middle of the twentieth century, when that great atheologian, Nikita Khrushchev, proclaimed that Uri Gagarin, the first Soviet cosmonaut, had finally "disproved" Christianity by going around in the heavens without once encountering God or the angels, his claims were met with mere amusement from religious believers. Modern religious people had by then so firmly modified their religious ideas, now to include the Copernican Revolution, that Khrushchev's blustering was no threat at all. Most religious believers found nothing theologically damaging, either, in our American expeditions to the moon, even though they brought back samples of rock and dust that would have driven Galileo's critics to frenzies of rebuttal.

It is extremely important to our topic to notice that this can happen. It has happened over and over again. Religious ideas have had to accommodate the age of the earth being stretched by science from roughly four thousand years to roughly four billion years before Christ, and, embraced by that millionfold increase, these ideas have had to make room for a geological understanding of our planet that has nothing to do with hell, and with vast biological evolutionary changes that do not cohere with stories of the special creation of a literal Adam and Eve.

Some continue to fight, of course, and the battlefront surges back and forth over specific issues. But the essential point of my allegory—and of this story of the parallel experience of Christendom at the hands of its great science "professors" like Copernicus, Galileo, Lyell, Darwin, and Freud— is that religious ideas are not condemned to be static in the face of science. Over and over again, scientific findings challenge religious ideas; but, with equal regularity, religious believers find ways of refining their ideas to maintain what they then can affirm as no less adequate—perhaps more adequate—to the essentials of faith. Science has forced major changes in religious ideas, but to date science has not come close to eradicating religion, even from among the most highly educated groups of modern society. The more intelligent the believers, and the better educated, the more capable they are of dealing with scientific challenges on the level of intellectual content. There are intellectual strategies, forged over the centuries, to deal with such intellectual threats.

Threats to religion, however, are by no means always intellectual ones. This is one of the greatest significances of technology for our topic, quite apart from science. Remember the alarm of my father's Swedish preacher at the spread of lightning rods among his rural flock. Technology puts power into human hands. Consider the simple lightning rod as symbol for human empowerment. It is a pretty good symbol for science-led technology: First, it is based on at least partial human understanding of what is going on in nature — lightning recognized experimentally (thanks to Benjamin Franklin) as electricity tending to arc across the potential between cloud and ground — and, second, while it may not work all the time, such technology attempts to channel vast forces according to our interests. It gives us something intelligent to do about cosmic forces, perceived as natural phenomena, rather than leaving us absolutely helpless and dependent on them.

But Friedrich Schleiermacher (1768–1834), who is often called the father of modern theology, defined religion itself as "the feeling of absolute dependence." What could be a more direct challenge to religion, so understood, than implements of human empowerment, designed to reduce our state and feelings of dependence? To the extent that our feelings of dependence are reduced by technology, it would seem that religious *attitudes* are undermined, even though religious *ideas* may not be directly challenged. This would seem to hold true for any technology; but if modern, science-based technology is more and more empowering, directly in proportion to the increasing penetration of scientific understanding into the natural order on which we depend, then science poses another indirect threat to religion, not so much through its theory as through its application.

Long before the age of scientific technology, important religious strands within the Jewish and Christian traditions were deeply suspicious of the attitudes of human mastery represented by crafts and inventions. This perennial suspicion is dug deep into the biblical tradition. We find it vividly in the story of the Tower of Babel. There human technological prowess is depicted as a challenge to God. The tower, which was to have its "top in the heavens" (Gen. 11:4), was just a sample of what human beings could do if they should remain united on a technical project:

> And the Lord said, "Behold, they are one people, and they have all one language, and this is only the beginning of what they will do; and nothing that they propose to do will now be impossible for them" (Gen. 11:6).

Such prowess was clearly not permissible, so self-evidently wrong that no reason is thought necessary to be given for its impermissibility. More generally, the technologies of civilization itself — the word *civil* in "civilization" coming from the Latin for "city" — are deeply suspect in the early stories of scripture. Who, after all, is responsible for the first city? It was the major artifact of the murderous Cain.

> Then Cain went away from the presence of the Lord, and dwelt in the land of Nod, east of Eden. . . . and he built a city, and called the name of the city after the name of his son, Enoch (Gen. 4:16–17).

Thus civilization itself bears the mark of Cain. The theme of the wicked city — Sodom, Nineveh, Babylon — runs like a deep organ tone through the biblical saga. We are situated by these stories just outside the urban technological enterprise, positioned with the viewpoint of a suspicious desert nomad looking askance at the corruption brought about by too much ease and by too much fancy know-how.

Now, however, practical know-how is instructed by theoretical science, and civilization is incomparably "fancier" than in early biblical days. The whole thrust of modern technological society has been to take charge of the universe, to assert human mastery over all things, and to struggle out from under oppressive feelings of dependence. There has never been a civilization less ready to accept dependence on anything. We dam the course of mighty rivers; we leap over distances by our airplanes and satellite dishes; we light up the night in our cities; we defy the cold and heat in our hermetically sealed buildings; we force the land to give forth food in unprecedented abundance; we create new species at will for our convenience or amusement; we hold death at bay with organ transplants and dream of cheating death altogether with cryogenic resurrections into future ages of still higher technologies. If the essence of religion is to be found in feelings of absolute dependence, there has never been a less religious civilization, in practice if not in profession, than our own.

Perhaps real, functioning religion is to be measured, not in degrees of dependence-feelings but in what might be called our absolute commitments. That is, if, instead of judging by Schleiermacher's standard of "absolute dependence," we considered the religiousness of our civilization in light of Tillich's "ultimate concern," ours might turn out, paradoxically, to be one of the great ages of faith. It has not been a faith based on feelings of dependence but on commitment to independence. Our modern society has been shaped by unlimited faith in ourselves, particularly in our capacity *to know* by the methods of modern science and our ability *to control* the world by embodying that scientific knowledge in our technologies.

Paradoxically, the typically modern worship of absolute independence — its world-picture drawn in cool formulae of science and its ultimate concerns expressed in warm commitments to technological progress — has by the very immensity of its own triumphs brought modern civilization to a dawning awareness of limits that were always there, and has roused feelings, again, of utter dependence. The language of apocalypse is again being heard and increasingly heeded. Nuclear winter remains one realistic hell, whose jaws will gape for us, despite the end of the Cold War, as long as the means of atomic holocaust remain in existence and our increasingly fragmented globe is ruled by political units expressing collective selfishness, hatred, and fear. Another apocalyptic scenario, as we all know, flows from the destruction, by human technologies, of the protective ozone layer high in the atmosphere, without which all life as we know it could be endangered. The damage may already be irreversible, with the consequences of past releases of chlorofluorocarbons, those already in the environment, still working their way into the atmosphere. Or, perhaps, the apocalypse of vast, uncontrollable climate changes awaits us, with warming or cooling effects that may force evacuation of coastal cities and completely change the zones of arable land. Or, speaking of land, perhaps the erosion of land and the poisoning of water, worldwide, has already carried us over the brink at which long-term food supply for the earth's growing human population becomes unsustainable and the gaunt Horseman of famine will ride among us as never before. Or, might another apocalyptic Horseman, a plague of unprecedented proportions, against which we have no natural defenses, sweep us away as a result of our unwise injection of genetically engineered organisms into the biosphere?

This cheerless litany could go on and on. I recite an abbreviated version only to remind us of the new sense of limits to which we as a civilization have been brought by the characteristic triumphs of modern technology. One of our greatest scientific and technological achievements was in the discovery and splitting of the atom. But that way we see nuclear nemesis. Our air conditioning and our automobiles are among our most typical artifacts. But those are among the more prominent causes of ozone depletion and climate change, respectively. The productivity of modern agribusiness has been one of our proudest boasts. But ruin of land and loss of genetic diversity looms that way. Biotechnology is one of the newest flowerings of our civilization. But unknown hazards lurk and the public remains fearful. As a civilization we are rapidly discovering that to make human empowerment through technology our ultimate concern is to worship an idol that does not finally have the power to save. Such technolatry[1] is being exposed in our time as folly. We are being forced instead to learn the appropriateness of attitudes of dependence on the powers that "limit and bear down on us";[2] we are being required to learn the urgency of policies of interdependence with other humans, other species, and the earth.

REBUILDING A POSITIVE RELATIONSHIP

If we are truly in a mood, at last, to consider these things, what shall — or should — be the contributions of science, technology, and religious ideas to the new world that needs to emerge from the modern? What should each contribute to a chastened "postmodern" scientific, technological, and religious civilization that has learned to live with limits and to blend personal responsibility with the acceptance of mutual dependence?

Rebuilding a positive relationship between technology and religious ideas should start with the recognition that religion has a still more complex relationship to technology than we have seen so far. One side of the relation is, as we have seen, well symbolized by suspicion of lightning rods. Christian doubts about technological faith are old and deep.[3] But there is another side of the relation to technology that rests on something else we have also noticed: the ancient sense that the human species is somehow special, with unique powers and unique responsibilities. That sense is symbolized in the story of Adam and Eve, as we noticed earlier, by their depiction as being specially created and being given dominion over the rest of creation.

Much depends upon how the elements of that story are taken. In an age of scientific knowledge, the story of Adam and Eve cannot be interpreted literally by religious persons who care about intellectual integrity, but the story loses none of its spiritual depth on that account. What does it mean to have a sense that the human species is in some ultimately important way unique, set apart from everything else in our known universe? What does it mean to have a sense that nature, in some very fundamental way, is "ours"? More important yet: Is it *right* to have this sense and to act on it?

Taken pridefully, the story of special human creation coupled with the doctrine of human dominion can encourage disregard for the natural environment and a rapacious policy toward the earth. This has doubtless been one of the sad legacies of one interpretation of the religious ideas found in the Genesis story. A huge literature debating this question has been generated since Lynn White's scathing indictment of Christianity's "heavy burden of guilt" for the present environmental crisis, appeared more than two decades ago.[4] Arrogant anthropocentrism, a domineering attitude toward other species and the resources of our planet, are possible lessons to be taken from a selective reading of these scriptures. Even though such lessons are unbalanced distortions of the full Jewish and Christian approaches to the human place in nature, we must not forget that basic and important religious ideas encourage human empowerment even as other religious ideas warn against its spiritual perils.

Both sides are important and true. The human species, though fully part of nature (as symbolized by Adam's being fashioned out of "dust from the ground" [Gen. 2:7]), is also unique within known creation because of our powers of awareness, reflection, and anticipation. We are indeed "special" as the only animals who, as far as we know, can in any major way conceptualize the natural order in which we find ourselves (as symbolized by Adam "giving names" to all creatures [Gen. 2:19–20]). We are also "special" as the only animals who, as best we can discover, can deliberately alter nature according to our long-range plans and by means of our purposefully designed implements. In those apparently unique powers we are godlike, relative to all other parts of nature. In that sense we see ourselves functioning in the image of God.

The religious legitimization of human powers of intervention in nature is an important theme to develop in the current debate over the shaping of the postmodern world. The modern world has bequeathed huge practical problems to the next generation, insoluble without new technologies of the most sophisticated sort. It is fortunate that spiritual wholeness need not necessarily be in conflict with technological inventiveness as such.

On the other hand, our fateful powers create for our species, uniquely in the known universe, the moral imperative to invent and intervene *respon-*

sibly. So far as we know, none of our fellow creatures are blest—or saddled—with moral responsibility. If beavers build a dam that blocks a stream and destroys a primal forest, they carry no burden of guilt. If we humans decide to do the same thing, we must stand answerable for our actions. It seems unfair! But that is the glorious agony of our human condition. We have the powers of remembering our past and contemplating our future; we can anticipate (and, with science, increasingly accurately predict) the consequences of our actions; we can deliberate about conflicting principles of right and wrong; we can (and sometimes do) restrain our heedless impulses for the sake of greater long-run good and/or for the sake of justice in the distribution of the good we seek.

Here religious restraints against unbridled human empowerment work to keep us in balance. Our interventions into nature are not to be taken without a healthy sense of moral accountability. The creation is "good." Our special powers within it give us special opportunities to name and nurture it, to make a garden, but as stewards of the higher, wider good, we are not morally free to pillage and destroy. The pressing human task of creating a new postmodern global garden, with wildness, too, preserved in it, will need both the encouragement and the restraint of these religious ideas.

But are these basic religious ideas compatible with the best in science? Are these ideas not only *needed* and *beautiful*, but also open to belief as *true* without the sacrifice of intellectual integrity? As my questioning father's son, I too must finally ask these questions of truth. We have seen that conflicts between religious ideas and science often have been resolved by the gradual untangling of religious ideas from unacceptable factual claims. Are there new potential conflicts here, in fundamental religious ideas about human *freedom and responsibility*, and in key religious ideas about the *wider goodness of creation*, from which science will force us to retreat?

This is a complex question, on the unpacking of which I have spent much of my career. Before answering it, it seems to me that there are three simple, but wrong, positions that need to be set aside. The first of these is the popular dodge that holds, in effect, that scientific and religious ideas are each fine in their own domain, but have nothing logically to do with one another. On this conflict-avoiding proposal, religion and science constitute different "language games," structured by incommensurable logics and insulated from each other like island universes in empty intergalactic space. On first appearance this seems an urbane and comfortable position, but it suffers from two fatal defects. First, in real human life there are no hermetic barriers between interests and activities. Consequently, our ideas overlap and crisscross in countless ways. Settling for separate logics would be settling for permanent fragmentation, not only in language but also in thought and life. A second defect in this position is that it fails to account for the historical facts of conflict between religious and scientific ideas. Copernicus, Galileo, and Darwin knew that their ideas would clash with accepted religious ideas, and of course they did clash. The agonies of conflict, including those within my young father's mind, were not simply based on the misconstrual of the logics of scientific and religious discourse. They were not pseudoconflicts. And yet, as we have seen, the blazes of conflict can and do die down, leaving the landscape changed but healthy. Religious ideas, refined in these fires, can be revised and improved without essential damage to what motivates religion. This shows that the island-universe theory of conflict-avoidance, though wrong about the total independence of science and religion, has something important to contribute to the answer to our question. The logics of science and religion, though not completely out of relation to each other, are significantly different in function. One, science, is especially concerned for accurate description of empirical regularities and their coherent understanding. The other, religion, is especially concerned for adequate focus of valuations and their relation to living within the context of ultimate reality. Both care about how things are; that is their unavoidable point of contact — and conflict. But each approaches from a different primary concern.

A second wrong position, to which many today are still tempted, is the view that religion can and should challenge specific scientific ideas, like the age of the earth or the evolutionary account of the origins of human life, on the basis of particular doctrines or dogmas. If the danger of the first proposal lies in fragmentation, the danger of this second is fanaticism. Frontal assault on the empirically fortified positions of science by the children of faith is suicide of reason. In the long run, such self-blinded assaults on confirmable fact will earn contempt and isolation for faith, too.

The third wrong position, one that by default might seem the only one left, is the view that science by right rules religious ideas, that influence between science and religion flows only one way — from science to religion — and that whatever scientists say should therefore be meekly accepted by religious thinkers as the ground and horizon for whatever else they might be permitted to say. This view tends to forget history and thus to distort the logic of science. Historically, science has grown and flourished only within a larger worldview that permitted and nourished it. What we now call science, as I argued in the previous chapter, could not have emerged in a world dominated by the religious conviction, for example, that empirical experience is systematically illusory, fundamentally irregular, or impenetrable by mind. That the world of experience is real, regular, and important enough to spend a lifetime studying — these are not themselves scientific ideas but rather the metaphysical and valuational ground needed for scientific ideas to germinate and survive.[5] As fundamental expressions of what is taken to be most real and most important, these are religious ideas functioning as superparadigms, or ontological models,[6] to allow for the possibility of science. In the absence of these supportive ideas, or in the presence of incompatible religious ideas, scientific work would wilt. The flow of influence from religion to science therefore has been not merely important but literally constitutive for science.

Logical consequences for present and future relations between religious and scientific ideas follow from these historical facts. We must of course be careful not to misstate what these consequences are. It does not follow that scientific ideas must literally agree with ancient religious stories or that theological doctrines based on interpretations of these stories (in the absence of scientific information) are entitled to contradict scientific reports of empirical regularities or well-established ideas that theoretically extend our mental vision far beyond the empirical data. But it does follow that issues of the *intelligibility, lawfulness, and importance* of the world are vital and relevant to what science is and shall be. Thus where religious ideas themselves rest on profound experiential grounds that bear on those fundamental matters, those ideas, too, are logically entitled to be heard in the debate over the adequacy of scientific ideas in depicting and shaping this still far-from-understood world in which we all find ourselves thinking and living.

Let us get back down to cases. The present discussion of the mutual relationships of scientific and religious ideas was prompted by worry about whether religious ideas, like the "goodness of creation" and the "moral responsibility of human agents," which may be beautiful and may even be needed to contribute to the nurturing of a better world, are in the end compatible with science. A skeptical answer would not be surprising. Modern science, after all, was founded in a spasm of revulsion against the value-laden science of Aristotle in which qualitative considerations dominated quantitative ones and in which purpose, known as "final causation," was an essential element. Galileo and his followers successfully reversed both features of premodern science in the great revolution that founded modernity. Thus, if modern scientific ideas were to be radically abstracted from qualitative features of the world, like colors, harmonies, textures, and the like, and instead focused on the formal, quantitative aspects of things, how much more remote and alien would scientific ideas need to become from issues like the "goodness of creation"! And if modern science were to exclude all notions of teleology from the world, where would notions of "morally responsible free human agency" fit? Indeed, they do not fit within paradigmatic modern science. The great, constitutive abstractions of modern science, which have shaped our view of the world and guided the development of our technologies, magnify the quantitative and work to persuade us that the qualitative dimensions of human experience are, in principle, properly reducible to mind-dependent properties of quantifiable energy functions. And in the study of mind, so conceived, for some hypermodern thinkers there remains no conceptual place for "folk psychological"[7] terms like "freely chosen purpose"[8] or "morally responsible agency."

These are the same triumphant abstractions that have given us the technologies of quantification: bigger, faster, more efficient—above all more powerful and profitable. In the modern civilization shaped by this world-view, the "bottom line" becomes the fundamental criterion of significance. What counts is the countable; the resulting ugliness of rusting automobile graveyards moldering between endless rows of filling stations, fast-food joints, and neon, is, after all, "only the mind-dependent product of secondary qualities." Ideals of social justice, harmony with nature, are "just" ideals, alien and negligible within the formulae of the modern scientific world-picture. They do not compute.

If this is so, then modern science and its associated technologies need the challenge of religious ideas. The funded human experience of freedom and purpose, as well as the importance of morality, beauty, and the holy, needs to count, too, in the critique and construction of frameworks for thought and life. All thinking, of course, requires abstraction, but some abstractions are more remote from life and experience than others. The more remote an abstraction is, the more powerful it becomes, for some purposes, since it can include more. This power to abstract has been the genius of modern science. But the more remote abstractions become, the more richness of specific content they must exclude and ignore. Sometimes in that richness there are elements that can be omitted from careful consideration only at great peril.

The science of ecology has taught such a lesson. Study of the interactions of organisms and chemicals in a tank of water — even a very large tank — may seriously mislead us, for example, about these interactions in the incomparably richer environment of a natural river system. Other lessons have been taught by the new, "subversive science"[9] of ecology, as well. To take a second example, it is fruitless and self-defeating to omit the natural teleological tendencies of organisms when studying the stability of systems. For a third example, it is hard or impossible to get along without qualitative concepts like "health" and "equilibrium" to which quantitative methods contribute but can neither define nor exhaust. And, for a fourth example, unlike the paradigmatic modern sciences, human involvement in what is studied by ecology cannot be excluded from the full picture. Here we have the makings of a new, postmodern paradigm for science: a sophisticated science using all the modern tools of quantification and analysis, but using them in the context of less remote abstractions open to qualitative richness, and using them fundamentally in the service of systematic understanding of prior existing, interactive wholes; a science hospitable to recognition of purpose and value in nature; a science by its scope and inclusiveness non-alienating between nature and humanity, the known and the knower.

It may be mere coincidence that there is currently a triple convergence: (a) our need for new technologies to shape a postmodern world, (b) traditional ideas and values supported by religious ideas of purpose and value in the creation, and (c) the framework ideas of the new science of ecology. They converge, however, at a moment in history when many are beginning to recognize that the magnificent abstractions of modern science have all along been too simple to hold the answers to what the world is like, and that the time for another revolution — perhaps as profound as the revolution that brought in the modern world — is upon us. Religious ideas change, mellow, are refined and burnished in the fires of controversy with science. Scientific ideas, too, are subject to change, sometimes to deep change. In recent centuries we have observed most of these changes in science to result from unsolved anomalies and other internal scientific challenges, but it may now be time when profound reforms in science will rise from reexamining its superparadigms and accepting external aid from religious ideas, as well as from recognizing nagging internal anomalies. The example of subversive sciences, such as ecology, will help. Whatever happens, science, technology, and religious ideas — though no longer expressed in the simple terms of hellfire or lightning rods — will be intimately entwined in the shaping of our future.

3.

New Metaphors for Technology

What's in an image? A lot! That blunt reply is one of my main theses, as will become obvious through the remainder of this book. As we now circle deeper into an examination of the technological phenomenon, considering especially how practical technologies relate to the spiritual dimensions of life, it will help to consider a variety of alternate metaphors through which we may view our topic.

TECHNOLOGY AS MIRROR OF HUMANITY

No human societies, however ancient or primitive, have existed without implements, techniques, or artifacts of some kind. At a minimum, every society shows through its technologies (whether these be hand axes or blow-guns, dug-out canoes or pottery vessels) what it *knows how* to do. Such knowledge does not, of course, entail any theoretical knowledge explaining why the techniques work. Practical knowledge without theory may be honed to a fine edge simply by trial and error, apprenticeship, and imitation. Fortunate discoveries of successful methods — how to obtain temperatures hot enough to fire pottery, what proportions of materials to use for desirable results, and the like — were preserved by oral tradition for millennia before the invention of writing. Such genuine practical knowledge preceded accounts of *why* these methods should be successful. Sometimes theories were generated, as in alchemy, to account for the powers of known techniques. But always, until recent years, technological knowledge led the way.

Even at the dawn of modern science, practical knowledge of glass working led the way to Galileo's telescope and Torricelli's barometer. Today, multiplied by many orders of magnitude, science would be literally unthinkable without its vast embodiment in the instrumentation provided by those who know how.

But priorities in leadership respecting practical and theoretical knowledge are now radically reversed for those who live in the modern era. Today *theoretical* knowledge suggests and shapes our practical surroundings. It was only after Heinrich Rudolf Hertz had conceptualized the electromagnetic wave, for example, that the successful technologies of radio and television could follow. It was only after the famous linkage of matter and energy by Albert Einstein's $e = mc^2$ that the awesome practical possibilities of nuclear power could be pursued.

Technology has always reflected the character of the human knowledge of its era. Now the materialized products of our civilization's knowledge surround us, wrapping us in a technosphere born of the late marriage of theoretical with practical intelligence. But the situation is further complicated by the fact that in many ways practical intelligence, though not in the lead in the old way, still presses ahead of theory. Today the vast bulk even of "pure" science is big, expensive science, wholly dependent for its existence on the largesse of those—in government, in industry, and also in education—who may care more for practical fruit than for theoretical flowers. This is not always bad. Result-oriented research into the cure of disease or into better ways of feeding the hungry, for example, is not wicked. But it reminds us that to recognize technology as reflection of human knowledge is, even today, not to find the image of pure theory alone.

This is to say, of course, that technology reflects human values. When we look at our artifacts, we see implicit in them our hopes and fears, goals and aversions. If a culture fears bad weather, these negative evaluations will be seen in its housing and clothing technologies. If a culture values meat eating, its weapons and traps will reflect its preferences.

By the same token, the technologies of an era will reflect what is taken as licit, i.e., not taboo in the working value-system of the human agents whose knowledge and values are being brought to bear on daily life. A vegetarian society will manifest a different food technology from a society specializing in animal husbandry or the hunt. A society taking for granted the legitimacy of judicial torture or the agonizing execution of witches will apply its knowledge to the refinement of deliberately pain-producing instruments and devices that would be unthinkable in other value contexts.

Perhaps it will be granted now that the collective technologies of an age reflect the dominant values and knowledge of the time. This need not in any way imply unanimity in valuing or uniform distribution in knowledge. On the contrary, the technologies of whips and chains in a slave society will be valued far differently by masters than by their slaves. Value conflicts in human societies are commonplace, and conflicts over technological embodiments of values must be expected. Likewise, knowledge is by no means uniformly distributed in many societies. The function of medieval guilds, for example, was to perpetuate *and guard* the practical secrets of a craft. Deliberate monopolization of knowledge or restrictions of access to it is a frequent feature in human societies, including our own.

Recognizing such knowledge restrictions and value conflicts helps to interpret much debate over technologies in our own time. Sometimes the

case against one or another technology—or "technology in general," whatever that could mean—is put as though technology were something alien,
inhuman, demonic. But this cannot possibly be the case, since all technologies are reflections of human knowledge and values. The charge that technology is "inhuman," if intended literally, rests on a conceptual confusion.
It might more properly be said that the technology under attack is perceived
as reflecting values that are keenly disapproved of, or as reflecting knowledge of which the protester has been kept in alienating ignorance, or both.
It might further mean that the protester has a view of "the human" that is
too restricted and idealized. One often finds the concept used normatively
to rule out, e.g., torture and destruction, heedlessness, suicidal mania, or
the like, as "inhuman." Indeed there is much in our technologies that is
inhumane; there is much that is foolish, self-destructive, tragic. But to this
extent we see reflected, there in our technologies, inhumane, foolish, self-
destructive, tragic aspects of the human creature. Our knowledge, lofty and
admirable though it is, is yet imperfect. Our values, sometimes noble, are
often short-sighted or worse. In our technology we see reflected the heights
and the depths of what we are.

TECHNOLOGY AS LENS OF HUMANITY

A mirror is one metaphor for technology. A lens is another. A mirror is
meant to reflect accurately, both blemishes and beauty. A lens, in contrast,
can both magnify for vision and function as burning glass for power. So
technology can bring aspects of our knowledge and values into clarifying
focus and can turn them into effective instruments for deliberate social
change.

Picking up the lens metaphor for modern technology, we may see features of our current knowledge and values as never before.

Modern science is the leading supplier of the theoretical knowledge that
has led the development of technology in our civilization for approximately
two centuries. It is not surprising therefore that our current technologies
hold a magnifying glass to the qualities of that knowledge. We see, for
example, modern technologies as specialized, devoted to solving specific
aims and goals. Generating electricity is one such goal. Cleaning grime out
of clothes is another. Providing rapid, comfortable private transportation
is still another. We are used to technologies that aim at a few clearly defined
effects. This focuses the fact that the methods of reasoning, the qualities
of thought that have gone into the development of such technologies are
themselves *specialized, linear,* and *specific.* Modern science adopted from
Descartes one of his most important rules: to conquer each problem separately by concentrating on solving each component part. This preference
for the precision of specialization and analysis has consequently permeated
our culture and its artifacts. But, magnified by the lens of contemporary

technology, it is evident that just such "rifle-barrel vision" has resulted in technologies that, in producing their intended results, produce other, objectionable results as well. Enormously effective electric power plants, if coal-fired, pollute the atmosphere; if nuclear, threaten the environment with immensely dangerous wastes over immensely long time frames. Chemically engineered detergents clean our collars wonderfully well, but (to our culpable surprise) overfertilize our water systems to the point of eutrophication and environmental death. Private automobiles, brilliantly designed for comfort and speed, clog our cities, overwhelm our landscape with their required pavement, and contribute to the death of forests and lakes through acid rain. Through the magnifying lens of contemporary technology's ambivalent successes—a train of specific triumphs purchased at the cost of disastrous "side effects," which our favored ways of thinking did not encourage us to anticipate—we recognize the latent defects in linear, specialized modes of knowledge.

Many important values of modern society are also sharply focused when seen through the lens of our technology. We see, for example, large segments of modern technological society in quest of quantified efficiencies: factories measured in numbers of units produced, in "bottom lines" of profits and endless growth. Behind much of technology's built-in drive for quantity we find, not surprisingly, the preference for the numerable over the qualitative at the root of modern scientific thought itself. Concerned by the quantitative goals of much dominant technology, however, poets and others have long warned of the dangers in downgrading imponderable considerations, moral and aesthetic, and of taking "more" as equivalent to "better." Likewise, we can vividly see in our powerful technologies, which attack the earth and nonhuman species as mere resources for our human comfort and exploitation, the anthropocentric bias that has led us to claim complete dominion over the world of nature. Our dominant values, like our characteristic modes of thinking, are brought to sharp and challenging focus by a thoughtful look through the lens technology provides.

If a lens can focus light for illumination, it can also focus for energy. Philosophers who, through contemplating technology, have raised to new clarity pervasive modes of knowledge and habits of valuing are in a position not only to criticize but also to offer alternatives for constructive social change.

What would a mode of knowing be like that looked for understanding not primarily through dividing and conquering its questions but through setting them in fuller context? Can the science underlying our future technologies be simultaneously rigorous and holistic? The science of ecology may be a hopeful model. To understand its proper subject matter—living organisms and their complex interactions within complete environments—scientific ecology, while using analytical tools, must stress the primacy of wider and wider patterns. Technologies reflecting such scientific knowledge would avoid the rifle-barrel vision that ignores "side effects" as though unanticipated negative effects were not all along part of the full range of effects to be considered.

Since ecology deals with the health of ecosystems, it cannot avoid qualitative considerations, inasmuch as health itself is a normative concept. Quantity plays its due part, but always a subordinate part, in such norm-guided thinking. Technologies designed with a stress on quality above quantity would reflect a greater readiness to seek optimum rather than maximum results; they would lead to balance and sustainability.

Finally, scientific ecology includes the human race as one important species in the global biosphere, as one among many. Technologies reflecting such ecological knowledge and values could not be engineered in heedlessness of the other inhabitants of the globe. Our alienated modern civilization would evolve, through such thinking and valuing, into a civilization more intent on designing artifacts that express respect for nature's wisdom and for including nonhuman interests as important practical goals. Such a civilization, holding before itself the mirror of new technologies that reflect such postmodern forms of knowledge and values, would behold a more beautiful human face than ours today.

TECHNOLOGY AS INCARNATE KNOWLEDGE

The metaphor of "incarnation," drawn from religion, may show still more aspects of technology. For example, the technologies of a culture embody — incarnate — the state of *knowledge* within that culture. This need not be theoretical knowledge, on my understanding of "technology," since I grant the term to all practical implementations of intelligence, no matter how rudimentary or merely traditional in character.

Intelligence, however, must be an ingredient in anything properly classified as technological. This requirement rules out purely instinctive practical constructions — e.g., bee hives, birds' nests, and the like — that are imprinted or "hard-wired" into behavioral patterns regardless of changing circumstances. Still, intelligence need not be *theoretical* to be genuinely intelligent, i.e., to make appropriate responses to environmental circumstances by taking account of ideal possibilities and implementing them.

Characteristically, intelligence mediates behavior through *methods,* which are themselves nothing but sets of formal possibilities for disciplined action under specifiable circumstances. But a method, as a set of ideas for behaving, can be learned either by direct imitation or from theoretical principles. This merely means that some technologies may be transmitted by rote, rule of thumb, or apprenticeship (in a word, by *tradition*), while others may be transmitted by insight into broader abstractions from which specific methods may be deduced (in a word, by *theory*). In both cases, such technologies embody a kind of knowledge, whether it be "knowing how" or "knowing that." I do not, of course, suggest that "knowledge" of this sort entails *truth*, since effective methods may well be deduced from false theories. But in this historically relativized sense, the technologies of an era or a culture clearly embody its state of knowledge.

TECHNOLOGY AS INCARNATE VALUES

Second, the technologies of a culture embody its *values*. As we saw above, these need not be the "official" values of the culture, as expressed in ethical codes or religious *mythos*. But at a minimum, one can see from the methods and artifacts in use what sorts of means are not taboo, what sorts of ends are considered licit. One finds embodied in technology, in other words, the implemented values of a culture—the ones that override when all is said and done.

There is, of course, no technology without values. Knowledge alone, unharnessed to human valuing, would not result in technology any more than valuing alone, lacking the requisite knowledge, could find effective embodiment. Both are necessary conditions of the technological phenomenon. It would not be wrong, and it might be revealing, to say that technology is the offspring in *praxis* of the mating of knowledge with value, of epistemology with axiology.

In our own culture, the epistemological base of technology has for the past two centuries been increasingly pervaded with theoretical intelligence, as modern science has fulfilled the Baconian dream of translating knowledge into a torrent of "helps" for the human condition. As this new knowledge has provided us with power to do hitherto undreamed of things, our actual values have been revealed in proportion to the vast expansion of possible actions open for our value-laden choices. The overriding, governing values that have emerged incarnate in our artifacts—in our assembly lines, our weapons, our means of transportation and amusement, and in all the other implementations of the modern industrial world—are often in tension with our traditional accounts of what our supreme values are supposed to be.

This clash between overriding value-systems is what gives the incarnational approach to technology in fact its powerful religious dimension. Religion is above all a domain of intense and comprehensive values. It expresses what is taken to be most worthy of worship, what is sacred. It is a community's way of organizing, expressing, relating, and reinforcing its most intense and comprehensive valuations. Thus, if in our culture the principal source for technological knowledge is science, and if our actual practices and institutions embody our society's basic values, then the technologies that surround us are nothing less than incarnations of characteristically modern science and religion.

TECHNOLOGY AS "ALL TOO HUMAN"

One advantage of such an incarnational metaphor for technology is its total elimination of the false dichotomy between the technical and the human that plagues much popular and academic thinking. At one level this dichotomy shows itself in the pigeonholing of issues as either "scientific and technological," on the one hand, or as "humanistic," on the other. In many universities, there is hardly any communication across these invisible but impenetrable boundaries. On my own campus the problem is vividly incarnated in brick and stone. The sciences are housed in ugly, efficient buildings on top of one treeless hill, while the humanities enjoy beautiful, if decaying, buildings on an ancient, shaded hilltop—with the football stadium wedged menacingly in the gulch between. The few faculty who want to fraternize with their opposite numbers must pay twice the normal fees for parking, though (if not afraid of walking) they can meet on neutral ground for lunch.

At another level this imagined dichotomy manifests itself in the confused sense that technology and science are somehow autonomous, inhuman, or antihuman forces. The image of the machine out of control, the robots ruling their designers, the dominance of tools over their makers, is a familiar (and in many ways compelling) one. Charlie Chaplin's frantic struggles to keep up with the production line and his entrapment in the feeding machine in *Modern Times*, along with the countless other variations on this theme, from Fritz Lang's ravenous Moloch-engine in *Metropolis* to Stanley Kubrick's paranoid H.A.L. in *2001*, are all part of the cultural *mythos*.

The incarnational metaphor for technology need not obscure what these images suggest, that our technologies are fearsomely potent and can go wildly out of control. It merely makes it harder to say or think that technologies—even when raging loose and feeding on their designers—are in any way "alien" to the human. What we see when we see Chaplin trapped in the feeding machine, for example, is a victim in the clutches of incarnated human values yearning after maximized profits by eliminating the "inefficiencies" of the lunch hour. When the machine sputters and spills the soup, what we see are incarnate limitations of the current state of knowledge. The machine is finally rejected ("not practical"), not because of the greedy goals it incarnates, but because of its cognitive defects. What we see, to take another example, when we see the monstrous power plant in *Metropolis* devouring its workers, is the readiness of the rulers above to exploit without compunction the labor force below.

If technology is the incarnate blending of fundamental knowledge with fundamental values—the joint implementation of whatever is current science with whatever is functioning religion—then our appraisals of the goods and bads of technology will at root be appraisals not of something alien but of human virtue and vice. Science itself, after all, is fully a human activity. It is properly included among the liberal arts. Its intellectual roots are deep in the philosophical quest for understanding the universe. Its theories and models are in dynamic mutual relationship with metaphysical ideas and cultural presumptions; it is shot through with value considerations, from the accepted norms of good thinking to the approval of peer reviewers. If scientific values tend systematically to ignore the values of tenderness, love, or concern for the objects of investigation, then we discover that human beings do not always value as fully as they should. If scientific thinking tends characteristically to lose sight of important complexities by reducing frames of discourse or to sunder vital relationships in the process of analysis, then we realize that human beings do not always think as well as they should. Similarly, if technologies distort human existence or exacerbate economic injustice by forcing obedience to unfeeling rhythms or by centralizing control over the goods of life, we learn how selfish, short-sighted, cruel, or heedless we human beings can be. And if our technologies destroy us in the end, we shall prove how foolish a creature was Homo sapiens.

The incarnational metaphor for technology would gently draw us to see that we should not blame alien forces for our ills but look instead to ourselves. We find out who we are, in part, by the technologies that we allow and applaud.

But doom and blame need not be our last words. On the contrary, if all the artifacts around us could be re-seen, re-felt, re-thought as the embodiment of someone's intelligence and someone's values, the world would not only begin to look different to us, it might become more plastic to our considered hopes. What would a world be like in which the dominant methods and typical artifacts incarnate the values (say) of Christian charity or Jewish observance or Islamic faithfulness or Hindu inclusiveness or Buddhist moderation or Taoist equilibrium? What sorts of things would we need to know in order really to incarnate such fundamental values in our implements? What sorts of artifacts would be unthinkable is such a world? What sorts would beg for invention and implementation?

There is no need to be utopian, however, to recognize the advantages of the incarnational metaphor for technology. Its main benefit is to shift the emphasis away from the external hardware and toward the central significance of our technologies. As an image to assist criticism and assessment, it offers a way across the fact-value, science-humanities, technical-personal abyss. As a guide to a postmodern—but still an inevitably technological—future, it may help us to concentrate more intelligent attention on clarifying those ideals that genuinely deserve incarnation.

4.

Technological Faith and Christian Doubt

Someday historians may look back on the twentieth century as an age of unusual faith. I am not now referring to the dramatic revivals of fundamentalisms, Jewish, Christian, and Muslim, in the latter decades of the century. Those revivals I take to be primarily reactions against the dominant faith of the century. That dominant faith itself has been an all-pervading and blissful trust in technology. There are many among us in the West (or global North) who still hardly recognize the degree to which technological faith has characterized our age, but this obliviousness tends to confirm the thesis, since ages tend not to be self-aware of the basic premises on which they stand.

A broad section of humanity, it should be added, had a much more ambivalent attitude toward Northern technological faith. Many such societies in the so-called Third World (or the South, as it is more often called today) feared the power that technology had conferred on Western civilization and considered its technological faith to be hostile to their cultural values. They also harbored deep reservations about its dehumanizing qualities and often found their misgivings were warranted. They, as peoples, seemed always to be judged less than fully human because they were not technologically advanced. A sense of superiority engendered in Westerners by their technology in the final analysis almost assured that most colonial administrators, their military lieutenants, traders, and (alas) missionaries never really encountered the humanity of the objects of their efforts. In virtually all cases, these individuals—mostly cultural Christians—were wholly unaware of their underlying technological faith.

TECHNOLOGICAL FAITH

The gradual awareness of a ubiquitous faith generally emerges together with challenges to it. This was spectacularly true in Christendom at the time of the great Lisbon earthquake, for example, which was used by Voltaire in *Candide* as an occasion for satire against Leibnizian theodicy. Equivalent massive shocks to naive technological faith have been administered to our culture recently by the epoch-marking events we remember as Three Mile Island and Chernobyl. How could these have happened? How could "they," the experts, have allowed such a breakdown in the order of things? The same sort of pain and searching, amounting to nothing less than a crisis of faith, is observed after major air tragedies, when the computerized efficiency of the air transport system betrays us. Above all, the agony of the Challenger explosion before the horrified eyes of millions, with its still-continuing aftermath of recrimination and soul searching, may stand as symbol of the spiritual torment of our time, caught unwillingly as many are in recognition that a worldview is in jeopardy. The efforts of the priesthood of the established order, the parade of NASA officials and astronauts and the President himself, reaffirming the creeds of technological faith and urging the continuing validity of technological imperatives, have done little to provide needed balm.

So much has been staked on technological faith that the levels of anxiety produced by discovering that it has, indeed, been faith all along are inevitably high. It would be tedious and unnecessary to enumerate the ways. One obvious example, however, is the faith our society has shown in the ability of the technical experts to cope successfully with nuclear wastes that are now building up and have built up for decades without any really effective solution for the inconceivable long run over which they need to be safely stored, insulated from the biosphere for tens of thousands of years. Despite warnings, we went ahead with nuclear technology, creating these wastes at an ever-accelerating rate, with the blissful confidence that "they" would come up with a solution; it did not matter that "they" themselves did not ("yet") know just how it would be done. What could be a more touching act of faith? Not only was it a *sacrificium intellectus*, it also showed a readiness to sacrifice the future safety of all life on the planet on the blessed assurance that a technological fix would somehow, over more millennia than any civilization has ever been sustained, take care of us and our progeny to the end of time.

Other examples could be given, like the faith that environmental degradation, acid rain, the ozone hole, the greenhouse effect, resource depletion, food production, population control, protection from accidents of biotechnology, the answer to AIDS—all can be entrusted to technological providence. But more examples are not necessary. It is abundantly clear that our civilization is grounded deep on faith and has committed itself, far beyond lip-service, to its creed. When we think about death, our immediate recourse is to medical research. When we think about sin, we turn to technologies of behavior modification and chemical cures. When we think about providence, we trust in technological progress. We even find evangelists for fusion energy competing with other cults in airports, our contemporary temples. The twentieth century may indeed be remembered as an age of unusual faith.

CHRISTIAN DOUBTS

Against this faith there has been a long tradition of Christian doubt. Sometimes it appears in amusing ways, as in the earnest debates experienced by my father as a young man in Minnesota over lightning rods (see chapter 2). The theological depth of a position that worries about omnipotence being hindered by a piece of metal and a grounding wire may be questioned, but the general doubt about placing one's faith in technology comes through loud and clear.

This perennial worry is dug deep into the biblical tradition, as we observed in chapter 2. My honored professor of Old Testament, the late Philip Hyatt, extended this viewpoint still further, arguing (in a Vanderbilt Divinity School class in 1955) that the "knowledge of good and evil" against which Adam and Eve were warned in the Garden of Eden could not have been knowledge of *moral* good and evil, since to have been able to know that it was "wrong" to eat the fruit of the forbidden tree required prior *moral* comprehension of exactly the same sort. Instead, the forbidden fruit had to be a kind of knowledge that both characterizes God and might be considered wrong to fall into human possession. This double criterion rules out the silly notion that *sexual* knowledge was at issue, since such knowledge could hardly lead to becoming "like God" (Gen. 3:5). If not sexual and not moral, then perhaps the essence of the forbidden fruit was *technical* knowledge—*how* to do "good and evil" things, as God only properly should know how to do. The original sin, on the Hyatt hypothesis, would be technical hubris.

This is, of course, highly speculative. It is an interesting speculation, despite its variance from the received tradition in which moral, not technological, innocence was lost in Eden. It does cohere well with many other biblical themes, and with myths of other cultures, like the Prometheus story in which fire, the symbol of technological capacity, was stolen from heaven at great cost for human benefit. If it is at all correct, it would place biblical religion on an unalterable collision course not only with technological faith but also with technology itself.

THE GREAT DEBATE

Christian doubts about technological *faith,* as a rival religious commitment, have not always led Christians to reject the technological *enterprise* as such. On the contrary, among recent articulators of Christian faith there are strong defenders of the legitimacy of, even the theological mandate for, technology.

One of these voices was that of Harvey Cox. Though Cox himself has become more cautious since *The Secular City* was published in 1965,[1] the book stands as a reminder that Christians may not always feel obliged to stand aloof from the technological world—what Cox calls the "techno-polis"—to which they have contributed so much. In fact, if Cox's reading of scripture is correct, biblical spirituality was the key factor in freeing the human spirit from domination by local goblins and allowing the full technological expression of human intelligence to get under way. In the Hebrew-Christian scriptures it is made perfectly clear that God, the only proper object of worship, is not nature but is the transcendent creator of nature. This liberating realization of the transcendence of the sacred had the effect of "desacralizing" the natural resources needed by technological society. God's clarion call to humanity, that we "subdue the earth," made Christianity the primary spiritual vehicle for the coming of the present age.

To Cox's Protestant position can be added Norris Clarke's Roman Catholic views. Clarke chooses a different theological starting place. He does not begin with the "disenchantment" of nature but with the story of the creation of Adam and Eve in the "image" of God. If humanity is to live up to its status, reflecting in a lesser way the character of God, then the human mission must include God's aspect both as contemplator and as creative worker. As Clarke writes:

> . . . God is at once contemplative and active. He has not only thought up the material universe, with all its intricate network of laws, but he has actively brought it into existence and supports and guides its vast pulsating network of forces. God is both a thinker and a worker, so to speak. So, too, man should imitate God his Father by both thinking and working in the world.[2]

The lesser human role is indicated by the fact that we do not, like God, create *ex nihilo*. Our materials must first be found and then refashioned. But the analogy between our technological work and God's making and doing remains valid. More, Clarke points out, the biblical story of creation includes the human vocation to cocreate with God. The first humans—significantly, before the Fall—were given a garden to "till and keep" (Gen. 2:15). The incarnate God-man, too, was depicted as a tool-user.

> Thus the labor of the young Jesus as a carpenter in Nazareth already lends, in principle, a divine sanction to the whole technological activity of man through history.[3]

Clarke is conscious of the tendency of humans to abuse technological powers and to exploit them for selfish advantage. Cox, too, mentions this tendency but sets it aside as just immature, "essentially childish and . . . unquestionably a passing phase."[4]

Clarke, in contrast, takes a darker view, acknowledging that theological interpretation of technology must not omit warnings against sin. Christians cannot be naive. Every aspect of human life and practice is subject to distortion and abuse. This is the sad legacy of the Fall. But, Clarke argues, such a warning is properly against the *misuse* of technology, not against the technological enterprise as a whole or in principle. A proper balance needs to be struck, he argues, so that

> the alert Christian, alive to the full implications of the Christian vision of man, will look on technology with a restrained and carefully qual-ified optimism, seeing it as at once a great potential good for man by nature and yet in the hands of fallen and selfish human nature an almost equally potent instrument for evil.[5]

A forceful theological counterattack against any sort of technological optimism, "carefully qualified" or not, comes from Jacques Ellul, who founds his wholly different evaluation of technology on a different render-ing of some of the same scriptural passages noted by Cox and Clarke. Ellul, a Calvinist, makes much of the radical break that entered history with the Fall. In Paradise, before the estrangement that forced us to survive by the sweat of our brow, there was no laboring, no use of tools. It is impossible for us now, with sin-laden minds, to think back across the bottomless chasm of Original Sin to imagine how Adam and Eve "tilled and kept" the Garden of Eden. But Ellul uses a *reductio ad absurdum* argument to show how wrong it would be to imagine Adam and Eve working with tools in the Garden, as Clarke seems to suppose. "Keeping" or "guarding" Eden (dif-ferent versions of Genesis translate this word differently) could not—cer-tainly not in *Paradise*—have involved the use of swords or spears or other weapons. That much is ruled out by the total inappropriateness of arma-ments in God's pre-Fallen, perfect environment. But if "guarding" allows of no weapons, then "tilling" allows of no farm machinery. If one is absurd, so is the other. If Paradise is to be even gropingly thought about as a true Paradise, Ellul concludes, we must resolutely omit technology from the picture. "No cultivation was necessary, no care to add, no grafting, no labor, no anxiety. Creation spontaneously gave man what he needed, according to the order of God who had said, 'I give you . . .' (Gen. 1:29)."[6]

Technology, then, is *tout court* in the domain of sin. It had no place in Paradise and arose only because of the Fall. To think of human efforts as "co-creating" with God, Ellul holds, is blasphemy. God's creative activity before the Fall was not in need of completing or perfecting. We must not, in our pride over our human technological abilities, forget that "creation as God made it, as it left his hands, was *perfect and finished*."[7] We put on airs when we tell ourselves that we are "working along with" God. If it had not been for human sin, there would have been no need for technology, because "God's work was accomplished, . . . it was complete, . . . there was nothing to add."[8] Ellul's theological condemnation of the technological imperative is complete. In his well-known sociological analyses he makes further important distinctions between the tools of the craft traditions and the all-devouring efficiencies of modern "technique." The former are less objectionable, though by no means theologically mandated; the latter are demonic and out of human control. Both as sociologist and as theologian, Ellul provides no comfort and gives no quarter to the defenders of technology.

Such an uncompromising prophetic voice seems to harmonize well with the Hyatt hypothesis and the chorus of suspicious or negative biblical attitudes we noticed earlier. But there is one serious defect in Ellul's position from a Christian standpoint: There is no final word of good news, no balancing affirmation of redemption to match the stern warnings of judgment and sin. A more balanced position is sought by Egbert Schuurman, another voice from the Calvinist tradition, when he argues that Ellul leaves us with despair, but that despair is not biblical. As Schuurman puts it:

> It is a constant consolation to know that man on his own and by himself cannot make the meaning of creation, the Kingdom of God, impossible. On the contrary, the fact that the Kingdom of God is already on the way means that at any moment people may be converted and led once again to seek the Kingdom—even in a technological society.[9]

REFINING THE ISSUES

This swift survey of differing Christian views on the proper Christian stance toward technology and the technological society makes clear how urgently we need to develop our thinking in this area. Theologians can hardly set themselves a more potentially fruitful task than thinking deeply, in a sustained way, about the technological phenomenon from the standpoint of ultimate commitments. Christians seem unable to live comfortably with the technological dimension; equally, Christians today are certainly unable to live without it.

A generally acceptable definition of the concept of "technologies" would help this thinking process. To some, the concept seems self-evidently associated with the "high tech" of the twentieth century, entailing that all tools and methods prior to the industrial revolution be relegated to "crafts" instead of "technologies" proper. To others, the concept seems self-evidently associated with tools of any kind. To the former, technologies are indissolubly linked with science, with all the attitudinal ambivalences this linkage carries. To the latter, technologies are more pervasive, for better or for worse, in the character and typical expressions of the human species.

Without attempting to go into the arguments in any detail here,[10] perhaps I may offer a reconciling suggestion: When we speak of "technologies" in general we must include all the ways in which intelligence implements practical purposes. To include less would be to create a conceptual bifurcation between past and present ways of implementing our purposes that would be insupportable by the evidence on objective reflection. Modern automobiles are different but not absolutely different, after all, from horse-drawn carriages or chariots. On the other hand, it is neither ethnocentric nor myopic to insist on recognizing the vast changes introduced into our practical means by the rise of modern science. A radio bears some but not much similarity to a jungle drum. Therefore the *genus,* "technology," will stand for all practical implementations of intelligence; the *differentia* will be the kind of intelligence involved, whether habitual-traditional on the one hand ("craft" technologies) or analytical-scientific ("high" technologies) on the other.

Having a definition that firmly roots the technological phenomenon in human purpose and intelligence helps make it clear to the theologian that technology is nothing alien to the categories of theological discipline. Indeed, looked at in this way, coming to terms with technology is part of the age-old task of Christian faith coming to terms with culture itself. Christianity, and more generally biblical religion, has yet to complete the long process of defining itself unequivocally with respect to the works of human hands. The prophetic tradition, standing outside culture and thundering against its perceived defects, contrasts with the priestly tradition, serving inside culture and seeking to relate the ideals of religion to the realities of social life. Both are part of the fabric of biblical faith. How shall Christ be related to culture? What has Jerusalem to do with Athens? Sharply varying answers have long been given over culture in general, and varying answers should likewise be expected over technological culture, embodying, as it does, the characteristic values and knowledge of human beings at a given time and space.

Asking the question in a new way, with a new sense of urgency, may elicit fresh degrees of clarity. When the question is put today in terms of perennial Christian doubts and modern technological faith, some things newly emerge. Above all, it becomes evident that the extremes will not hold for Christian thinkers. First, Christians cannot, without grave danger to their own faith, embrace the pagan quasi-religion (better, the alternative *real* religion) of "technologism." Its anthropology is uncritical; its soteriology is unidimensional; its cosmology is reductionist. Placing unqualified confidence in the works of human hands is technolatry[11] unworthy of Christian conscience. But, second, Christians cannot, without abandoning vital aspects of their faith, participate in wholesale gnostic rejection of intelligent methods for dealing with the material order. Gnostic rejection of materiality is tantamount to the rejection of the reality of incarnation. Gnostic absolute dualisms of good and evil are tantamount to despair over the redeemability of all creation. Somehow the balance for Christians, between remembering human disobedience and trusting in divine redemption, between acknowledging the Fall and accepting the mandate to till a garden and fill a world, must be maintained. Anything less lacks something of the warnings—and the promises—of the full Christian message.

TOWARD CHRISTIAN TECHNOLOGIES

A deeper, sustained meditation on the relationship between Christianity and technology, however, will need to press theologians and Christian philosophers to go beyond merely refining their reactions to the actualities of contemporary technological culture. Could Christian styles of knowing and Christian fundamental values inform the technologies of a future culture so pervasively and characteristically that it would be possible to speak of "*Christian* technologies" as well as "modern technologies" or "high technologies"?

The question rings oddly at first on our ears. We have no logical place for phrases like "Christian mathematics" or "Christian physics." How, then, could there be a use for an expression like "Christian technologies"? And yet all technologies, as the practical implementations of intelligence, embody characteristic *values* that always go before and define practical aims. Every artifact is the incarnation of some value, positive or negative. The value may be obvious and widespread, like a preference for protection—from weather and predators—and the embodiment of that evaluation in housing technologies. Or the value may be more esoteric, like the appreciation of a certain level of sonic quality embodied in digital recording technologies. Every technological item is the implementation in this way of some aversion or adversion. The mere fact of it shows that someone, at some time, considered those values permissible and pursuable. By studying classes of technologies in this way we can discover what values are characteristic of a given culture, what sorts of things are at least not taboo. Our aviation technologies, for example, show that as a civilization we do not feel it illicit to break into the heavens.

Values are one necessary condition for technologies, but values alone are obviously not sufficient to account for them. Simply valuing something will not automatically give us a means to its achievement. Every artifact is the embodiment not only of some value or values but also of some level of *knowledge*, if only the knowledge of an inherited tradition or rule of thumb. The style, what I have come recently to call the "epistemic norms," of such knowledge shows in its technological embodiment. Scientific knowledge, especially, with its emphasis on precision, on quantification, on analysis, may be seen incarnated in the high technologies of our time.[12] These technologies have tended to be justified as powerful and efficient ("efficiency" is itself a concept and a value that reflects the style and norms of scientific knowing[13]), pursuing a clear, often quantitative, objective with singular focus. But our high technologies, invented with this Cartesian logic, have tended to produce "side effects" that no one was well-positioned to fore-see — largely because of the narrow methods of knowing that were used in designing them. These unwanted effects, in turn, require still more tech-nological solutions, mocking with fine practical irony the way in which the answers of traditional modern science have been praised for leading end-lessly to further unanswered questions.

If Christianity is truly a distinctive way of thought and life, then what is wrong with Christian thinkers attempting to imagine together what tech-nologies might represent the practical embodiment of characteristic Chris-tian cognitive styles or epistemic norms and of distinctive Christian values? This, perhaps, is the sense in which it might after all be meaningful to speak of possible "Christian technologies."

Is there a characteristic Christian cognitive style? The question is debat-able, since there are so many strands of thought woven into the Christian tapestry. But it might be argued that Christian knowledge, whatever else might characterize it, would at least be *respectful of the integrity of the object known*. This entails that the cruel ways of knowing used by the officers of the Inquisition were not Christian. If this is a paradox, so be it. But if it is correct, the normative Christian cognitive style would be compassionate and warm, not remote and cool as has been the approved paradigm for modern knowers since Descartes. It would also, in consequence, be reluc-tant to cut up wholes in an effort to know the parts out of their relation-ships. We might call this cognitive style *compassionate holism*.

Is there a distinctive dominant Christian value? Again, debates may be expected, since visions of the essence of Christianity differ. But one long tradition, to which I adhere, has held that *agapē*, self-forgetful concern for the other, is the one norm by which all the rest are to be measured. If this stress on *agapē* is accepted, the technologies of a Christian future would be very different from those of the global North in the last three hundred years. Private profit as a motivating value would be replaced by community well-being; synthesizing concern for the interlocking multiple effects of technological interventions on society and on the natural environment would replace linear, analytical solutions; qualitative rather than quanti-tative considerations would rule decisions; the unquestioned dominance of the "bottom line" and of efficiency would be balanced by other concerns.

These thoughts are not predictions of anything likely to come about — surely not without a miracle or a catastrophe or both. They are, rather, designed to suggest the sort of criteria that Christians might well use today and tomorrow in assessing the technological society of which they are, willy-nilly, a part. The technologies that surround us are not all of a piece, cognitively or valuationally. Values embodied in one artifact or system may not at all resemble values incarnated in another. Christians may — should —

be selective and discriminating in their evaluations and participations. The powerful technologies of *eros* are today in the ascendent, but if it is not impossible to imagine future technologies of *agapē*, we may by the same standards be able to identify and strengthen present technologies of compassionate holism. If a "cup of cold water" can be laden with ultimate significance (Matt. 10:42; Mark 9:41), then support for a community's water purification system can be given also in Christ's name. Technology is not remote from religion. It is where we live and breathe and have our worldly being. It is the present practical meeting place for the perennial dialogue between faith and reason.

Christian doubt of technological faith in our time is justified. Technolatry represents an overweening and frighteningly shallow approach to life and reality. Christian doubts of technolatry are grounded in a much older alternative faith: trust in divine love that does not scorn embodiment in matter or in historical praxis. Thus sensible Christian doubt of technolatry does not need to lead to despair of all technology. Much human intelligence has, we know, been implemented for purposes that are ego- and pride-driven. These have resulted in offenses to community both within nations, between rich and poor, and among nations in the global North and South. They have resulted in abuses of creation. No Christian, aware of the powers of sin in ourselves, will find that distorted outcome surprising. Equally, and on the same grounds, no Christian is likely to suppose that a utopia of Christian *agapē*-technology awaits us in any realistic historic future. But technology, like human intelligence, is not an all-or-nothing matter. Compassionate holism is a standard Christians can use to measure the technologies of our culture. Then, by combining Christian love with persistent Christian intelligence, it may be possible to look toward a modified technological future with chastened Christian hope.

PART 2

SCIENCE AND ULTIMATE BELIEF

5.

Explanation in Science and Theology

Is the idea of a theology of nature intelligible in an age of science? Is the formulation of an ecological theology a legitimate undertaking that can be defended on methodological grounds? Might theology have something significant to say about nature—or is nature the exclusive domain of science? We must try to answer these basic questions about the justification of the theological enterprise itself before we can attempt in subsequent chapters to formulate specific details of a theology of nature.

My aim in this chapter is to consider what we are trying to do when we seek to understand our world as scientists, philosophers, theologians—and, more important, as whole persons concerned about the whole earth. Ecological awareness has taught us, among other things, that there are too many compartments in our society and in our thought. We must think, and think wisely, if we are to find an adequate philosophy for living together on this small planet.

This chapter will aim therefore at clarifying what I believe to be the proper relationship between the kinds of thinking done by scientists, philosophers, and theologians. It will do this by analyzing various kinds of "explanation." The chapter will also challenge the common assumption that explanation and evaluation must always be kept in compartments sealed from each other. An epistemology suited for an ecologically conscious age must learn how to relate not merely different facts, not merely different modes of explanation, but different essential aspects of our own human consciousness itself. Only when we come to terms with the attitudinal component always effective in our fundamental modes of thinking about the universe will we be able to recognize and use the very human logic of ultimate explanations.

To the reader unfamiliar with the discussion among philosophers of science in recent years, the first part of this argument may seem uncomfortably dry. I ask such readers, however, to bear with the next few pages. Scientific explanations are the key to our culture's understanding of explanation itself; thus without seeing how the interests of scientists themselves create a deeper thirst than some philosophers have been willing to recognize, we would miss seeing the essential human continuities between proximate or limited explanations and the larger explanatory forms toward which we are fumbling—with such urgent need—today.

One of the more nerve-shattering challenges to theology from science — or what has been widely supposed to be from science—has been the raising of grave doubts about the logical possibility, or the intellectual propriety, of dealing in what I shall call "ultimate explanations." This challenge arises from a view of scientific method rather than from any substantive discoveries made by the sciences. It is therefore better thought of as a challenge coming from scientists and philosophers reflecting on scientific procedures, rather than from science directly, yet this challenge is nonetheless a serious inhibition to one of the traditional roles of religious thinking, particularly in regard to a theology of nature, as long as it is able plausibly to claim the authority and prestige of first-order scientific practice to support it.

EXPLANATION AS DEDUCTION FROM LAWS

The attack consists in two claims, both of which I intend to dispute. The first claim is that an explanation *within science* is always analyzable into a deductive pattern in which the statement of what is to be explained is derivable as a conclusion from a set of premises, premises usually containing particular statements of initial conditions and always containing the statement of at least one general law. According to this view "subsumption under a law" is crucial for every scientific explanation. In agreement with widespread usage, therefore, I shall call this first claim the "covering law" view of scientific explanation: A scientific explanation is provided if and only if the event or law to be explained is brought under, or "covered" by, a law expressing a general regularity of nature. For example, the bursting of one's frozen water pipes might be explained in this manner by reference to the universal proposition that *all* water expands upon freezing.

The second claim is that scientific explanations, as conceived by the covering law view, are the *only genuine explanations*. Anything else is, at best, only an "incomplete explanation" in which whatever is put forward as explanatory—whether it be similarities with already familiar domains, "understood" personal motivations, or the like—will have "explanatory value only if it involves at least tacit reference to general laws."[1] Mere familiarity, for instance, may give us a comfortable feeling or a sense of being at home with the subject matter, but according to the covering law view, this is both potentially misleading[2] and logically irrelevant ("the extent to which an idea will be considered as familiar varies from person to person and from time to time, and a psychological factor of this kind certainly cannot serve as a standard in assessing the worth of a proposed explanation"[3]). Likewise, a sense of understanding motives may give emphatic vividness to an explanation of personal behavior, but this is cognitively unreliable and really nothing more than a special case of the appeal to familiarity, familiarity that comes from our own experience of purposive behavior.[4]

It is claimed, in short, that *every* sound explanation must subsume the event to be explained under general laws.[5] Since theological thinking is not engaged in the enterprise of formulating general laws of nature, it must be supposed that any explanation offered by theology will be methodologically unsound.

Now it is not my heroic—but absurd—intention to deny that many theological explanations of the total scheme of things have been unsound, since I suspect that a great many such candidates for ultimate explanation have been egregiously faulty, for a variety of reasons. But I believe that the wholesale disposal of them is at least equally unsound, and that the dismissal of all efforts at constructing ultimate explanations (culminating, as I shall argue, in religious forms of ultimate explanation) does injustice to the flexibility and power of human thought on several fronts, the scientific as well as the metaphysical and theological.

Let us start by looking at the sciences themselves. The covering law view has serious defects as a "reconstructed logic of scientific method,"[6] and these have been the subject of an extensive literature. For our purposes three areas of weakness are particularly pertinent. First, it is doubtful whether one can long maintain that *only* when a covering law is known can we claim to possess a genuine explanation. We may, I think, agree that *often* the deductive scheme portrayed by the covering law view is present in scientific explanation, particularly in such fields as physics or astronomy. We may even admire the precision and rigor of such deductive explanations and begin to wish that all explanations could be similarly patterned. But it becomes costly to insist that unless our explanations in science conform to these few fortunate ones, they are not really scientific explanations at all. In light of the actual situation within recognized and responsible scientific enterprises, it becomes increasingly evident that such tenacious holding to the covering law view slips quietly into techniques of persuasive (i.e., emotion-charged) definition for "explanation."

What is the actual situation? The simple but unavoidable answer is that a great many of our explanations in science cannot provide laws of the sort deemed necessary by the covering law view. The explanatory power, for example, of the concept of evolution—including even the so-called law of natural selection—does not function in the way we would expect if only subsumption under a specific natural regularity qualified for scientific explanation. These principles do not permit deductive prediction of the specific course of the history of biological forms, though they do greatly aid our understanding of it. Even more obviously, social and psychological sciences must function without recourse to such covering laws from which (taken together with statements of initial conditions) the phenomena could be uniquely deduced. Laws permitting us to deduce the outbreak of civil war in a society, or the falling in love of a particular couple, are not even a realistic hope on the horizon. Even an author who has defended the covering law view acknowledges that in the sciences of human behavior we simply lack covering laws that will fulfill the supposed requirement, and (he adds significantly) "it is worthy of note that we do not deny ourselves the claim that we have explained . . . because of this."[7]

It appears, then, that there is a wider but still legitimate and needed use of the concept "explanation," even within science, that is not included in the covering law view. Subsumption under a law may indeed form an important kind of scientific explanation, but it turns out not to be a necessary condition for all such explanation. The weakness of the covering law view is hidden, for a time, behind the vague assertion that the general laws need only be implicit. But where it becomes evident that there simply are no known laws of the sort called for in the appeal to "at least tacit reference to general laws,"[8] the case either fails or is driven to the high but barren ground of a priori dogma.

Second, even the presence of general regularities of nature may not, by itself, be sufficient to provide a complete scientific explanation. That an event can be shown deductively to be an instance of a more general pattern of events observed in nature very often will not satisfy a scientist that it has been explained. Why is *that* pattern found and not some other? What is it that *accounts* for this general regularity? Sometimes, perhaps, the answers will be sought, as the covering law view holds, in subsuming the law in question under some still more general law, deducing the regularity from other wider regularities, just as one might attempt the "derivation of the general regularities governing the motion of double stars from the laws of celestial mechanics. . . ."[9] But sometimes even this will not be enough to answer the scientist's quest for explanation. The scientist wants to have some idea of the structures, the underlying mechanisms, by reference to which the observed regularities may become intelligible rather than merely arbitrary. All the available laws, together with a full grasp of their deductive relationships, may not add up to a single explanation in this fuller sense of the word. On the contrary, the natural regularities themselves, even the widest observed, may become the problematic phenomena crying out for explanation rather than supplying it. The covering law view thus fails in its account of the scientific enterprise, since it may be possible to have laws in abundance but still not to have an explanation.

THE EXPLANATORY POWER OF THEORIES

This consideration brings us, then, to the third and most revealing defect in the covering law claim I am criticizing. This defect is the failure to make adequate provision for scientific *theory* in the "reconstructed logic" of science. It would be dangerously misleading, as much current discussion has shown, to make the distinction too sharp between the laws and the theories of a science. What we observe is deeply influenced by what theoretical language we employ, just as our theories are scientifically useful to the extent that they remain in fruitful touch with observation. Still, in the covering law view there is a strange neglect of the differences between what constitutes the statement of an observed regularity of nature and what constitutes the statement of an inferred "regularity" of a theoretical entity or structure. This neglect is illustrated in the following passage:

> To an observer in a row boat, that part of an oar which is under water appears to be bent upwards. The phenomenon is explained by means of general laws — namely the law of refraction and the law that water is an optically denser medium than air — and by reference to certain antecedent conditions — especially the fact that part of the oar is in the water, part in the air, and that the oar is practically a straight piece of wood. ... But the question "Why?" may be raised also in regard to general laws. Thus ... the question might be asked: Why does the propagation of light conform to the law of refraction? Classical physics answers in terms of the undulatory theory of light, i.e., by stating that the propagation of light is a wave phenomenon of a certain general type, and that all wave phenomena of that type satisfy the law of refraction. Thus, the explanation of a general regularity consists in subsuming it under another, more comprehensive regularity, under a more general law.[10]

What is evident here is the running together of two quite different types of laws. The first is a law that we may say, roughly, is a law of gross observation. We see oars as "bent" regularly under certain circumstances. We see refraction effects of other sorts, inside and outside the laboratory. But neither in nor out of our laboratories do we see light waves being propagated like water waves in a pond. We can, indeed, observe regularities of various sorts — interference patterns and the like — that are highly encouraging to our theories that light can sometimes be represented as being in certain ways like "wave phenomena of a certain type." The point is, however, that in moving from explanation by subsumption under *observable* natural regularities (what Comte called positive general facts[11]) to explanation by reference to *supposed* regularities of structure (which make sense out of the given observable regularities of nature), the step has been taken to a logically very different type of explanation. The crucial importance of this step is obscured by the covering law view.

There is a practical consequence, too, embedded in this logical distinction. There is a difference between, on the one hand, treating nature as a black box, the behavior of which we note, generalize upon, and predict with considerable effectiveness, and, on the other hand, approaching the world with additional interests in understanding what may be behind the visible structures and behaviors. If we ignore this distinction, we may be lured uncritically into the false belief that the discovery of uniform correlations between events is the most important part of our cognitive endeavors. And this may, as a practical consequence, lead us to focus attention too fixedly on the quest for uniformities and still more uniformities in nature—to the neglect of the search for theories and models through which alone these uniformities can be made intelligible to us.

The methodological point here at issue is the difference between what Henry Margenau calls the *correlational* and the *theoretic* procedures within science,[12] or what Stephen Toulmin more vividly, and with perhaps more glee, contrasts as "natural history" (or "mere bug-hunting") versus "physics." The former is interested in finding "regularities of given forms," whereas the latter is in quest of "the form of given regularities."[13] This distinction—of the greatest importance however it may be phrased—is ignored and indeed denied by any proposal that "to explain an event is simply to bring it under a law; and to explain a law is to bring it under another law."[14] Such an account would send us hunting on the surface of our experience for more empirical regularities, whereas actually what may be most needed (even for eventual practical control) are what Margenau terms the "subsurface connections," always most highly acclaimed by working scientists.[15]

Illustrations of the enormous difference of explanatory power exhibited by these "subsurface connections" as contrasted with "uniformities" are not difficult to find. For example, practical knowledge of the relationships holding between the lengths of the sides of the three-four-five right triangle long antedated the Pythagorean theorem; this regularity of form was used for surveying land before the time of Pythagoras as well as after.

> Yet we pay homage to Pythagoras' mathematical demonstration. . . .
> Why should it be so important to devise a proof which adds nothing
> to the empirical knowledge already available? What distinguishes the
> Greek philosopher from the careful observers in Egypt? The answer
> is: Through his act a theory was born; the surface of mere correlation
> was broken, subsurface explanation had begun.[16]

The usefulness of theory, on the basis of which we may give *reasons* for a particular event happening or for a particular correlation, is further illustrated by the explanatory advance represented by Niels Bohr's theory-cum-model of the hydrogen atom, an advance that gave *reasons* for the success of Johann Jakob Balmer's formula in stating the "uniformity of nature" discovered in the absorption lines of the hydrogen spectrum. "Again, in the proof, a theory of the atom was born. An internal luminosity suddenly shone through the empirical formula."[17]

What is it about a theory-cum-model that provides our higher-level explanations with this "internal luminosity" that is denied to less powerful explanations limited to statements of empirical uniformities? The answer centers on the *connections in thought* provided by theories, the finding of shared patterns in widely diverse concepts about quite varied phenomena, the fittingness of our ideas together according to the canons of logic, and the discovery of analogues where previously none had been evident—in sum, in the replacement of sheer multiplicity with coherence, the substitution of imaginative acquaintance for opaque strangeness, the elimination or diminution of the sense of the sheerly disconnected and arbitrary.

Perhaps we may have discovered at this point the correct logical place of "familiarity" in explanation. The covering law view was no doubt quite correct in rejecting the oversimple appeal to the familiar; such an appeal would, if allowed, short-circuit the entire theoretical enterprise by demanding that explanations be forbidden to venture beyond the already known. But granting the dangers implicit in premature concern for the familiar, we may also recognize the large role that familiarity—of pattern, of operation, of conceptual relation, and the like—plays in the logic of explanation. True, familiarity is a relative notion, but explanations, likewise, must explain to *someone* if they are to function as explanations at all. To this extent, explanation is also a relative notion; but in this sense—in which all language is relative to some user/interpreter—the relativity of both notions becomes decidedly innocuous.

EXPLANATORY PARADIGMS IN SCIENCE

The battle for understanding is none other than the war against "unfamiliarity," in its widest sense of incoherence and arbitrariness; science is the human spirit's most carefully constructed and consciously invented instrument for the waging of this war. Thus the internal demands of all the sciences press toward wider and still wider models and theories. The special sciences themselves, as we shall see, cannot remain true to their own particular role in humanity's cognitive quest and at the same time respond to the drive toward theories and models of *unlimited* comprehensiveness. But the push toward such all-encompassing theories is implicit within the sciences, and therefore the rationally disciplined attempt at forming such schemes of unlimited scope is continuous, though not identical, with the goal of the sciences.

That the special sciences are in search of explanations that would be *basic relative to their own fields of application* has long been recognized by philosophers of science. *"Basic"* here does not need to involve "finality" in the sense of "never-to-be-superseded"; basic explanations are not usefully defined as "incorrigible" ones. Instead, they should be recognized as "final" in the sense that although accepted they themselves do not call for, or admit of, further explanation. That such explanations have in fact been part of the logic of the special sciences, and that these explanatory paradigms have not proved incorrigible, has been reemphasized, among others by Stephen Toulmin and Thomas Kuhn.[18]

Toulmin points out that underlying the lesser explanations of the sciences have always been what he calls "ideals of natural order."[19] It is on the basis of some such ideal that the scientist is content to rest. Ideals may vary with the era, but the reliance on them is undeniable; the ideal of natural order represents what the scientist considers to be beyond the need of explanation. For Copernicus, Toulmin shows, this self-explanatory principle was uniform circular motion. "He felt no need to look for interplanetary forces in order to explain why the planets follow closed orbits: in his opinion, a uniform circular motion needed no further explanation, and would — in the nature of things — continue to maintain itself indefinitely."[20] Scientific explanations may seldom in practice be pushed back to these bedrock concepts, but

> about any explanatory theory . . . we can always ask what it implies about the Natural Order. There must always be some point in a scientist's explanation where he comes to a stop: beyond this point, if he is pressed to explain further the fundamental basis of his explanation, he can say only that he has reached rock-bottom.[21]

Still, the ideal of natural order that serves the scientist as a basic explanation within a special field (e.g., "The natural state of motion is circular") will never — so long as it remains a scientific conception — be a totally inclusive one (e.g., "All events happen as God wills"). The reason for this is that the scientist qua scientist has contracted for the task of discovering "why this happened *rather than that*, and the theological explanation will not enable him to make this discrimination. . . ."[22] To protect the very *specificity* of the *special* sciences, it is essential that even their most wide-ranging "ideals of natural order" renounce every pretense at providing a basis for the coherent understanding of *all* things. In a sense, perhaps, this reminder may be no more than a tautology: that the special sciences have specialized jobs to do. But if it is a tautology, it is an important one to keep in mind. And it has practical consequences: e.g., that the physicist qua physicist may properly remain aloof from certain phenomena that the biologist qua biologist finds extremely important, and, in like manner, that a thinker is no longer acting simply qua special scientist when the connections are considered between all that lies within the purview of each of the sciences. Every special science contributes toward our understanding; but no one should too quickly suppose (nor is it any part of the special scientist's job to claim) that all things can be understood in terms of the explanations, even the basic explanatory paradigms, of any such science. It may have made sense to Copernicus, for example, that the only "natural and self-explanatory" notion would be circular; but this had to do with motions and not with "the sum of things entire." For Newton and for ourselves, his descendants, the one form of motion not requiring further explanation (straight-line motion in a vacuum) is of a quite different character. The consequences for physics of the change in these explanatory paradigms are of the highest importance; yet the difference between the Copernican and the Newtonian notion of "rock-bottom" for the explanatory regression remains a difference *within physics*, with clear physical implications and clear conceptual boundaries.

We may here note in passing that although such concepts as these remain part of the explanatory logic of the special sciences, the means of testing them is considerably more elaborate and indirect than is often acknowledged by many popular analyses of scientific procedure. John Hospers, for example, insists that every concept used as an explanatory premise in a science must be open to empirical falsification. "Without this condition it would not be considered an explanation in any science."[23] True, but the meaning of falsification — once one admits the role of theories as well as experimental laws, and explanatory paradigms of natural order as well as theories — must be enriched beyond the simplistic look-and-see concept of the "crucial experiment" that has hobbled the philosophy of science — though not the sciences themselves — for far too long.

The means of verification or falsification of these most far-reaching concepts or models of the natural order depend upon the scope, the coherence, the consistency, and the practical effectiveness of the entire theoretical structure of the science founded upon them. "Such models and ideals, principles of regularity and explanatory paradigms, are not always recognized for what they are; differences of opinion about them give rise to some of the profoundest scientific disputes, and changes in them to some of the most important changes in scientific theory. . . ."[24] The substitution of Newton's view of straight-line motion as needing "no explanation" in place of Copernicus' satisfaction with the "self-explanatory" character of "natural" circular motion had more to do with the entire schemes of thought of which these models were a basic part than any simple empirical observation. And the adoption of Galileo's fundamental concept of impetus in place of Aristotle's was (despite the "Leaning Tower" myth) more the result of cerebration than observation.[25]

METAPHYSICAL EXPLANATION AND THE SEARCH FOR COHERENCE

But, at last, when the most wide-ranging concepts of any science — those to which other explanations keep returning — are "verified" by the cognitive and practical effectiveness of the articulated science, there remains nonetheless an element of the arbitrary and the disconnected. The logical element of disconnection must haunt the basic concepts of every special science, as we have seen, *just as long as these sciences defend their specificity*;

and the sense of the arbitrary must cling to every notion that is accepted as rock-bottom, to which one can only shrug and say, "That's just the way it is." Something in all of us dislikes this shrug. That something is what initiated the cognitive quest and initially set the sciences their task: to bring us understanding. Must the quest end here?

Hospers believes that it must, and although he cautions us against prematurely supposing that we have *found* a basic law or a rock-bottom explanation, he points out that if we did actually have a basic law, it would not only be a waste of time but would also be logically self-contradictory to request an explanation of it, since such a move would be "a request for explanation in a situation where by one's own admission no more explaining can be done."[26] The demands of theory, that "basic" must mean what it says, would seem to lead inevitably to the frustration of our unquenchable thirst for understanding! Hospers adds:

> Like so many others, this point may seem logically compelling but psychologically unsatisfying. Having heard the above argument, one may still feel inclined to ask, "Why are the basic uniformities of the universe the way they are, and not some other way? Why should we have just these laws rather than other ones? I want an *explanation* of why they are as they are." I must confess here, as an autobiographical remark, that I cannot help sharing this feeling: I want to ask why the laws of nature, being contingent, are as they are, even though I cannot conceive of what an explanation of this would be like, and even though by my own argument above the request for such an explanation is self-contradictory.[27]

To account for this psychological dissatisfaction, Hospers blames habit— the mere habit of asking "Why?" even when it makes no sense to do so.

But perhaps the source lies deeper. Our previous analysis of the concept of explanation in terms of the drive to theoretical coherence and completeness may dissuade us, first, from accepting Hospers' identification of the source of our unrest as *merely* psychological. Perhaps there is a built-in drive within the logic of explanation that refuses to be quieted until satisfied; perhaps the human mind properly declines, therefore, to accept the boundaries often proposed for its cognitive aspirations. Perhaps it must so decline, for good reasons, despite acknowledgment (with Kant) that the terms of its explanatory paradigms can never be known to be meaningfully applicable in precisely the same ways as are those of its less ambitious theories.

But, second, granting that there are "psychological" sources to our reluctance to abandon the quest for ultimate explanatory satisfaction, the existentialists direct our attention—possibly with some perceptiveness—to a less trivial human basis than "habit." They point to human anxiety in the face of (what used to be called) its "contingency," and to fear of the abyss of meaninglessness that yawns behind the starkly arbitrary. But it is here, poised over this abyss, that the special sciences are entitled — and obliged — to leave us. Whether all people actually feel or are capable of feeling or latently feel (deep down) such "ontological anxiety" is not a question that needs to be answered in this chapter. It is enough to note that at least some people find their cognitive aspirations reinforced by profound anxieties about what we have learned to call the human "existential situation." And they discover that even the broadest explanations of the special sciences are unable to answer fully either the cognitive or the personal demand.

Still, the creative energies behind the human struggle against arbitrariness and disconnection have not been exhausted in giving birth to their offspring, the sciences. Prior to the development of the sort of rational inquiry that gave rise to the sciences, conceptual syntheses were frequently attempted — and with sometimes impressive results. But we shall find that adequate ultimate explanations for our own time cannot be divorced from the principles and findings of the scientific method, undoubtedly the most significant intellectual fact of our modern world. How, then, can we proceed responsibly beyond the special sciences in quest of cognitive satisfaction?

First, to overcome "disconnection" by coherence and to provide familiarity of pattern in the place of sheer diversity, theories and models drawn from the special sciences as well as from other sources are quite often used outside the methodological restrictions of scope imposed by their strictly scientific uses. Julian Huxley's or Pierre Teilhard de Chardin's concepts of "evolution," for example, or Alfred North Whitehead's thoughts on "organism" — one could multiply examples — these are in their new contexts given conceptual functions as all-embracing interpretive principles for thought, feeling, and behavior that far transcend the boundaries of their original employment. As a result, these new uses are as vulnerable as fish in a barrel to the accurate fire of those[28] who proceed to demonstrate that these new uses, in attempting to bring coherence to reality as a whole, no longer have the right (in this new employment) to claim the authority and precision of the special sciences from which they were borrowed.

These critics are right — of course. This much is built into the very nature of the case. What is not so clear is whether such a line of criticism meets the relevant issues: *Must* all explanations have no more than specialized scientific uses? May not concepts be put to work in disciplined ways to bring coherence to our account of reality-as-a-whole as well as to reality-as-delimited-by-our-departments-of-science? The demands for conceptual coherence are surely not prima facie irrelevant to the *whole*, though relevant to the *parts*, of our account of reality.

Some more profound point must lie behind these recent criticisms than the mere platitude that attempting to explain the whole is not the same thing as attempting to explain the part. It may be that underneath such criticisms there still persists the view — residuum of more exciting "principles" from positivist days of not so long ago—that "explanations of the whole" *cannot* be put to work in a "disciplined" manner, since "discipline" implies "testing," and "testing" (here lurks the ghost) implies "looking and seeing." But this assumption is false. Disciplined inquiry does demand tests, but there are conditions under which the tests, on their theoretical side, must be extremely general and, on their experimental side, must be extremely indirect. We have already seen examples of this indirectness and generality of verification in connection with basic explanatory paradigms in the special sciences. We should be prepared for a like situation—intensified—when we turn from models and theories that are taken as "basic relative to a given field" to evaluate models and theories that are offered as ultimate for all knowledge.[29]

Supposing, then, what is at least possible, that our account of things has (to some extent) been unified and given coherence through the disciplined employment of a conceptual synthesis of some kind. We will have overcome (to that extent) the enemy of "disconnection." What, though, of the threat to cognition posed by "arbitrariness"? There are those who maintain that the latter is inescapable and that we shall do well to settle peacefully for the greatest degree of coherence we can find. Whitehead puts it:

> In a sense, all explanation must end in ultimate arbitrariness. My demand is, that the ultimate arbitrariness of matter of fact from which our formulation starts should disclose the same general principles of reality, which we dimly discern as stretching away into regions beyond our explicit powers of discernment.[30]

ULTIMATE EXPLANATION AS VALUATIONAL

Shall we rest content with this verdict? From the viewpoint of pure theory, it is probably the most that can be said, especially if we may also hope, as Whitehead does, that "the sheer statement, of what things are, may contain elements explanatory of why things are."[31] But the human cognitive quest, although carried on in the terms and by the canons of theory, is not for the sake of theory alone. The sense of values and the need for action are as much a part of the demand for explanation as the thirst for theory. It may even be the case, indeed, that all theory is for the sake of the life-oriented domain.[32] And if so, then the very concept of cognitive satisfaction at its ultimate levels may require analysis in terms that include the *whole* person's quest for understanding, i.e., not only the defeat of disconnection through logical coherence among our concepts but the victory over arbitrariness as well.

Is this, though, to embark upon a journey without hope of arrival—or worse, as Hospers tells us—to begin a search for the answer to a senseless question? What "answer" could *possibly*, in principle, satisfy the insatiable demand? Would we recognize the answer if we found it? On the plane of pure theory, I acknowledge, there can be no such answer, no such "arrival," no such satisfaction. In theory it is possible to go on asking the question "Why?" as Hospers says, forever.

The notion of the arbitrary needs further inspection, because its poignancy extends beyond the theoretical domain. We tend to be bothered by the arbitrary when confronted with that which seems either void of meaning or downright *wrong* (note the overtones of the phrase "brute fact"). Whatever is *right* or valuable, on the other hand, needs no further justification for its being. Our ultimate cognitive resting place as humans—whole people who are valuers and agents as well as thinkers—would seem to lie nowhere short of that elusive point where ultimate *fact* is seen also as perfect good, where our most reliable account of "the way things are" shows also the ultimate rightness of things. Such rightness, of course, is properly predicable only of the *whole* state of affairs referred to in our ultimate explanations. It would be not only methodologically self-defeating but also logically a category-mistake to characterize partial or proximate explanations as though they were ultimate ones. We can allow no shortcut to the termination of the cognitive process through premature appeals to value considerations; but, equally, we shall find no cognitively satisfying termination of this process at all, apart from a vision of the whole of whatever is as also that which *ought* to be.

But wait a moment! If we adopt this view, are we not in danger of begging the question about the character of reality as a whole? To say that explanations of unlimited generality *must* show the "rightness of things" to avoid the irrationality of arbitrariness may, at first glance, seem to be a blatant begging of the question concerning what may be the case. Such a supposition, however, would be mistaken. There is no claim made here that any logically coherent and experientially grounded explanation of unlimited generality *will* in fact exhibit the unity of *is* with *ought*. It may even be that constructing a conceptual synthesis, relevant to the formidable (and growing) mass of contemporary knowledge, undigested, incoherent, and unstable as it is—a conceptual synthesis, in other words, that succeeds merely in overcoming the single enemy of disconnection—may prove (though perfectly legitimate in principle) practically impossible at the present moment in history. And even if, by dint of generous efforts from geniuses as yet unknown, a fortunate model should prove fruitful in the development of such an omnirelevant account of things, it would still *remain to be seen* whether this account answered our nontheoretic (practical and valuational) thirst for explanatory satisfaction. It may be that the arbitrary, at the furthest reaches of our conceptions, will never be eliminated from the human situation. But if so, this is a discovery to be made, not an axiom to be assumed. And inasmuch as the arbitrary *is* ever genuinely overcome in cognition (as is my contention), the victory will go to the ultimate explanation that combines the unsparing standards of theoretical success with the fruitful satisfaction of human aspiration.

It is here that we discover again the profound insight into the human cognitive situation displayed by such giants of conceptual synthesis as Plato, Aristotle, or Spinoza. In each of their attempts at offering ultimate explanations, the Real is inseparable from the Right; the *is* and the *ought* are seen *sub specie aeternitatis*, one and the same. The arbitrary is overcome; brute fact is seen not to be just "brutal" but to display a necessity that is also acceptable; the demand for understanding comes, for a time at least, to fulfillment.

Plato, Aristotle, and Spinoza will not, of course, satisfy our conceptual needs today. The concepts that they were attempting to bring into coherent relation are not our own; human knowledge, thanks very largely to the spectacular successes of the special sciences, has vastly increased. It is our own knowledge, not the concepts of an earlier day, that we demand to see "steadily and whole." But these thinkers, though chosen only as examples, are properly of more than antiquarian interest. Their diagnosis of the cognitive demand was basically correct, although their specific prescriptions for its treatment no longer satisfy. In thus stressing the *continuing* nature of the quest for ultimate explanations—frankly recognizing these to be corrigible, like their distinguished forerunners—we embark upon this philosophic enterprise perhaps more adequately forewarned concerning the logical character of our task. As long as human knowledge continues to grow and human judgment to develop, the search for fresh and fuller syntheses will be required. The cognitive demand for ultimate explanations is not a threat, therefore, to the wholesome excitement of the hunt. The satisfactions of the search are no less genuine than the pleasures of possession. Ultimate explanation in our interpretation is no enemy, then, to free and searching minds; instead, the common enemies of responsible thought at all levels are dogmatism, prejudice, and that unadventuresome temper so bound by orthodoxies, and by what David Hume called "modes," as to shun the risks always present in creative "venturing far out." Every ultimate explanation, religious or secular, is an invitation to take a chance.

THEOLOGICAL EXPLANATION AND PURPOSE

Finally, we may at last explicitly consider the status of theological explanation in the light of what I have been arguing. In a sense, those are right who scornfully curl a logical lip at explanations of the nature of things via appeals to "God's purpose." It is true, as far as we can tell from anthropology and studies of infant logic, that animism and the attempt to account for all things in terms of purpose are, as Hospers tells us, the most primitive conceptions of explanation.[33] But the case may not be left on this level. If ultimate explanation, to be cognitively satisfying, demands a union of fact and value, the explanatory model of a perfectly good personal purpose joined to creative sovereignty over all being may deserve our philosophical attention and respect. But this respect will be deserved only if the model is rigorously articulated, coherently related to all knowledge, and successfully defended against prima facie incoherences. The fact that explanations in terms of purposes are ubiquitous would then prove to be significant for positive as well as for negative reasons. The most primitive concept of explanation is, perhaps, best qualified to be our ultimate basis for explanation as well. Just as familiarity may be seen to reflect victory over disconnection, so also benevolent purpose in the last analysis may turn out to represent our most effective weapon against arbitrariness.

If this is so, however, it will not be so because of the appeal of *purpose* alone or even primarily, but because purpose, taken as an explanatory model, proves capable both of undergirding a successfully coherent conceptual synthesis and of being recognized as *good*. In a footnote of his discussion of the blank contingency of ultimate explanations, Hospers writes:

> Explanation in terms of divine purposes again will not help: if we are told that the laws of nature are as they are because God willed it so, we can ask why He should have willed it so; and if here again an answer is given, we can once again ask a why-question of this answer.[34]

Who is to tell Hospers that he is wrong? Of course one can do as he describes, asking over and over again the theoretical "Why?" or rejecting every stopping place as theoretically arbitrary. But to shift the emphasis so that theological explanation is seen not so much in terms of "divine *purpose*" as "purpose that is *divine*" — and to understand the "divine" as that which is worthy of our worship — this (or something of this *kind*) may conceivably offer a way through which persons can responsibly cope with the cognitive bottomlessness of the arbitrary.

Those who take the procedures and practical aims of the special sciences as determinative for all respectable cognitive endeavor will in all likelihood be shocked by this injection of value consideration into the notion of explanation and hence into cognition. There is little recognized room in the methodology of the special sciences for consideration of value — at least when it comes to choosing between proffered explanatory schemes. The franchise of the scientist is vast but not carte blanche. It is to give us understanding for the sake of coping with nature, and for this pursuit our role as valuers remains normally and methodologically subordinate (though not entirely inactive, as witnessed by the importance of such aesthetic values as "elegance" and such practical values as "simplicity," in our decisions between scientific theories).

The franchise of the philosopher is also to provide us with "understanding," but not alone for the sake of coping with nature. The postanalytical, ecologically aware philosopher who determines to move carefully, self-consciously, and rigorously toward synthesis will attempt—not only with the aid of the specialized scientist but also with the aid of the artist, the moralist, the theologian, the business person, and the poet—to construct a coherent and effective conceptual context within which the philosopher and other investigators may cope with *all* of their environment and the *totality* of their experience, including felt demands of value and of action. To deny ourselves the right to engage in this synthesizing explanatory activity is to deny the possibility of substituting a rational and responsible for an irrational and irresponsible means of coping with life as a whole and the earth as a whole.

Finally, the theologian deserves to be drawn back once again into a rightful place in the thoughtful community. If my account is correct, it is only the theologian disciplined by science and philosophy—or the philosopher prepared to venture into the theological domain of ultimate value commitments—who will bring the cognitive quest to whatever temporary resting place may be hoped for by any generation. It may be that the current situation is ill-suited to our generation's hopes of cognitive satisfaction; it may be that in turbulent times synthesis is less needed than a constant alertness to the ever-changing data—data of value as well as of empirical belief. But if the human spirit continues, as seems likely, to demand ultimate explanations, we shall at least be in a position to ask certain crucial questions of any candidate for our acceptance. First, is this proposed explanation *in keeping with the best findings of the special sciences*, explanatory models and theories of which lie at the beginning of the quest for understanding and may not be ignored without cognitive peril? Second, has the candidate for explanation *overcome the disconnection of separate explanatory paradigms* in the various special sciences by some coherent principle of theoretical unification that is also adequately inclusive? And, last, has the *value dimension implicit in the explanation been seriously considered* and tested against humanity's most profound intuitions of ultimate worth? It is by these criteria, I submit, that a theology of nature must be evaluated. The functions of scientist, philosopher, and theologian in explanation are not identical; they are, I believe, continuous. Therefore if we continue to hope for understanding as whole persons, we shall wish success to each.

6.

Organizing Images and Scientific Ideals

The potent affinities between metaphor and religious vision have a long history and have been recognized since the time of Plato as worthy of serious critical attention.[1] My aim in this chapter is to focus upon a particular form of metaphorical imagery—I shall call it the "religious world model" (RWM)—which I believe is immensely influential but inadequately noticed by philosophers of religion. If I am correct, these metaphors hold vital sway over the consciousness of any age, including our own supposedly "secular" one. I shall argue that they arise from various sources, not only from well-recognized religions like Christianity but also (very importantly for our civilization) from such vigorous expressions of creative imagination[2] as the sciences.

My aim, therefore, will be to introduce this needed concept, the religious world model, and to sketch a pair of examples of what I take to be significant RWMs, one drawn from a traditional and the other from a scientific ground. Finally I shall conclude with a brief consideration of the importance of such consciousness-shaping RWMs for the understanding of our contemporary world and of possible future trends.

WHAT ARE RWMs?

I define a *religious world model* in terms of its *representational* (i.e., referential) *capacity*, its *comprehensive* (i.e., world-inclusive) *scope*, and its intensely *valuational* (i.e., religious) *potency*. Any image suggesting how *all things fundamentally should be thought*, which also *expresses or evokes profound value responses*, will be considered an RWM for the purposes of this discussion.

What, in contrast, is not an RWM? I exclude metaphysical models, qua metaphysical, on the one hand, and value-laden images, taken merely qua images, on the other. *"Metaphysical* models," as I understand them, are world models taken without stress on their value-resonances. Value-laden images, taken in their own right and not considered as lenses for viewing another subject matter, are not (as I use the term) *models*[3] at all, though if the values invoked are sufficiently intense and comprehensive, they will be "organizing images" of religious import.

This use of the term *religious* may be objectionable to those who are accustomed to thinking of religion primarily in doctrinal terms (the content of belief rather than the quality of the believing) and, even more, in terms of familiar biblical doctrines (e.g., belief in God, the Ten Commandments, an afterlife, and so on). My plea to such readers is to remember that religion is not identical with Christianity or Judaism or other familiar religions of our culture; that well-recognized religions exist with very different beliefs (classical Buddhism, for example, has no place for God in its scheme of things); and that what ties all religion together is *worship*, the acknowledgment of some compelling value ("worthship"), rather than specific *doctrine*, which tends to arise in support of and rationalization for intensely felt value.

The significant mark of all religion, as I see it,[4] is its power to affect the whole range of human life, both personal and social, by rising from some sense of supreme worth (the sacred) to mold how people act, feel, perceive, and think. Anywhere we find such power, however dissimilar it may be to the familiar religions of our culture in other respects, I propose to call it "religious."

Whatever the names we use, it is clear that we are deeply influenced, today as always, by value-laden conceptions of what the world is like. More and more people are becoming conscious of the degree to which our relations to each other and to the environment—both as individuals and as a civilization—have been shaped by a vision of nature and humanity's place in it that is not the only one possible for human beings to adopt.[5] It is tragic that such awareness of the presence of RWMs in the background of social and environmental practices has had to wait so long—until the burden of inequity against our fellow humans and insults against our environment had grown so heavy as to threaten our current way of life and, possibly, civilized life itself on this planet. The further pity is that vast numbers of people are still unaware of the religious roots of the cultural and environmental crisis-time into which we have entered. They are half-blind, therefore, to their own participation in the problem and to their own potential role in its outworking.

My basic thesis is that RWMs function profoundly in the ordering of society itself. This seems to me clearly true. At one level, for example, every social structure has implicit within it a vision, laden with great valuational significance, of human nature. What are people really like, at root? What are they capable of? What effectively influences them, and the course of history? What are the overriding interests that society must protect at all costs?

Still deeper, one's basic picture of what it is to be human arises out of yet more basic convictions as to what it is to be *anything at all*. Can there in principle be such a thing as an afterlife? Are material interests the only real ones? Can "human nature" be changed? If so, do we best appeal to reason (pride? aesthetics?), or should we merely manipulate environmental conditions?[6]

For the limited purposes of this chapter, those more general metaphysical issues will need to remain in the background, requiring independent development elsewhere.[7] But it should be kept in mind that they remain there, even while we concentrate here on certain more specific issues.

HERE DO RWMs COME FROM?

I do not intend to offer an exhaustive picture of the origins of RWMs, either historically or psychologically. There may be a number of sources to which a full treatment would need to attend. Historically, the potent, comprehensive, idea-generating images we are interested in may well have come from agricultural practices or sexual preoccupations or hunting concerns; and to this list we could add today's political imagery, economic pressures, or aesthetic intuitions. Psychologically, it would be fascinating to speculate about the two hemispheres of the brain and whether in some cases our RWMs are more readily traceable to our right-hemisphere engagement with patterns, while in other cases they may be better interpreted as extensions from our left-brain hunger for linear explanation.[8] Since the burden of this essay is to suggest that RWMs arise both from myth and from science, the latter suggestion is attractive, but it cannot be pursued here.

Instead, I shall be content to trace the parallel and contrasting ways in which traditional mythic metaphors received from one direction, and central scientific ideals, drawn from another, become potent RWMs that deeply influence our daily lives. The important point is not to catalogue every source for RWMs, but to show that in fact they come by different paths from more than one source and that one of these sources for our society is science. If this can be done, then it will be clear that science is even more significant in our culture than is normally recognized, because science contributes vitally not only to our knowledge and technology but also to our ultimate vision of things. At the same time it will become clear that religion is even more pervasive and influential in our civilization than modernity's brash secular front might suggest, because religion shapes not only our formal worship and our official ethical codes but also the basic attitudes and real policies with which we approach each other and the world we live in.

Traditional RWMs

Human beings are myth-making animals. By "myth" in this context, I do not of course mean to imply anything false or outmoded. I mean, rather, to refer to the network of stories that provides a framework of intelligible order and moral guidance for the originating, story-telling community (and for others who may make them their own). Such stories make use of familiar value-laden images to help us cope with the strange and threatening. They include stories about the very first beginnings or the very last endings of things; about the final realities behind all confusing appearance; about the underlying authorities impinging on humankind, on one's own tribe or nation, and on one's self. Some of these stories are aetiological (like ancient "just-so" stories), providing an explanation for the origin of a tribe's special practices regarding, say, a holy place or an ancient feud. Some are more comprehensive, depicting the gods (or God or other ultimate powers) and the circumstances of creation itself. Most important, all such stories are deeply freighted with values for those who rely on and find personal or group significance through the images they evoke.

I believe that these images, which may be called "organizing images" because of the role they play in organizing the perceptions and values of those who dwell on them, may become in the full sense *models* for the understanding of the world if, in addition to their several value roles, they are also taken seriously for *thought* as well. This thought-guiding function need not always surface. A metaphor, for example — such as the Lord as my "Shepherd" — may be evoked mainly for emotional needs. I choose this image from Psalm 23 because it is plainly and explicitly poetry. Like any metaphor, it must be acknowledged as false on the literal level. But it is an image of proven power to attract and comfort. It helps one feel, behind the often contradictory appearances, a companion who cares; it assists those who take refuge in this image to perceive the world — their life's career — as a journey with a strong companion and a secure destination. It gives needed encouragement.

But often, in addition to the evocative powers of such metaphors drawn from the mythic tradition, we find that these metaphors provide aids for generalized thought. The organizing image, that is, becomes a *model for thinking* as well as a *metaphor for feeling and perceiving* the whole of reality.[9] The Lord is not only "Shepherd," he is also "Shield of Abraham," and "Rock of Ages." These metaphors are mythopoetically coherent but literally inconsistent: a shepherd obviously cannot be a rock; useful shields are not made from stone. Yet if such metaphors are taken seriously within a faith-community at the level of valuation, there is a strong tendency to take them seriously also at the level of thought. What is it that this typical mosaic pattern of images can be thought to be saying about the general nature of things? Is it not saying at least that *there is protection*; that we are not naked before the vicissitudes of life; and that the protector is personal, caring, aware?

As an *organizing image*, a metaphor's power of stirring values is vested in its vivid concreteness as it captures attention and consent. As a *model*, a religious world model, the metaphor's function is to suggest general respects in which the profoundly real may be thought to resemble features of the familiar and treasured. In this way the image becomes a model and the model gives rise to theory, i.e., to a structured and logically disciplined effort to conceptualize the unknown out of the materials of the known.

Religious theory, on this view, functions as metaphysical theory but is always derivative from the value-drenched imagery that constitutes its heuristic metaphor. The highest flights of theological construction, no matter how coherent and adequate they may be intellectually, return for their religious authority to earth again in poetry, whence they were launched. One can see this with especial clarity in connection with doctrines about God that spring from the key Christian metaphor of God as Father. The image is vital to the Christian RWM: it is dramatized in such parables as the Prodigal Son; it is reinforced in Christian liturgy with the constant repetition of the Lord's Prayer beginning, "Our Father, . . ." God is not literally a father at all, of course, and yet the metaphor has great point both for the stirring of potent feeling (as organizing image) and for the stimulating of profound thought (as model). And, as we shall note, it has an important social impact, as well.

What are the features in respect to which we might be entitled to *think* as well as to *feel* this vital image? One respect must have to do with the generative function of literal fatherhood: the doctrine of creation stems from this general feature, and with it all the subtle discussion of the similarities and dissimilarities between human creative activity and the divine *creatio ex nihilo*. Again, another respect in which we can think of the fatherhood image is in terms of moral authority and rule making for the family: moral theology arises from this general feature. Still another respect modeled by the fatherhood image is that of continuing power: doctrines of providence root here. More than this, the father is a unifier of his family: theology of the Church, ecclesiology, as well as ecumenical theories of humankind find footing in this feature. And finally, paramount to the Christian metaphor itself as stressed by Jesus (particularly but not exclusively in the Fourth Gospel), is the feature of God's fatherly love: soteriology (theology of salvation), eschatology, Christology, and more, arise from attempting to think appropriately in the light of essential Christian imagery.

In sum, the potent valuational image is primary to the RWMs that derive from the ancient mythic tradition. Insofar as these images are effective in organizing lives and profoundly influencing feelings, there is strong motivation also to think as generally and as consistently as possible in their terms. In that role, as undergirding the effort to construct an intelligible pattern of relationships among familiar things for the sake of representing fundamental reality, such metaphors that offer organizing images become what I have called religious world models through which we see and relate to our world.

Science-generated RWMs

It is less often noticed that RWMs spring also (by a different route) from modern science. Science seeks to explain as well as to control the world we live in. Its aim, despite positivist denials,[10] is toward understanding as well as prediction. But explanation is an inherently open-ended process. The principles used for explanation are subject, themselves, to a demand for explanation. Once this is supplied, by invoking further principles, these, too, will be subject to still more explaining. The quest for understanding would seem forever unattainable. But this frustrating situation—though apparently theoretically inevitable—seems not actually to have come about. Scientists at any given time *think* that they understand tolerably well what they are studying. They do not suppose that they have ultimate explanations, but neither do they give up their efforts in despair over the logical truth that every explanation remains unexplained as long as the whole hierarchy of explanations remains without a theoretical anchor. Instead, working scientists take for granted certain principles[11] as not requiring explanation, as being understandable "straight off," as it were, on their own credentials. These principles, which Stephen Toulmin calls "ideals of the natural order,"[12] just stand to reason, are felt to be transparently appropriate. When one gets to one of these ideals of the natural order, one has reached the end of the line, one has hit the bottom deck in the quest for understanding.

In Newtonian physics, for instance, a body will continue in uniform motion in a straight line (or remain at rest) as long as no forces are acting on it. Changes in motion—starting, stopping, speeding up, slowing down— need explanation, but in the absence of such changes, uniform straight-line motion just "stands to reason." What *else* would a body do with itself? That is just the way nature is, ideally, when all the perturbations and confusions of daily life are removed. We may never be able actually to experience such a state of affairs (that is what is meant by its being an "ideal" of the natural order), but we can approximate it. As we do, no further comment or explanation is called for.

That this readiness to accept some stopping place in the otherwise infinite regress of explanation is not without its historical risks is shown by the fact that ideals of the natural order are subject to displacement. This happens with difficulty, for reasons that will become apparent, but it happens. To illustrate, prior to the Newtonian ideal of unaccelerated *straight-line* motion as "standing to reason," astronomers took as wholly natural and without need for explanation the ideal of uniform *circular* motion. Nicolaus Copernicus declared:

> . . . that some sorts of natural happenings stand to reason, being self-explanatory, natural, and intelligible of themselves. The task of astronomy . . . was complete only when all the celestial motions were displayed as explicable in terms of "the principle of regularity." What was this principle of which Copernicus wrote? It laid down that, in Nature, all bodies which are in their proper places move uniformly and regularly—and this, for him, meant that they moved along tracks

composed out of circles, each of which was revolving at a constant
angular rate about its own proper centre.[13]

And Galileo, too, who came close to anticipating Newton's law of inertia
in picturing the motion of a ship to be just as "natural" as its being at
rest—it takes the imposition of a force to slow down a moving ship just as
much as it requires a force to speed one up—still retained the ideal of
circular motion as being directly intelligible.

> For what he envisaged as his ideal case was a ship moving unflaggingly
> across the ocean along a Great Circle track, for lack of any external
> force to speed it up or slow it down. He saw that uniform motion
> could be quite as natural as rest; but this "uniform motion" took place
> along a closed horizontal track circling the centre of the earth; and
> Galileo took such circular motion as entirely natural and self-explan-
> atory. He does not seem to have regarded the ship as constrained by
> its own weight from flying off the earth on a tangent—the image which
> can clearly be found in Newton.[14]

Thinking of circular motion as "natural" is vastly different from taking
a similar view of straight-line motion. On the first position, no questions
need to be raised about what keeps the planets in their chosen orbits or
what keeps massive bodies moving along the curved surface of the earth.
Those would not be phenomena to be accounted for; they are simply natural—the way things ought to be. But on the second position, that of Newton and his followers, the provision of a force, gravitational attraction, was
necessary for proper understanding. The ideal of what ought to be in nature
was different. What simply "stood to reason" for pre-Newtonian thinkers
had been penetrated to a new "lowest deck," and the content of explanation
had to be adjusted appropriately.

Ideals of the natural order set the challenge for explanatory science,
then, at any given time. They are vital to the explanatory process both in
posing the basic problems that are acknowledged as needing to be answered
and in providing the stopping place of intelligibility in what otherwise would
be an endlessly frustrating abyss of unexplained explanations.

But beyond this, making possible these basic functions, ideals of the
natural order are intimately related to still broader value-laden assumptions
drawn from the cultural context out of which they arise. The Copernican
ideal of natural circular motions, for instance, did not by any means orig-
inate with him. On the contrary, it was a pre-Ptolemaic, pre-Aristotelian
ideal of astronomical explanation set by Plato[15] as a challenge to his successors: to account, by appealing to none but "perfect" uniform motions,
for the complex appearances of the heavens. Behind Plato's challenge was
both a philosophical and a deeply religious motive. First, only the perfect
forms are fully intelligible; and, second, the heavens, being divine, would

be desecrated by being thought in any terms short of perfect motions. Still earlier than Plato's views lay another great tradition, that of Pythagoras, who had earlier taught his followers to think of the real as identical with the perfect intelligibilities of number. Deeper yet, enfolding much of Greek thought and perception, was the cultural premise that the perfect forms were the closed or limited ones. Why is a circle more "perfect" than a zig-zag or an endless straight line? To the culture that built the Parthenon, with its firmly limited lines and graceful, closed proportions, the answer was obvious. In the context of ethical thought stressing the avoidance of the hubris of excess, preference for the limited above the unlimited, for the self-contained circle above the alarming craziness of erratic motion — all these were too plain to require argument. Behind the explanatory ideals of Copernicus and Galileo, therefore, and far below the conscious surface of the scientific specifics being investigated, were profound visions of the nature of the world and visions shot through with intuitions of basic value.

On the other side, with Newton and the ideal of straight-line motion, equally deep implications for ultimate reality and value can be seen. True, scientific specifics were the immediate reasons for Newton's shift in ideals; he was interested in explaining a wider range of data in one set of principles than could have been done without penetrating below the ideal of uniform circular motion as simply "standing to reason."[16] And he was successful in this; his revolution in ideals was not on its face a clash of underlying philosophical and religious worldviews. But the clash, nonetheless, was real and deep. The image of the straight line, without beginning or end, as the ideal form of motion, had its own roots in early Greek thought. This tradition was defended by Democritus, who pictured the universe as a collocation of atoms falling endlessly in the void of space; it was continued by the unorthodox speculations of Nicholas of Cusa on the infinity of space; and it was dramatized by the martyrdom of Bruno, burned for his belief in an infinity of worlds. No longer ideally bounded by the sedate limits of form, space had to be assumed to be infinite in the Newtonian scheme;[17] bolstered by Newton's prestige, the concept of infinity itself could be embraced as something good and exciting rather than unthinkable and threatening. The cathedral, with its asymmetrical vertical lines aspiring heavenward, thrusting ideally forever up and out, could provide a religious analogue for this shift of sensibilities, contrasting portentously with the firm-lidded temples of the form-loving Greeks. Likewise the "excessive" saints — seeking ecstasy in hair shirts — were far from the moderation of the Classical ideal. Here we see a value-universe that is open-ended, not curved in upon itself. And the religion of progress, faith in human culture ascending forever on the endless inclined plane of historical development, would soon follow the Newtonian shift from the bounded to the boundless ideal of the natural order. To this social implication we shall return.

In this way we see illustrated the emergence of RWMs from the explanatory logic of modern science. The process is the reverse of the one we traced earlier, in which organizing images, as we saw, come first from value-laden mythic consciousness and then are put to work as models for thought that aims at making the world as a whole more intelligible within the framework of those values. In this second case, the requirements of explanatory theory lead first to ideals of the natural order which, in turn, have powerful implications for shaping or reinforcing basic values as well as for providing the groundwork of intelligible thought about the nature of reality. But the product of either of these processes is a religious world model, representing the fundamental nature of things by a set of general ideals drawn from some domain of familiar experience and expressing profound and powerful values that have great bearing on how we organize our priorities, perceive the significance of ourselves, and relate to our fellow human beings and our natural environment.

HOW DO RWMs MATTER?

The importance of noticing our RWMs is — their importance! Our ultimate values are pervasive in shaping society, and our key religious metaphors provide the keys to our becoming more self-aware, as individuals and as a civilization, as to why we have become as we are and where we may be headed. In the remaining space of this chapter I can hope only to illustrate this final point from a vast selection of possibilities.

I shall take two examples: one RWM from a traditional source in organizing imagery, and the other from an ideal of science. Then, after these have been noted, I shall conclude with a little speculation about possibly emerging RWMs that may have a bearing on our future.

Patriarchalism

One of the great and basic organizing images that we had occasion to notice in a previous section is that of Fatherhood. The paternal values are profoundly part of human experience and were functioning to organize families, villages, and nations long before our biblical tradition incorporated and modified such father-imagery into what we think of today as the Fatherhood of God. From Sky God to Zeus, from Jehovah to our Father in heaven, the high concepts of rule and responsibility, moral principle and generativity, the brotherhood of Man under the cosmic Father, and similar values, were expressed and reinforced by traditional organizing imagery centering around the phenomenon of paternity.

It would be difficult to overstate the pervasive influence of this RWM, older than Christianity but strongly supported in Christendom by the theology, the liturgy, and the spirituality of Christian faith. The language of prayers and hymns, despite feminist attempts at reform, seems ineradicably masculine. Our taken-for-granted political structures, whether presidential or judicial or congressional, are deeply hierarchical in structure. So are the structures of our economic and academic institutions. Indeed, so are the conceptions we internalize about ourselves, in a world of rules and authorities and father-figures. Interestingly, it seems not to matter whether a woman is filling the place of the father-figure in the judicial robes or in the pulpit or in the prime ministership — the structures and standards themselves are paternalistic.

In the theological literature of the final quarter of this century,[18] there has been at last significant discussion of patriarchy as a problem for our spirits and our society. This is not the place for reviewing that literature, but in essence the charge is made that our stress on *hierarchy* leaves *community* underattended, that our emphasis on *rules* leaves *insight* undernourished, and that aggressive, competitive, masculine values lead to conflict, exploitation (of persons and of nature), and to the horrors of war.

This charge is a serious one and must be attended by those who are concerned for the spiritual health and future course of civilization. Have our traditional RWMs overemphasized the masculine values at the cost of the feminine? Should there be more recognition of the phenomenon of Motherhood, and all that this stands for, in our society's institutions? Has a traditional RWM led us astray toward the rape of the earth and the brink of nuclear destruction?

These questions cannot be answered lightly, and it will need to be enough to ask them at this time. But if the question is whether and how RWMs "matter," the simple putting of the questions provides a start toward the answer.

Progressivism

Another characteristic of our civilization is its dynamic trust in the future. Unlike most human cultures, the global North has operated with an open-ended sense of possibility and without much consciousness of limits. Led by the dynamic example of science, with its endless vistas for refinement and cognitive growth, and driven by the industrial power of science-led technology, our modern civilization has assaulted the future with aggressive confidence in its destiny.

Behind all this, allowing it and encouraging it, is the vision of the universe as likewise open-ended. As we saw in our earlier discussion, the Newtonian revolution was not only a change in theoretical dynamics but also a shift in sensibility: Space itself becomes homogeneous and infinite so that the straight line of endless motion can become the ideal of natural order, replacing the closed figure of the circle both in theoretical principle and at the center of modern consciousness.

Again, only recently, we have begun to question the values generated by this science-based RWM. The classical faith in inevitable progress began to fade, of course, at the beginning of this century, with the tragedy of the

First World War, but it has taken until the present to absorb the more fundamental shocks to our culture's mythic faith in growth.[19] Can we continue our patterns of exponential growth without destroying the earth and ourselves, either by pollution or overcrowding or exhaustion of natural resources? Has the heady image of limitless motion along an endless line proven, as an RWM, to be dangerously limited? Was it applicable only to an unusual era of ample resources and empty spaces? Will its influence destroy our biosphere, and us with it, unless alternative RWMs can be found to guide our basic perceptions and practices in the building of a postmodern civilization that can live more gently on the earth?

It is not necessary to attempt an answer to these pressing questions here in order to see how enormously important they are to our daily lives and to our future. The importance of our RWMs is indeed their importance: They are vital to everything we are and do and hope. Are there emergent RWMs that may give us some ground for fresh hope in a world battered and torn by the old?

Organicism

If patriarchal and progressive values have been dominant in our modern civilization's history, and if they are now the occasion for deep reconsideration among those concerned about our spiritual and physical survival, other RWMs may be emerging in our time that have promise for a very different postmodern world. It is hard more than to speculate about such large questions, of course, but it is vital to be alert to the larger shifts in imagination and value-consciousness that may be occurring around us and within us.

One possibility that I glimpse is of an emergent organicism in thought and value that may be (in part at least) generated by the new science of ecology. Not since the Newtonian revolution at the start of the modern age has the valuational overtones of a science so captured the imagination of so large a segment of society. The ecology "movement" in the United States and Canada, the phenomenon of the "Greens" in Germany and elsewhere in Europe, coupled with the widespread sense of malaise and disillusionment among great segments of the population of the modernized nations, makes it thinkable that the immense historic phenomenon of "the modern world" — its social structures shaped by paternalistic values and its mighty military and industrial machine patterned after Newtonian progressivist images — may be giving way to a new order with fresh, contrasting values and images.

The religious world metaphors that arise from ecology as a pioneer postmodern science guide thought and feeling toward mutuality rather than hierarchy and toward cycles rather than open-ended lines. First, consider the emerging RWM of *mutuality*. Against the image of the Sky God, always associated with paternalistic, hierarchical religions, again is posed the image of Mother Earth. The model of infinitely complex interaction among symbiotic organisms replaces the picture of kingly rule. The internal evolution of richly supportive ways of living together contrasts with the external enforcement of decrees. The political consequences of such revolutionary changes in basic ideals are difficult to anticipate in detail; but it is clear that if ecology-generated RWMs become typical of a future civilization, these consequences will be profound.

Second, imagine the difference to our economic life that would be made by substituting the RWM of the circle for the progressive, infinitely extensible line. Ecologist Barry Commoner struck a profound chord with this image in his widely read book, *The Closing Circle*.[20] Nature *will* close the cycles that humanity attempts to force open with progressive, dominating ways. The question is whether we shall cooperate with the wisdom of nature or be crushed. Newton's infinite line may be an ideal of the natural order for physics (and even so, for pre-Einsteinian cosmological theory), but it is no viable ideal for a world grown aware of ecology. Sufficiency, balance, equilibrium, fulfillment within limits — these are the new ideals from ecology that may be in the process of replacing the progressivist RWMs of the modern era.

In this way, by drawing attention to the ultimate values implicit in the great, global metaphors-in-conflict that surround us, philosophy may broaden our awareness of the ultimately religious dimensions of contemporary "secular" society. In addition, philosophy can bring its critical tools to bear upon these various contending religious ideals and help put them into the context of traditional, recognized religions, like Christianity, so that the current clash of faiths may be subjected to the scrutiny of reason.

7.

Religious World Modeling
and Postmodern Science

Modern science has dealt notorious blows to person-oriented Western religions. In a series of retreats, theologians have been forced to concede specific issues like the peripheral location of the earth in the universe, the kinship of Homo sapiens with the ancestral ooze, the depths of human unreason, and even the molecular basis for valued traits. But by far the most anguishing effect of modern science on the religious confidence of the civilization built by its technologies and shaped by its values lies deeper. It is the sense of alienation from responsible agency, from community with nature, and from personal inwardness. The images of the universe that are naturally drawn from the ideals of modern science — ideals contributory to three centuries of intellectual and technological achievements — provide no home for such qualities.

IDEALS OF MODERN SCIENCE

I stress the images and the ideals of modern science because these are the evocative and value-laden aspects of the scientific phenomenon that flow most directly into the religious consciousness of an age. Science cannot function without ideals. Every measurement, however carefully taken, is laced with error and only approximates the ideal of perfect precision. Every significant theoretical concept reflects an idealization — point masses, frictionless surfaces, instantaneous velocities, and the like — not directly met in the unkempt world of experience. And every explanation finally depends on what Stephen Toulmin calls an "ideal of the natural order,"[1] that gives the scientific reach for understanding a stopping point for the incessant "Why?" by offering a sense of the rightness or appropriateness or inevitability of the answer given.

These ideals, as we saw in the previous chapter, generate images of how

things are. For example, the important scientific ideal that things be perfectly regular, despite the apparent randomness of much in crude experience, suggests the image of the Perfect Machine. By it the universe is
thought—and felt—in terms of an ideal clockwork mechanism in which
nothing ever goes awry and in which every part is determined by the springs
and gears that drive its every motion. The ideal is fundamental to scientific
activity; it is hard even to imagine a science in which apparent disorder
might be accepted with a shrug at face value. And the world modeled after
the Perfect Machine supports that ideal and encourages the devotion of
years to the search for the hidden regularities and what Henry Margenau,
as we saw in chapter 5, calls "subsurface connections"[2] that make up the
triumph of scientific genius. The world model of the Perfect Machine has
further consequences: It gives a sense of the ideal unity of all things, organized in principle within one great system; it also gives a sense of the kind
of security that comes from feeling that all things are working together and
are continuing as they must without accident, flaw, or mischance.

These last consequences, of course, are religious attitudes. The images
that evoke or embody them are what I christened religious world models
(RWMs) in the previous chapter, when such images are used not only to
focus attitudes toward the world but also to think about it and to grapple
with it through policies of life rooted in a vision of what that world is like.

The image of the Perfect Machine is only one of several RWMs generated from the ideals of modern science as they have contributed to shaping human consciousness since the seventeenth century. Another important
example is the image of the Ultimate Particle. The method of analysis
sponsored by Galileo and codified by Descartes is basic to modern science.
This method requires the dividing of problems into their smallest components, reducing the issues from the complex to the simple and solving them
separately. In like manner, looking for explanation tended to become a
quest for the smallest unit, something simple underlying all other things. If
only the fundamental particle (or particles) could be identified and understood, then those complexes built up from the ultimate particles in combination would also be thoroughly understood. Explanation would proceed
by reduction. To know what a thing really is, in terms of this ideal, would
be to know as much as possible about the parts that make it up. The lure
of the atomic theory, and deeper yet the lure of subatomic particles and
finally of the quark (if the quark is indeed that from which all other particles
derive) is the ideal image of the Ultimate Particle. It represents Being in
and of itself. Its properties define those of reality; all other properties are
mere appearance. To discover its nature is to stand before the deepest
secrets of what all things are like in essence, which turns out to be most
austere. It excludes color, sound, texture, or quality of the sort we are
accustomed to experiencing in the everyday world. Those are joint products
of "reality" interacting with subjective mentality. Mentality itself has no
secure place in the image of the Ultimate Particle; it is something different

from the rest of what counts as reality. Perhaps it, too, is merely derivative Appearance?

A third image, that of the Pure Object, reinforces the other two. One of the principal ideals of modern science has been to rid the world of the merely subjective, whether it be at the level of scientific belief (where objectivity must rule the tendency to whim and delusion) or at the level of subject matter (where remnants of Aristotelian "final causation" must be rigorously excised in every area). The objective is highly valued; the subjective is shunned. Even laboratory ritual, such as the highly impersonal manner of writing up results, as I noted in chapter 1, obeys and strengthens the ideal of commitment to the objective and the Object.

Unfortunately, the RWMs that spring naturally from these ideals of modern science are not easily reconciled with profound human cravings. If we venerate the qualities implicit in the image of the Perfect Machine— those of regularity, predictability, control—we lose the values of spontaneity, creativity, responsibility. And those are the values of the personal. If all reality should be seen and felt as perfectly regular clockwork, with each happening being determined by its preceding circumstances, then we are not free to do otherwise than whatever it is we find ourselves actually doing. Then we are not responsible agents, capable of initiating chains of events, but are only necessary links in the causal sequence that looms indefinitely into the future and ties us remorselessly to the conditions of the past. Then we can never truly say, with the former U.S. President Harry Truman, that "the buck stops here." The buck never stops; all events are conditioned in a Perfect Machine by the state of the machine in its previous moment, and so on, ad infinitum. Personal responsibility falls victim to the deterministic ideals of regularity and predictability. And with this loss come serious social and psychological consequences for modern civilization. Human beings, perceived as without essential responsibilities or need for personal creativity, will more easily be placed into economic bondage to assembly-line production techniques; overwhelming bureaucracies will show less compunction in mechanically administering our lives not only without spontaneity but (worse) without personal assumption of moral accountability from birth to burial.

The consequences of the RWM drawn from the ideal of the Ultimate Particle are no less depressing. The reductionist vision sees the whole as an aggregate of the parts and what the parts are, so the whole is. Nature, thus modeled, is in reality "a dull affair, soundless, scentless, colourless; merely the hurrying of material, endlessly, meaninglessly."[3] If we value reality and disdain mere appearance, we shall on this RWM build the Ugly Society, since aesthetic values are merely in the subjective eye of the beholder, and commitment to reality is best acted out through single-minded devotion to the amassing and manipulation of material. Further, since physical nature has no mentality or values of its own, we are free to treat all of our environment, without compunction, as a resource pit and garbage dump. Even animals, as Descartes assured us, deserve no more consideration than would the chemicals which compose them.[4]

Thus the reductionist ideal, although vital to science since Descartes, leads quickly to a "nothing but" attitude toward our surroundings and, together with the discounting of the qualitative aspect of experience and the loss of place in the universe for mentality, drives us to a state of deep alienation from the universe in which we live.

Likewise, we find the influence of the ideal of the Pure Object leading to dismaying consequences of spirit and action. By worshiping the Object at the cost of the Subject, this RWM alienates us from our own inwardness, from our own intuitions of meaning and our own structures of purpose. Not only are we cut off from the world of nature, but the world of other persons becomes the domain of I-it perception, and the stage is set for both the great and the little atrocities of modern life.

The French reductionist biologist Jacques Monod, who embraces the key religious world models of modern science and advocates them despite acknowledging their incompatibility with profoundly rooted human needs and values, summarizes the painful religious legacy of modern science by urging that if the human race truly accepts the import of modern science:

> then man must at last wake out of his millenary dream; and in doing so, wake to his total solitude, his fundamental isolation. Now does he at last realize that, like a gypsy, he lives on the boundary of an alien world. A world that is deaf to his music, just as indifferent to his hopes as it is to his suffering or his crimes.[5]

ALTERNATIVES TO MODERN SCIENCE

What I have been calling "modern science" is of course only one of many possible approaches to the problems of "natural philosophy" (as science used to be called, until this century), and alternatives to it and its ideals have not been lacking. Modern science was itself an alternative to premodern forms of natural philosophy, mainly rooted in the thinking of Aristotle. It is a verbal matter whether we choose to call such approaches, including the highly developed astrological and alchemical traditions of the Middle Ages and the Renaissance, "premodern science" or "prescientific." I prefer the former, because I believe that modern science, with its bleak value consequences, does not deserve a monopoly on the whole meaning of the honorific word *science*.

Something importantly new, however, came into the world with modern natural philosophy, and (despite the yearnings of some, like Theodore Roszak[6]) there is no going back to premodern forms of science. The requirements of empirical testability, for one thing, and the powerful linkage of explanatory theory to mathematics, for another, have brought us too far and given us too much unprecedented control over (and responsibility for) nature to be simply "gotten round"[7] as merely another mythology. However humane they were (and this point itself is debatable), premodern sciences like astrology and alchemy cannot on value grounds alone compete with the demonstrable results of three centuries of scientific achievement.

Indeed, the proper role of intellectual regulation in the governance of belief is a question of basic values; as such this question falls within the domain of the religious if religion, as I believe, is primarily a value phenomenon.[8]

The posture of some religious traditions, we know, is indifferent or hostile to the values of critical intelligence. Some strands of Christianity, which has in the main tended to value the virtues of the mind, view the intellect as a temptation, something to be mortified rather than fulfilled. The *sacrificium intellectus*, however, is always subject to ethical assessment. A religious stance that requires the mutilation of any great aspect of life is to that extent in my view faulted. The richer the wholeness that religious imagery supports in individuals and in communities, the better.

If this is so, then for religious adequacy itself there must be found a place for the values of critical intelligence. It is possible to scoff at the demands for logical consistency and coherence, or for evidential relevance and adequacy, but only at the expense of the human capacity for thought itself, including even that of the scoffer. Although religion's root is in the life-oriented domain of practical reason, it is pushed by its own drive toward comprehensiveness to include the values of theoretical reason as well. In principle, therefore, an enterprise devoted to the support of intellectual needs should be valued positively within an adequate religious framework; science, on its deepest intention, is such an enterprise; therefore science, for any valuationally comprehensive religion, will be acknowledged as having just claim on the loyalties of religious persons. An antiscientific religious posture shows its valuational inadequacy on its face.

If there is neither cognitive nor valuational justification for abandoning modern science for premodern modes of thinking, but if at the same time the images and values of modern science are threatening to the spiritual health—and indirectly even the survival of contemporary civilization, then our best hope will be the emergence of a postmodern form of science that will preserve the virtues of rigorous thinking without absolutizing the alienating religious world models of Machine, Particle, and Object. Is this a futile hope?

Some, like Jacques Monod, argue that science shows no signs of weakening in its headlong antihumanistic tendency, and that it cannot escape being perceived as a danger to contemporary society.

Here, I am not referring to the population explosion, to the destruction of the natural environment, nor even to the stock pile of megatons of nuclear power; but to a more insidious and much more deep-seated evil: one that besets the spirit. One that was begot of the sharpest turning point ever taken in that evolution of ideas. An evolution, moreover, which continues and accelerates constantly in the same direction, ever increasing that bitter distress of the soul.[9]

Monod's proposed solution is to try to root out the craving for meaning and purpose despite the depth of its hold within the psyche. But this solution calls for capitulation to alienated consciousness and depersonalized society. Is there no alternative? Are there no grounds for hope for genuine science and human meaning at once? I believe it is possible, first, to challenge Monod's assertion that the evolution of science is in fact linear, accelerating "constantly in the same direction" and, second, to see what implications important changes in direction from modern to postmodern ideals and images might have for generating religious world models appropriate for our lives now and for our future.

It is easy to see how a scientist like Monod, steeped both in modern scientific ideals and in the Cartesian cultural tradition, might see the historical development of science as a clean, straight line leading from the heroic days of seventeenth-century quantifiers, analyzers, abstracters, and reducers through the Newtonian mechanists, to his own highly reductionist and analytical science of molecular biology. Not only Monod but a great many persons today see the wave of the scientific future in the study of the Ultimate Particles drawn from living things considered as collections of physical and chemical parts conforming to the ideal of the Perfect Machine and treated as approximating the image of Pure Object. From huge new plans for fighting cancer to genetic engineering, and from test-tube babies to rumors of cloning, the news columns are filled with discussions that suggest the potency, for good or ill, of this scientific development and its associated technologies. All this seems new and startling as it vaults into public consciousness.

And yet from another perspective there is nothing quite so familiar. Molecular biology and its offspring sociobiology are the fulfillment and at the same time the apotheosis of tendencies central to the old ideals of modern science. As we have noted, these are powerful ideals, well-designed to bite deeply into hitherto unknown territory. Since this is the case, we should not be surprised at the effectiveness of these well-honed ideals and abstractions when they are directed at the pertinent aspects of living things.

We need not suppose, however, that every aspect of living organisms is interpretable through ideals and images, no matter how powerful, that have their historical origin in astronomy and physical dynamics. These specific ideals are both limited and accidental. They are *limited* in ways I have discussed at the outset and shall return to, by way of contrast, in what follows. They are *accidental* for science, but not in the sense that it is difficult to understand just why astronomical subject matter, with negligible frictional disturbance giving rise to its great simplicities and highly visible regularities, became a paradigm for clocklike explanatory representations; or why physics, with its relatively uncomplicated, inert, and docile subject materials, became the fountainhead of reductionist and objectivist presuppositions. These make sense in the historical context of a nascent science, but precisely this historical context reminds us that there is nothing logically essential in such ideals for all science in every period or mode of development. They may, indeed, be essential to the understanding of the specific cultural phenomenon of modern science in the tradition of Galileo and Newton; without these ideals and images we would have a very different science. But they are historically accidental so far as science itself, taken simply as a logically controlled and empirically responsible way of understanding, is concerned. Different interests, alternative research paths, might have led to other, less abstract images and ideals.

TOWARD POSTMODERN SCIENCE

To demonstrate that this is no empty possibility in the current scientific world, we find among us bona fide sciences that have broken sharply with the ideals and assumptions that have been identified with modern science for long centuries. These postmodern sciences are the really exciting developments in the evolution of science, culture, and value today.

Harold Schilling writes of a "new consciousness" breaking out in all of the traditional disciplines, including his own field of physics.[10] His evidence is welcome that postmodern concepts and values are becoming pervasive, if not by any means yet dominant, in the various sciences. For the purposes of illustration it is possible to examine the science of ecology as a young but immensely significant specimen of a postmodern science.

Ecological science, first, involves a whole *way of thinking* that is radically different from the epistemological model of modern analytical science. Ecologists need and use analysis, of course, in their methodological toolbox. They need chemical analyses, such as of complex compounds, and geophysical analyses of estuarial systems. But for the ecologist these analyses always become means to a wider end, the end of conceptual synthesis that preserves awareness of living systems in dynamic interaction. As the leading ecologist Eugene P. Odum puts it:

> . . . it is important to emphasize that findings at any one level aid in the study of another level, but never completely explain the phenomena occurring at that level. When someone is taking too narrow a view, we may remark that "he cannot see the forest for the trees." Perhaps a better way to illustrate the point is to say that to understand a tree, it is necessary to study both the forest of which it is a part as well as the cells and tissues that are part of the tree.[11]

The science of ecology does not, then, reject analysis. It incorporates and employs all the rigor of modern analytical technique, but it neither stops with analysis nor worships antiseptic analytical values. It includes and transcends analysis in a holistic way that is essential to its conceptual task. Thus ecological science becomes a model for a postmodern consciousness that is neither reductionistic nor antirational.

Second, ecological science involves a *vision of reality* that is wholly at odds with the typically sterile, alien images generated from the modern sciences. The postmodern images of reality that come from ecology portray the world as an endlessly complex network of organic and inorganic systems locked in constant interaction.[12] In each system the lesser parts—far from being the basis for all explanation—are intelligible only with reference to the larger unities in which they play a role. These unities, in addition, are themselves not merely an assemblage of parts. Some of them are entities with interests and projects of their own. They need to be "let be" so as to allow for full appreciation of their importance in their own right and not merely in terms of human needs or concerns. There are nonhuman centers of value in the ecologist's world. At the same time alienation from the matter being studied is overcome; the ecologist is personally and inevitably part of the total subject matter.[13] The excitement from the sense of being involved, from *participating* in what is of scientific interest rather than being merely the disinterested observer, places the science of ecology quite apart from other sciences in obvious ways. It is no coincidence that there has grown up around it an ecology *movement* intent on reforms for present society and zealous with the inspiration of a new consciousness. It is ludicrous but instructive to ponder what a "chemistry movement" or an "astronomy movement" might be like, and why there is no reason to expect such movements to appear. Ecological science is essentially different, in content and in style, from the modern framework methods and beliefs from which it has departed.

Third, the postmodern science of ecology involves *a set of values* that differ sharply from the manipulative and Promethean values characteristic of outlooks inspired by modern science. By contrast, the values appropriate to ecological consciousness are modest, self-limiting, and integrative. Human exploitation is not accepted uncritically as a justification for bending nature to our will. Human intervention is, of course, acknowledged as a fact—and as a necessity as long as there is to be a human race. Ecological values are not misanthropic. But neither are postmodern ecological values anthropocentric, as the controlling consciousness bred by the alienating dichotomies of modern science has tended to be. The essential values of ecological consciousness acknowledge a variety of legitimate interests, human and nonhuman, interacting in dynamic equilibrium. The world is portrayed neither as a mere resource pit to be mined nor as a sheer wilderness to be preserved, but as a complex garden to be tended, respected, harvested, and loved.

The image of the Garden, then, bids to replace the RWM of the Machine in postmodern consciousness, if holistic ecology becomes the paradigmatic science of our future. Modern attitudes and values, however, are still overwhelmingly dominant in our universities, and it may be that the most vital religious struggles of our time are occurring within the discipline of ecology itself in the fight for the soul of this science. As Donald Worster observed in his study of the history of ecology, the internal reductionist counterattack, in the name of "responsible" (modern) science, may be winning the day.

> By the 1960s, orthodox scientific thought was virtually monopolized by thermodynamics and bioeconomics. The organicists' vision of relatedness was confined to the ecosystem model of the New Ecologists, who were quite as reductive in their way as Whitehead's *bêtes noires*, the eighteenth-century *philosophes*. From most professional circles, at least, the metabiological, idealizing tendencies of organicism had been firmly exorcised: Ecology at last had got its head out of the clouds, its feet on solid ground, and its hands on something to measure.[14]

But the battle remains in flux. "It was thought that, to qualify as a field of objective knowledge, ecology could have no further dealings with the private, muddled realms of value, philosophy, and ethics. How long the discipline will remain so carefully sterilized is another matter: Organicism has a way of gaining a foothold on even the most unpromising surface."[15]

It is not for us to prejudge the outcome. If the image of the Garden, in which humanity and nature interact with balance and mutual benefit, becomes a fundamental image for our world, it will of course be easier to see how the Machine can fit—as an inorganic simplification and servant of the organic—than it is now to understand how a Garden could come to grow in the cosmic Machine. The intellectual and spiritual fruits of this reintegration of understanding with valuational intuition will be immense; the consequences for social sanity will be beyond calculation.

But if these specific hopes are dashed within the field of ecology itself, as seems possible, there is still no need to capitulate to the values of the Machine, the Particle, or the Object. Religious insight into value should not dictate what the scientist claims as fact, but the profound attractions of the Garden are not likely to die. "There is no reason for believing that this science cannot find an appropriate theoretical framework for the ethic of interdependence. If the bioeconomics of the New Ecologists cannot serve, then there are other, more useful, models of nature's economy that await discovery."[16]

Once we see the religious world modeling functions of scientific ideals for what they are and succeed in distinguishing them logically from the more limited techniques and tentative findings of science as a human enterprise, then we are freed from the painful choice between respect for science as such and regard for essential values. Modern science, in giving us the Machine, alienated us from the purposive, the responsible, and the whole; the task for postmodern science will be to let us keep the modern tools of analysis sharp in their proper role as tools and to send us back into the Garden to work with respect and caution.

PART 3

MYTHS AND MODERNITY

8.

Limits, Myths, and Morals

As we move toward an increasingly crowded twenty-first century, we are much in need of relearning an ancient lesson. It is a lesson that seems suspiciously easy to forget—namely, the basic truth that we are not gods but merely men and women; that we are mortal; that it is the human condition to dwell as finite beings in a world that has boundaries we neither made nor can escape.

This is hard news to take. There is a strong human urge to reject all limits, to push back all boundaries, to find a way around all constraints, to be in control of all situations. This urge goes deep. Perhaps it is an expression of the restless, innovative nature of life itself. We are, as biologists are sometimes fond of saying, "evolution grown conscious of itself." Without the built-in urge to transcend the given, to break through all boundaries, to overcome all difficulties, the story of life on Earth would have been very different and very dull. If we abandon adventure against obstacles, we betray life itself.

But healthy life contains and acknowledges constraints, as well. Runaway, unconstrained growth of a species spells disaster, and most species have controls of territoriality or dominance or the like to prevent it; runaway, unconstrained growth of an individual leads to the painful problem of gigantism, and our organisms normally embody homeostatic constraints to keep that misfortune from happening; finally, runaway, unconstrained growth of a tissue is another name for the tragedy of cancer. The limits, as well as the love, of growth are embedded deeply within our being as living organisms and within our psyches as conscious ones. What is called for by life itself is balance.

Balance between creativity and constraint is hard to maintain, however; it is harder yet to achieve within a culture, like our own modern industrial civilization, that has been for roughly three hundred years tilting vertiginously toward the virtues of "growth," and "progress," and "human control," while largely ignoring or disdaining the profounder limits of the human condition itself.

Even environmentalist reformers, whose larger function has been to re-awaken us to the finitude of the human condition, have sometimes not escaped our culture's tilt toward images of human control over history. Often, and with the best of motives, they approach our problems with the attitudes and assumptions of what I call "historical engineering." Among the assumptions of historical engineering are the beliefs that the mechanics of historical change are knowable to a degree permitting generally reliable prediction; that technical manipulations can harness this machinery to deliberate human purpose; and that what is needed is more behavioral engineering, more manipulation of personal choices on a massive scale, more control over the levers of public policy to bring about programmed results.

But *is* history properly conceived as such a complex machine—humanly predictable, humanly controllable at will (however wise, however benevolent the controlling human will may be)? Even the weekly weather continues to baffle and surprise, despite our best efforts at prediction. Compared to the infinitely complex web of interactions among human beings—each acting within contexts of ambitions, fears, lusts, religious fervors, innovations, inhibitions, and just plain orneriness—the ever-treacherous weather is a simple problem! To assume that human history is in principle open to human prediction and control is not only to underestimate the powers of history to deal out surprises, but also to overestimate the cognitive skill and manipulative resourcefulness of the would-be predictors and controllers of history.

The ancient Greeks had a word for such unbalancing overestimation of finite human powers: *hubris,* the overweening pride that goes before the inevitable fall arranged by slow but sure-footed Nemesis. Would-be historical engineers from Alexander to Hitler, from Napoleon to Nixon, are object lessons in hubris. All show the same excess of confidence in their own powers of manipulation and control; all show the same naiveté regarding the engineerability of the future to conform to their pet blueprints.

We of the European cultural tradition all grew up with the funny but pointed story of the Sorcerer's Apprentice—the fellow who began something he could neither control nor terminate by himself, a process that turned out to be terrifyingly different from his initial amiable plans. And the great Jewish tale of Golem, the artificial man who dominated his human creator, has been universalized and branded on the consciousness of modern times through Mary Shelley's story of nobly intentioned Dr. Frankenstein who overreached human limitations by means of science and whose Nemesis stalked monstrously through the night to repay his hubris with fear and death.

The most instructive image of all, I submit, comes from the Greeks. It is the beautifully ambivalent story of Prometheus, the Titan who sponsored the human cause against Zeus, defying the gods themselves by stealing fire so that human arts and crafts could be founded and human progress could begin. Prometheus, the patron of technology, thus became a culture hero not only for ancient Greece but also for our progressive, industrial civilization. Wherever boundlessness is celebrated, wherever defiance of limits is preached, there the Promethean spirit is invoked. But in the original Greek myth, we recall, the hubris of Prometheus was punished cruelly by Zeus, who bound him to a rock for thirty thousand years (until finally released, with divine permission, by Heracles), during which time an eagle would devour his liver each day, an equal amount of liver being regenerated each night.

The Prometheus myth is instructive because it embodies the legitimate protest of life against arbitrary constraints. It rejoices in the creative powers. It celebrates human craft. But at the same time it vividly recognizes the painful penalties for overreaching. It is this latter side of the well-balanced myth that we (who, with the poet Shelley, prefer to imagine Prometheus unbound) need to recover. The Promethean spirit has been left unbound too long in our modern industrial civilization, and the footsteps of Nemesis are drawing near.

ALTERNATIVE HEROES

What, then, shall our responses be to this turbulent moment in history? If it is given the human lot to be able to discern possible dangers ahead but not to be in a position to engineer controlled historical solutions, what posture shall we, individually, take toward all this? What attitudes and actions are appropriate and responsible for those in the Northern nations on this globe during the present transition to the twenty-first century?

One flippant response is summarized in a cartoon showing two enormous dinosaurs munching weeds in a Jurassic swamp; one brontosaurus is saying to the other: "I say, eat, drink, and be merry, for tomorrow we will be listed under 'extinct' in the *Encyclopedia Britannica.*" This theme is certainly not one we can ignore. The temptations to self-indulgence are obvious. They are grounded in us at an instinctual level and are fed by the vast advertising economy in which we are all submerged. If to this we add the sense of hopelessness that may be one reaction to the truth that we cannot determine our destiny at will, the slide into hedonism is an easy one.

At another stormy period, in Hellenistic times, the followers of Epicurus took consolation in the immediate gratifications. Hedonism need not be grossly piggish. Original Epicureanism, indeed, was refined and moderate. It was a dignified retreat from the world of affairs into the garden of sensual pleasures, the fundamental aim being the avoidance of pain. (Epicurus' own paradigm of highest pleasure was a good digestion, of which, when it is working at its best, one is not aware at all.) Epicureanism was frankly selfish, though the circle of selfish interests was wide enough to include the more mutual pleasures of friendship among a few selected persons.

One criticism of the Northern version of the "eat, drink, and be merry" response, then, might be that it is not sufficiently Epicurean in quality. We tend to be Gargantuan rather than Epicurean. Our ideal of selfish pleasure leads to "more, more!" and "faster, faster!" and thus to constant need for Alka Seltzer to help us become unaware of our digestion, again. Epicurus would be appalled at the pain we create for ourselves in our frantic pursuit of pleasure. He would, I am afraid, think us not very bright hedonists, more the captive dupes of the capitalist production-line who are required to "get in there and consume" dutifully for the sake of someone else's profit. A wise hedonism would stop at sufficiency, would remain close to simple satisfactions of natural needs, and would never allow pain-causing artificial desire to be trumped up for ulterior motives.

Therefore, if hedonism is our response, I hope that it is at least of the wise variety. What a difference it would make in our world if Northern peoples, in growing numbers, were to become intelligently Epicurean in taste, attitude, and habit! No more consumer-slaves but free to enjoy simple, basic pleasures, such people would eat more wisely, lower on the food chain, and would waste less in a hungry world; they would diminish the market for such things as snowmobiles, distilled beverages (wine, in moderation, Epicurus found quite natural, but seven-to-one martinis would surely not qualify!), antacids, and handguns; they would not patronize the soul-torturing ugliness of Big Mac America or fling rubbish where they might be insulted by it again. A private, selfish retreat by many persons to intelligent hedonism would have beneficent public consequences. We could do worse — generally we *are* doing worse — than to follow, individually, the counsel of Epicurus.

But can we not do better? The trouble with Epicureanism is that it is such a fragile, vulnerable, introverted way of life. It depends on relative political stability and on an economic status quo in which the epicure has a somewhat comfortable and protected position. When the garden walls come tumbling down, the Epicurean is totally exposed. And even the *fear* of future collapse is enough to make Epicurean peace of mind a vain quest. It is hard to be a successful Epicurean today and still be aware of the world. The great multiplying masses of hungry humanity, even if one stifles all pain of compassion, pose a threat to selfish garden life, especially now that nuclear, chemical, and biological weapons are spreading into the hands of the desperate. The possibilities of economic catastrophe continue to loom on our horizon, how near or far being subjected to anxiety-producing debate.

Epicureanism seems unsuited to the times, after all. It is too passive: It leaves the painful work of political engagement to others, though it depends for its stability on the political outcome. It is too effete: It lives as a parasite on the system that supports its comforts. And in its gross form, as Northern Gargantuanism, hedonism is the quickest way to ensure collapse. The mindless squandering of energy and resources is suicidal. Obsessively eating and drinking oneself to death may at times look like fun, but it is rooted in despair. Hedonism begins in hopelessness and ends by verifying its own cynical expectations.

Another, better, alternative for individuals who recognize both the facts of our world and the finitude of human powers to design history according to plan, is the stolid determination to maintain personal dignity and virtue, come what may. What matters, on this response, is not what happens in the future so much as how we relate to any happening. As long as we keep our heads, as long as we maintain our humanity, the uncontrollable winds of history may bluster as they will without blowing in the worst. The worst would be not great suffering nor even the finally unavoidable end of the race itself; the worst would be the gradual succumbing of human beings to bestiality, to connivance with the corruption of what gives meaning to being human.

I was startled, once, to hear a learned speaker end his strong argument for the probability of imminent social collapse with the remark that, of course, such collapse was really not a problem.

"Not a problem?" I blurted.

No, he explained: *Problems* are defined as difficulties one can do something about, for which there are, in principle, "solutions." But some unpleasant states of affairs, like aging, belong to the class of difficulties we can do nothing about. The most we can do, and the best we can do, is to arrange our own spirits to meet them, when they come, with poise and dignity and sympathy and, if possible, a little humor. Historical times of trouble are like that, he continued. We need to resign ourselves and prepare to defend our humanity as best we can.

Such a personal response to troubled times has a lineage no less ancient than Epicureanism. Already in Hellenistic times the Stoics were staunch rivals of those who would sink into hedonism as the answer to their historical difficulties. Not escapist pleasure but firm duty, was and is Stoicism's watchword. The main point is not whether one succeeds in achieving one's hopes but whether one has tried to do the right thing. The historical outcome of one's efforts is always beyond one's control; and anything beyond one's control is not a proper object of concern, according to Stoicism. Therefore Stoicism (unlike Epicureanism) is capable of being a highly political philosophy, supporting one's engagement in the world of affairs (since duty must be attempted) but discounting in advance the pain of losing. The pain is not unreal of course, but it is unimportant for the virtuous person. Human solidarity is based on common rationality and common duty, not on sympathy, and the key to duty is endurance.

This is a possible philosophy for each of us. Besides its accent on personal nobility, the Stoic attitude would bring noteworthy public benefits to Northern life if large numbers were to live it. High among them is the spur it would give us to rise above the atomism of selfish interests and the pettiness of myopic pleasure seeking, for the sake of facing our enormous historical challenges with farsighted rationality and calmness of purpose. Robert L. Heilbroner calls for Stoic attitudes in *An Inquiry into the Human Prospect*, as he contrasts the dangerous mood of frustrated Promethean man with what is needed for our general survival. He puts the problem vividly:

> When men can generally acquiesce in, even relish, the destruction of their living contemporaries, when they can regard with indifference or irritation the fate of those who live in slums, rot in prison, or starve in lands that have meaning only insofar as they are vacation resorts, why should they be expected to take the painful actions needed to prevent the destruction of future generations whose faces they will never live to see? Worse yet, will they not curse these future generations whose claims to life can be honored only by sacrificing present enjoyments; and will they not, if it comes to a choice, condemn them to nonexistence by choosing the present over the future?[1]

And in his answer Heilbroner calls on another mythic figure to help turn attitudes toward the Stoic virtues and away from our species' destruction.

> At this last moment of reflection another figure from Greek Mythology comes to mind. It is that of Atlas, bearing with endless perseverance the weight of the heavens in his hands. If mankind is to rescue life, it must first preserve the very will to live, and thereby rescue the future from the angry condemnation of the present. The spirit of conquest and aspiration will not provide the inspiration it needs for this task. It is the example of Atlas, resolutely bearing his burden, that provides the strength we seek. If, within us, the spirit of Atlas falters, there perishes determination to preserve humanity at all cost and any cost, forever.
>
> But Atlas is, of course, no other but ourselves. Myths have their magic power because they cast on the screen of our imaginations, like the figures of the heavenly constellations, immense projections of our own hopes and capabilities. We do not know with certainty that humanity will survive, but it is a comfort to know that there exist within us the elements of fortitude and will from which the image of Atlas springs.[2]

We are capable of being Atlas-like, I agree, no less than of aping Prometheus. Stoicism remains a human possibility, though our culture has not done much to cultivate the spirit of Atlas in our recent past. But it is interesting to note that the ancient Greeks did not let Prometheus and Atlas stand in isolation. Both Titans were the sons of Iapetus, uncle of Zeus. Atlas and Prometheus, it turns out, are themselves linked by the closest of fraternal bonds. Polar opposites, as we have been seeing them until now, they yet belong together in whatever larger picture we finally achieve.

And this is as it should be. Stoicism is a noble personal posture, but surely it lacks something, even as a response to crisis. It is cold and stern, though human life also needs warmth and tenderness. It is solid, but it is not creative. It is universal, though sometimes we need to be very particular. Can we shape an individual response to destiny that somehow combines Stoic virtues with something fuller, freer, more zestful? Neither historical engineer nor despairing cynic will meet our standard; neither arrogant Prometheus nor stolid Atlas alone will satisfy our need. How shall we come to terms with the urgent demands of life? What myths may we live by healthily, into the uncertain future?

IMAGES FOR LIFE

I hope it is not necessary to belabor my central thesis of how vital—on public as well as private grounds—are the myths we live by. A myth, as I am using the term, is a story or an image reflecting the way things ultimately are, and incorporating or illustrating fundamental values. Their "magic power," as Heilbroner puts it, rests in their ability to focus primary aspirations, evoke deep response, represent ultimate beliefs. We all are influenced by myths, although we are not critically aware of the mythic images at work in our lives. Every culture has its stock of myths, and sometimes we are simply drawn by our culture into the images that define the basic values and beliefs of that culture.

In our scientific-industrial culture, the images of everlasting growth and progress have served a mythic function. Progressive science, seen as constantly bettering itself in its never-ending quest after total truth, has been the mythic matrix, the fundamental generator, of distinctively modern consciousness. Progressive technology, science-fed, has promised endless material improvement to match the upward march of science. Growth, betterment, and advance at every level—material, cognitive, moral, social— have literally been invested with theological significance as the myths of scientific-industrial society gradually replaced (as living religion) the once potent myths of Christendom. Thus when thinkers like Thomas Kuhn[3] challenge the progressive interpretation of the history of science (which most of us never thought of as an "interpretation" at all, so deeply were we caught up in our culture's imagery), and when analysts such as Dennis and Donella Meadows[4] cry halt to the technological progress-machines shared by capitalist and socialist societies alike (exposing a shared myth deeper than the lesser images that divide technological-industrial societies from one another), the horrified reaction is not merely based on disagreement with arguments presented but, much deeper, is rooted in religious revulsion against blasphemy. Apostasy, heresy, breaking the common faith is always an immensely traumatic matter—a matter for anathemas and anger as well as outraged rebuttals.

This happens because the issues are not over private faith alone, though individuals do find their personal frameworks of meaning threatened when their own implicit mythic imagery is called in doubt and sometimes strike back defensively; the issues of myth and cultural meaning have, as well, the most profound bearing on social decisions that must be made cooperatively if there is to be a society at all. Think of the many ways in which the fundamental images of progress and growth—with their particular manifestations in myths of the "endless frontier," myths of "Manifest Destiny," myths of civilization's ultimate imperative to replace the "savage" Indian, myths of the "invisible hand" of economic providence, and more—have been manifested in this nation's political, economic, and military policy.

Policy rests on perceived meaning, that is, on the union of factual circumstance (as it is able to be seen through the filtering framework of fundamental belief) together with ultimate values (as these are transmuted and particularized into preferences and attitudes). The basic shared myths of a society, therefore, as the sources of common meaning, give rise to the possibility of cooperative policy and thus to the possibility of society itself. The myths we live by are manifested not merely at the level of particular *decisions* (e.g., shall we break this or that treaty with this or that tribe?) but at the level of the fundamental economic, political, and technological *structures* (e.g., shall we have a market system that treats labor as a commodity; that equates "demand" with purchasing power?) through which any particular decisions are made. Nothing, therefore, can be of greater importance to a society than the nature and the quality of the ultimate springs of meaning and motivation that inform the lives of its people. Our myths matter. They are, indeed, the very standard of all else that matters.

Thus if our myths have been one-sidedly Promethean, with correspondingly unbridled economic structures, political appetites, and technological goals; and if the hubris of our Prometheanism has now brought us close to the point at which Nemesis awaits our whole civilization; then we have not our stars to blame, but our myths—or, more precisely, the values that our expansionist myths have supported and celebrated at the expense of the ravaged earth and of our exploited fellow humans. And if there is to be a reversal in our reckless course, it will be because individuals in sufficient numbers have learned new values reinforced by different myths.

These new values are, or should be, already plain to see. They are not, of course, really "new" values. They are the values implicit in healthy organic life: life that is in balance with itself and in harmony with its larger environment. I see these as reducing, at root, to three great principles.

The first is the value of *creativity* in life. It is the original inventive drive that energizes life from adventure to new adventure. In us it finds zest in risk and joy in accomplishment. It is the titanic force symbolized in Iapetus' son Prometheus, who stands for something precious as well as dangerous in full human existence.

The second great principle is dialectically opposed to the first, presupposing it but restraining it. It is the value of *homeostasis* in life. This recalls the presence of boundaries and limits within life, conditions for healthy balance that cannot be evaded. It is the equally titanic force we have symbolized by Iapetus' other son, Atlas, whose patient endurance serves as model and inspiration for the values of perseverance despite limits, the strength involved in maintaining dynamic balance.

The third great principle stresses the value of *holism* in life. Holism is the drawing together of differentiated parts into larger unities of interdependence. It is the principle of mutuality within difference. Every healthy organism has differentiated parts that work together, not despite but because of their differences, for the good of the organism as a whole. Complex, multicellular organisms like ourselves are vast symphonic arrangements of larger and larger mutualities of differentiated parts. We need those differences, but all such differences must also be held creatively together in the service of higher unity. Here the titanic forces of creativity and homeostasis come together in a dynamic fraternal bond that must not be broken. Prometheus and Atlas are brothers, and it is precisely in their brotherhood that holism finds its symbol. Prometheus, as creativity, reinforces the values of life's impetuous vigor; Atlas, as homeostasis, reminds us of the values of restraint; together, differentiated as they are, they undergird the values of holism in the service of new creativity.

These are the values our new world requires. They are the values of organicism, rooted in the requirements of life itself. Not surprisingly, such values may be found symbolized in many great myths of many cultures. If we seek alternatives to correct the imbalance of our scientific-industrial culture's one-sided worship of Prometheus and progress, there are numbers of images to which we may turn. Buddhist imagery, for example, deeply reinforces the vision of holism: harmony and restraint are enjoined not only within oneself but also among oneself, others, and nature. As a "middle way" between indulgence and ascetic denial, Buddhism has a place for the creative values of joy and zest in living, as well as harmony and restraint, though it supports much less of the Promethean spirit than global Northerners are accustomed to expect. Perhaps Buddhism, then, would make a good antidote for our failed progressivism. Many are finding this path. Perhaps many more will follow it in the days ahead.

We need not, however, leave our own culture and religious heritage to find mythic images capable of reinforcing the organismic values. Judaism and Christianity, though compromised by long association with and infiltration by exploitative attitudes, offer motivating imagery which reinforces the needed balancing values of homeostasis and holism. In chapter 15, "Remything Judaism and Christianity," I shall return to this possibility in some serious detail.

Other great myths may serve, also, to shape organismic consciousness for a new society suited to a better future. I personally find much inspiration in the two gods of Delphi, Apollo and Dionysus, who represent the dialectic between lucid order, on the one hand, with its calm boundaries and balances, and creative frenzy, on the other, with its own intoxicated joys. I am impressed at the need they had, and still have, for one another, and at the genius of the Greeks in alternating, at the same sanctuary in different months each year, the sublime paean of Apollo with the excited dithyramb of Dionysus. Others may be struck by yet other images: perhaps by the gentle, shamanistic vision of the world and humankind, all bound together in strands of cosmic meaning, derived from Native American lore; or perhaps by others neither old nor yet visible today, but on the way to consciousness.

What this amounts to for individuals, aware of this historical moment with all its uncontrollable uncertainty but at the same time earnestly concerned to shape our own attitudes and policies as wisely as we can, is the possibility of responsible pluralism of mythic expressions within a larger framework of life-centered organismic values. Pluralism is not only permissible, given the larger organismic framework, but it is also liberating, a needed alternative to the stultifying spirit of dogmatism that tends to confuse our limited representations of ultimate reality with ultimate reality itself.

Any image, by its very nature, defines and limits. Unless alternative images are available to show alternative ways of representing ultimate reality, a natural tendency is to suppose that one's own favorite myth exhausts what can be said, sensed, and felt about the real — to the impoverishment of one's deepest thought and experience. We need not fear or fight pluralism among organismic myths, then; we may welcome the vividness and excitement that multimythic consciousness allows. As I shall try to show in part 4, below, Multi-mythic Organicism will be suited to the age of pluralistic transition we sense ahead.

But the range of legitimate pluralism, though broad, is not unlimited. Multi-mythic Organicism is not to be confused with lazy relativism. Not all values, not all policies of life, are equally healthy. Beneath the multiplicity of possible representations remain the principles of creativity, homeostasis, and holism. This means that if you, in shaping your individual life, are drawn to Epicureanism, you should at least be a wise Epicurean. Learn the meaning of natural sufficiency (e.g., give up junk foods); avoid policies of life that only add to your eventual displeasure by fouling the nest in which you live (e.g., insist on returnable bottles); forestall later pain by paying early attention to the miserable who otherwise will one day shatter your tranquility.

If, on the other hand, you are inspired by Stoic firmness, spice your endurance with more zest. Risk a little frivolity; learn to dance or play the flute; if electricity someday becomes too expensive to use for running your stereo, don't just endure the loss, make your own music. Let the creativity of life manifest its inventiveness through you, even in tough times.

If Prometheus is your hero, add Atlas to your Pantheon; if Atlas attracts you, remember Prometheus. If you are a Christian, let potent New Testament images spur your concern for holism to the point of acting concretely out of love rather than worldly self-interest. If you are a Jew, expand the meaning of observance in your behavior to its full prophetic significance. And if your answers are still "blowin' in the wind," remember at least the values of life itself and shape your individual destiny, whatever your myths may finally be, by them.

One final thought: I have been emphasizing the personal responses each of us can (and unavoidably must) make to the historical moment. In one sense this is for each of us the bottom line. Responsibly shaping the most fundamental policies and attitudes of one's own life is the most basic and most important thing any one of us can do. But in another sense, hinted at before, there is still another level at which our bottom-line decisions may merge with those of others, and still others—friends and neighbors and far-flung strangers weaving, with their individual decisions, a strengthening web of societal commitments to constructive, life-supporting values.

Human destiny, at large, is surely not under human control. Even an individual's life-career is not, properly speaking, fully "controllable." But we do have it in our power, through the human gift of awareness, to influence our individual destinies. We can, within limits, determine whom we shall be by choosing what values we shall live by. And in so doing we shall not only be shaping our individual lives but also, to the extent that each of us constitutes a significant part of our society and our world, we shall be shaping the destiny of our civilization and of the human race.

9.

Myths and Hope for Global Society

The previous chapter was premised on the view that scarcity, learning to live with limits, facing the moral dilemmas of distribution in a wanting world, are an unavoidable part of our future, just as they have been for most people for the whole of human history. This will be the governing assumption of this chapter, as well.

With this assumption made, what then? What policies shall we adopt? What attitudes shall we cultivate? Shall we continue business as usual, with the foreboding sense that this way is likely to lead to slow or sudden catastrophe, but without hope that anything much can be done to avert our fate? This is one important—perhaps dominant—tendency today. It rests on a sense of helplessness before the larger forces of nature, human inertia, and history. It seems in 1988 to have been reflected in the "business as usual" vote for President Ronald Reagan's anointed successor. If this is our society's answer, and if Americans and others of the global North continue to temporize and evade hard choices, it may be too late for significant changes when they are finally seen as necessary.

Or, second, should the relatively prosperous nations prepare for scarcity in the world at large by looking to their own defenses: that is, by building a fortress North capable of insulating themselves from the plight of the South? This is another significant—and perhaps growing—line of thinking. It urges steps that would make the wealthy nations as self-sufficient as possible and cultivates attitudes that would support the remorseless task of letting the rest of the world fend for itself, even if this meant exercising "triage"—on the battlefield, an analogy that valuable resources should not be wasted on the hopelessly wounded—and letting whole nations perish of starvation and disease. If this is Northern society's answer, those who live there will have to replace humanitarian concerns with unflinching collective callousness and take unprecedented steps to organize to withstand siege by whatever means are necessary, probably in the process replacing familiar democratic forms of government with authoritarian leadership capable of such iron control.

Or, third, shall the North attempt to meet scarcity by sharing the burden, appealing to common humanity, and making more resources available to the desperately poor (while simultaneously assisting with long-term solutions to population and resource problems in the South) by adopting voluntary measures of restraint in consumption by the relatively wealthy? This is a rational way that would accord with basic moral sensibilities. It would react to reality vigorously while there is time. It would redirect vast resources otherwise needed for repression and defense efforts (efforts of doubtful efficacy in a world of proliferating nuclear means of terror and extortion) in order to manage cooperatively our common human problem. But is this third alternative, though incomparably more desirable, even worth discussion? Is it *possible* in principle? Can we hope for it without self-delusion? Are serious efforts toward such policies doomed from the outset by the nature of the physical world or human nature or the processes controlling human history?

Here, in answering these basic questions, is the point at which our most fundamental beliefs—or deeper, our preintellectual visions of how things are—become beyond all other matters urgent and practical. Here is where our mythic images of nature, of humanity, and of history shape the choices that together shape the future of our world. This is a time, therefore, for maximum attention to clarity about the mythic sources of our own motivations.

MYTHS OF NATURE

What is physical and biological nature really like? What sort of environment do we ultimately find ourselves in as we plan for the future? Our basic vision of the natural order will greatly influence our attitudes and our enterprises.

One image we find familiar is that of nature as Lady Bountiful, overflowing with gifts and pliant to every demand. It is a romantic vision of boundless possibility that supports, as well, the myth of the endless frontier. It is the nature of James Fenimore Cooper, abounding in beauty and in plentiful fish, game, and birds of all sorts. It is the cornucopia, the treasure house where "only man is vile." It is the mythic idyll of the Swiss Family Robinson.

Unfortunately, it is an image of nature that has not been able to survive the hard realities of other times and wider places. It was a specialized vision, suited to a narrow range of human experience. It left out the struggle for survival, the exhausting pain of battle with the elements, the grudging ingratitude of rocky hill and parched plain. It was a myth that failed because it saw nature with only one eye. It was therefore incapable of interpreting the full phenomenon, however much it might appeal.

In its place we have come to recognize a very different face of nature.

It wears the expression of implacable hostility, both biological and physical. On the biological level it is symbolized by the unremitting conflict of species, "red in tooth and claw," for survival in a world where teeming populations must always be held in check by merciless limitations on the means of life. On the yet more basic level of physics, nature is seen as indifferent—worse, ultimately hostile—to all of humanity's values and ambitions. On what might be called the Myth of Implacable Decay, the Second Law of Thermodynamics dooms all structures to inevitable dissolution in the "heat death" of the universe. As Bertrand Russell put it poignantly just after the turn of this century:

> That Man is the product of causes which had no prevision of the end they were achieving; that his origin, his growth, his hopes and fears, his loves and his beliefs, are but the outcome of accidental collocations of atoms; that no fire, no heroism, no intensity of thought and feeling, can preserve an individual life beyond the grave; that all the labours of the ages, all the devotion, all the noonday brightness of human genius, are destined to extinction in the vast death of the solar system, and that the whole temple of Man's achievements must inevitably be buried beneath the debris of a universe in ruins—all these things, if not quite beyond dispute, are yet so nearly certain, that no philosophy which rejects them can hope to stand. Only within the scaffolding of these truths, only on the firm foundation of unyielding despair, can the soul's habitation henceforth be safely built.[1]

Such a vision of the natural order, as Russell was quick to claim, is strengthened in a science-oriented society by being offered with the credentials and thus the authority of the sciences themselves. It is presented (and often taken) as nonmythological, as simply the "nearly certain" results of objective, responsible, and dispassionate thinking.

This is an easy mistake, but a serious one. It is a mistake, in the first place, because it neglects the logic of scientific assertion. All scientific laws, including even major laws like the laws of thermodynamics, insofar as they are being used scientifically, are relevant to a specific range of application. It is always speculative and risky to assume the extension of that range of application beyond the available evidence. It may be the case that the Second Law of Thermodynamics, whose scientifically warranted range of application is to ideal closed thermal systems, is also applicable to the universe as a whole; but, again, it very well may not be. Is the universe a closed thermal system? Are we sure that there are no sources of fresh energy? If we knew the answer to these questions, which would be a necessary condition for the applicability of the Second Law, we would know far more about the origin and nature of the physical universe than we can yet claim.

And even if we knew, or were "nearly certain," that the universe is finite and thermally closed, within the relevant meaning required by the Second Law, we would still not have the sufficient condition for automatically extending this Law's range of scientific application to include the universe as a whole. There is something logically odd about talk concerning "the universe as a whole" when uttered by scientists aiming at verifiable knowledge, since only particular and local observations are in principle capable of supporting or confuting their claims. At some point the vague boundary between highly general scientific theorizing and completely inclusive metaphysical speculation has been crossed. No one should deny scientists the right to metaphysical speculation, of course. As we saw in chapter 5, it is a natural extension of the legitimate urge to theoretical completeness, and it provides a needed context for the more specific explanations and understandings of the empirical sciences; but it must not be confused with the findings of those sciences themselves. As a metaphysical vision of the nature of the physical universe, Russell's theory should be given due respect, along with the other metaphysical alternatives with which it is in competition; but it has no logical right to coerce our assent with the enormous authority of experimental physics itself.

Taking Russell's vision of the universe as a "nearly certain" scientific image is a mistake, further, because, like the Lady Bountiful myth of nature, it offers only a one-eyed view that leaves much important data out of account. These data, on the level of physics, include the remarkable facts of the existence and evolution of life itself. In some regions of the universe, at any rate, and under some conditions, it is evident that the physical universe does not merely run downhill either in complexity or in levels of available energy. Somehow, outside the conventional range of applicability of the Second Law of Thermodynamics, parts of the world have become more organized, have devised ways of capturing and storing higher levels of energy. Somehow life has arisen, spread, and transformed the face of the earth. Looked at without the theoretical biases imposed by the Myth of Implacable Decay, we might say that there is somewhere in the universe an antientropic agency. Our conventional theories, as Whitehead says, "have omitted some general counter-agency."[2] We know this agency only by its undeniable effects: by the evolution of life and by the existence of physical order. But even though only indirectly known, Whitehead goes on to note, the need to postulate some such upward trend in the universe is clear:

> The universe, as construed solely in terms of the efficient causation of purely physical interconnections, presents a sheer, insoluble contradiction. The orthodox doctrine . . . demands that the operations of living bodies be explained solely in terms of the physical system of physical categories. This system within its own province, when confronted with the empirical facts, fails to include these facts apart from an act of logical suicide. The moral to be drawn . . . is that we have

omitted some general counter-agency. This counter-agency in its operation throughout the physical universe is too vast and diffusive for
our direct observation. We may acquire such power as the result of
some advance. But at present, as we survey the physical cosmos, there
is no direct intuition of the counter-agency to which it owes its possibility of existence as a wasting finite [system].[3]

Moving back to the level of the biological data, then, the image of Nature
Red in Tooth and Claw, like the Myth of Implacable Decay, though focusing on much that is accurate, omits large domains that are also important
for a fully balanced view. Cooperation as well as competition is a fact of
life. Symbiosis and even self-sacrifice are part of the living universe, too. A
vision of biological nature that ignores these aspects is no more adequate
than the rose-tinted romantic portrait that omits the reality of struggle. But
all this is obvious, once stated; it does not need long argument. Whence
then the powerful hold of images of cruelty and decay? Why should large
numbers of our contemporaries choose to look at nature through the single
lens of alien, implacable power?

Perhaps they do not "choose." Perhaps, in the end, the images of Russell
or of the metaphysical Darwinians on the universe should not be confused
with the relatively dispassionate deliverances of science because these
images function, ironically, to satisfy deep emotional yearnings in those
who are grasped by them. It may seem paradoxical that affirming the need
for "unyielding despair" could be done for emotional need, but the paradox
is not hard to resolve. There are powerful satisfactions in donning the
emotional armor (and displaying the image) of stern courage in the face of
the implacable foe. Similarly, the picture of oneself (and one's species) as
representing unique value in an otherwise alien and inhuman world is radically reinforcing to self-esteem. Again, even in the vision of the destruction
of all things there is the subtle relish for the apocalypse that Richard Rubenstein so effectively warns us to notice in ourselves.[4] And, not least, there
is the sneaking satisfaction one gets from announcing bad news to others,
when one has prepared oneself to "take it" and to feel morally superior
thereby, while the others suffer and scramble in vain for comfort.

These and other motives may help explain why images of bleak despair
have such attraction despite their very partial cognitive success in representing all that is important about nature. They are properly to be understood as functioning myths. They represent a way of perceiving, feeling,
thinking, and acting in reference to the universe. They underscore certain
values and deemphasize others. They are not required by pure, dispassionate intelligence but are adopted from many motives. They are negative, in
many ways, but not unsatisfying to the fashionable modern mood of anger,
betrayal, and despair. They elevate despair to among the highest virtues,
in fact, and undergird a cult of alienation that befits the ending of an
overconfident age.

If our task, however, is to remain critically alert to the underlying images that shape our attitudes and policies toward nature, we shall reserve judgment. The fundamental facts are much more complex than either Lady Bountiful or Lord Despair alone can handle. Nature presents us with mixed data. On the one hand, there is in nature an immense plasticity to purpose. Human intelligence has proven capable of penetrating many of nature's secrets (though how many more secrets remain continues to be a mystery), and human invention has given civilization the key to many of nature's treasure rooms. Our plans and hopes are by no means always unrequited. But, on the other hand, nature imposes on human purpose the rigors of responsibility. Not every purpose wins assent. If a student pilot really wants to learn the freedom of flight, he or she must learn natural limits and obey nonarbitrary rules. The alternative is a crash. And, to broaden the metaphor, so it is with civilization. Nature is plastic to purpose, but only within bounds not set by convention. Why should this be? Why should nature offer both promises of plenty and threats against excess? If there is a counteragency that lures the natural world toward an upward way, can humanity identify it and coordinate civilized purpose with cosmic construction? We need adequate myths of nature to shape our consciousness of how much ought to be attempted and how much human purpose should be restrained. Only in such a balanced vision, neither naively optimistic nor prematurely despairing, can reasonable hope and wise policy be grounded.

MYTHS OF HUMANITY

The responsiveness or recalcitrance of physical nature to our purposes is one fundamental issue on which our hopes for a constructive new era depend, but what about our purposes themselves? How shall we think, feel, and plan about human nature? All our policies must be grounded in some estimate — explicit or implicit — of what human beings are basically like and what they (or we) are likely to do. If we are to support wise policies we had better be clear on the major alternatives concerning human nature and about their major practical implications.

The quest for definition of human nature is notoriously difficult,[5] but images abound to guide our attitudes and expectations. One of these is the image of the Noble Savage: Men and women are basically good, beneath the superficial corruptions of social custom; if left to themselves they will act with generosity, reason, and restraint. Policy based on such an image of human nature would recommend trusting human decency in times of scarcity, especially if the distorting (competition-generating) structures of modern industrial civilization are husked away and people are left to meet and deal with other people on human-to-human terms. The ecologically sensitive, wise, generous, and trustworthy example of American Indian culture is often cited to support such an image of human nature.[6] The wisdom of the shaman is offered for our guidance.

The counter to this optimistic image of human nature might be given in another image. A generation ago William Golding's gripping and horrific picture of raw human nature in *The Lord of the Flies* was the one regularly referred to; now it is likely to be the nonfictional account of the African tribe called Ik.[7] These people, having been dislocated and dispossessed, seem to have lost all traces of sympathy, mutuality, or concern. Even a mother laughs uproariously at the sight of her baby rolling helplessly into the campfire; merriment is general when an old blind person, groping her way along a cliffside path, stumbles and falls headlong into the precipice. No thought is given to helping. On the contrary, lying and stealing are standard behavior; betrayal of the most intimate relationships is a way of life. Laughter and other symptoms of delight are the spontaneous responses to the pain of others.

The Ik image of human nature will be a potent and disturbing one. But is it basic? Is that "how human beings really are" at the depths? A currently widespread view of human nature would answer in the affirmative. This neo-Hobbesian view—that people are essentially and inevitably selfish but marginally capable of calculating their best interest—might welcome the image of the Ik as a warning of what bestiality threatens in the dreaded "state of nature." To avoid such a state, practically any political arrangement is warranted, and the stronger the better. The ruler on horseback will impose peace on the latently warring individuals within the body politic; the tough-minded garrison state created will defend the frankly selfish interests of its members against the universal covetousness of the rest of the world. Robert Heilbroner sees the prospects pointing to the need for "authoritarian" government to deal with the internal changes necessary in our society as we enter the parsimonious future. And Garrett Hardin advocates a national "lifeboat ethic" in which we fend off by any means necessary the desperate hordes who would, if they could, climb aboard our adequately supplied but finite craft, sinking us all in the end.[8]

These policy suggestions are logically consistent with the view of human nature that suggests them. If human beings are not capable of sharing their shortages voluntarily, and if society requires it, they must be forced. If the irrational nature of humanity prevents the creation of new modes of international cooperation, such as is urged in Mesarovic and Pestel's thoughtful study of the alternatives,[9] then we must expect (despite all its demonstrable disadvantages) a world of garrison states engaged in perpetual Hobbesian war with one another in a climate of increasing desperation. We may not like these prospects; we may honestly deplore them; but if human nature is capable of no more, then we must remember the Ik and expect the worst.

How cognitively compelling, though, is this image of humanity? Must we take the Ik as our symbol for ourselves and our neighbors? Is the neo-Hobbesian myth of humanity sufficiently adequate to ground our expectations and therefore our preparations for the future? If the data were uniform, it would be easier to agree, but it is far from uniform. Like physical and biological nature, human nature offers us an enormously mixed selection of evidence. The Ik exist, but so do the gentle Hopi, among whom benevolence and honor are practiced and selfish competitiveness, even in language, is discouraged. Crime exists, but so does heroism. There are cheating scandals, but there is enough trustworthiness in human beings to make honor systems possible and to make instances of cheating on them widely perceived as scandalous. There was the Beast of Belsen as there are many bestial torturers in the world today, but there were also those who even in the most extreme conditions of deprivation in the concentration camps maintained a noble dignity and shared their final crusts of bread. The amazingly positive images woven through Viktor Frankl's *From Death Camp to Existentialism*[10] are as vivid and important philosophically as the horrible ones from Richard Rubenstein's *After Auschwitz.*[11]

The evidence is far too mixed to allow ourselves — if we are attempting to remain alert to the importance of our basic images of human nature — to rest our policies on simple optimistic or pessimistic alternatives. Humanity is still a mystery to humans. There is in us a tendency to rebellion, destruction, and self-centeredness; there is also a capacity for sacrifice, cooperation, and creativity. Our policies for the future will be one-eyed and treacherous if we discount either aspect of our nature. As the Harvard psychiatrist Robert Coles comments on the deeper significance of the Ik:

> I am a psychiatrist, trained to be wary, if not downright suspicious, of people and their motives. Yet as I read this account of the Ik I saw them a people grimly, wretchedly, devastatingly debased, not as rock-bottom examples of what we all are at least trying to be: affectionate toward others as well as self-regarding, generous as well as greedy, reflective as well as driven or impulsive.[12]

Such a balanced vision of human nature would be well understood on Whitehead's theory of the person. On the one hand, all human persons are tremendously complex societies of societies bound together in organic unity. The "ruling occasion" at any given moment of personal experience enjoys the blended and amplified achievements of harmony and contrast that rise from the whole body and brain, and those in turn gain their specific content by drawing from the larger environment. Subjective satisfaction is the goal of everyone's subjective aim. On the other hand, persons are no less affirmed by Whitehead to be "superject" as well as "subject." There is a tendency to press beyond present satisfaction, both toward future, successor occasions in the life of the same person and toward the larger environment to which the subject makes a contribution. "The stubborn reality of the absolute self-attainment of each individual is bound up with a relativity which it issues from and issues into."[13] In this tendency lies the possibility of ethical impartiality, heroism, and finally "peace."[14]

Much depends, finally, on the quality of the images to which we give our consent. We are free to assess our imagery consciously and critically. We need not be trapped unaware into living with partially misleading myths about ourselves and our prospects.

MYTHS OF HISTORY

The interaction of physical nature and human purpose gives rise to history. As we stand, today, at a significant turning point in our civilization, wondering about alternative scenarios for our future, our basic theories about what really influences history become critical. All our thinking about historical probability, and subsequently about our own personal preparations for the future, depends upon our deepest hunches about what causes are at work around us. Myths of nature and myths of humanity both come importantly into play here, but incorporating both and adding a new dimension to them are also myths of history itself.

This is not the place to deal with even a fair sampling of the many views of history that might be influencing our preparations for life in a postmodern world. But it is easy to identify some of the principal contenders. One is the voluntarist theory of history in which it is deeply felt that human will should be depended upon to rise to any occasion. Some voluntarists[15] believe that history is primarily shaped by great persons, arising in response to historical need, whose will, intelligence, and personality turn the tide for all the rest. Others, instead, trust the rational will of the ordinary people to do the right and sensible thing, when required. Leaders, in this view, are really reflecting and focusing the common will rather than initiating major happenings. Still others, also voluntarists, envision the directions of history being set by scientists and inventors who, as the need arises, answer the historical question with a technological fix. In any of these variations, or others, the crucial belief is that human purposes (benevolent or not) are dominant over historical change. History is something for which humankind, collectively, is clearly responsible.

Like the voluntarist position, the opposite view, the involuntarist theory of history's perspective is really the name for a cluster or family of more specific theories, all of which have in common a key belief. This belief, for the involuntarists, is that history is caused by forces quite other than human will or purpose; rather, by profoundly compelling factors over which human beings have minimal control. Some older versions cited climate or geography as the determining factors in historical change. Marxists of all varieties unite in looking to the economic conditions of society for the real driving force of history. Freudian theories of history point to unconscious psychological compulsions, mass neurosis, and the like. Above all, in this involuntarist vision of history, there is no significant place for rhetoric about human ideals. Consciousness is merely epiphenomenal; purposes couched in moral terms are ideological or self-deceptive. What really runs history is more basic and more implacable. As Robert Heilbroner concludes: "Therefore the outlook is for what we may call 'convulsive change'—change forced upon us by external events rather than by conscious choice, by catastrophe rather than by education."[16]

The practical consequence of such a conclusion, of course, is that each of us had better look to his or her own defenses as best possible. The image is of standing on the control deck of a great ship speeding toward deadly icebergs. Frantic signals about the impending crash have been coming for quite a while from the radar operator, and even the on-deck lookouts are beginning to shout about signs of danger, but nothing can be done to change course or speed because, it seems, the impressive-looking controls have never really been connected to the engines or the rudder. What is to be done except to scramble for the life jackets and try to be first in line for the too few lifeboats—or to resign oneself to go down with the ship?

But is this image adequate or necessary? Must we choose between the voluntarist and the involuntarist visions of history? Or is it not the case that the data on historical causation—like those on nature and on humanity—are profoundly mixed? Climate and economics, changing technology and psychological pathology, geography and population pressures—all have certainly impelled historical change quite apart from our best laid plans. The voluntarist image of history is inadequate to the extent that it leaves the raw power of such irrational forces out of its portrait; the teachings of Marx and Freud cannot be ignored. Still, personal purposes, hopes, and ideals are also ingredients in the mix of historical causes. The ideals of human dignity and freedom played a part in the abolition of slavery no less than the cotton gin. Popular moral repugnance against the Vietnam War had an influence in the ending of that war probably greater than the length of military supply lines.

Such conscious influences work in different ways from the compulsions of natural forces. The former are far less visible, less easily measured, than the latter. The former tend to be much slower in their effects, though after working in human consciousness over long periods they may seem suddenly to burst forth with power. As Whitehead saw:

> We notice that a great idea in the background of dim consciousness is like a phantom ocean beating upon the shores of human life in successive waves of specialization. A whole succession of such waves are as dreams slowly doing their work of sapping the base of some cliff of habit: but the seventh wave is a revolution—"And the nations echo round."[17]

Ideals and compulsions work together to shape the course of history, and in the process they modify each other. Human purpose, finding nature plastic within limits, modifies geography by irrigation; the challenges of climate in turn modify human purposes. Ideals are shaped by social structures and conversely function to reshape society. Again Whitehead describes the situation:

> The history of ideas is dominated by a dichotomy which is illustrated by [the] comparison of Steam and Democracy in recent times to Barbarians and Christians in the classical civilization. Steam and Barbarians, each in their own age, were the senseless agencies driving their respective civilizations away from inherited modes of order. These senseless agencies are what Greek writers sometimes . . . call "compulsion" and sometimes "violence" . . . .[18]

Alone, however, Whitehead continues, this tells only a half-truth about historical causation.

> It is one task of history to display the types of compulsion and of violence characteristic of each age. On the other hand, Democracy in modern times, and Christianity in the Roman Empire, exemplify articulated beliefs issuing from aspirations and issuing into aspirations. Their force was that of consciously formulated ideals at odds with the ancestral pieties which had preserved and modulated existing social institutions. . . . Senseless agencies and formulated aspirations coöperate in the work of driving mankind from its old anchorage.[19]

If Whitehead's view is correct, then it need not be the case that our ship is completely out of control. Human intelligence, human ideals, may have an important influence on the course taken and the quality of the cruise. That does not mean that all troubles will be avoided, even when accurately foreseen. The inertia is enormous and it is not yet clear that the proper orders are going to the engine room — much less that the massive inanimate forces involved are going to respond quickly to such orders, even when given. But in the Whiteheadian view of history it is not necessary to despair of the ship and elbow our way to the lifeboats. In his bipolar theory we should respect the might of the involuntary and work to shape it to our purposes, so far as we can, by voluntary efforts in line with our highest clarified ideals. "Thus," as Roberto Unger puts it, "we are able to recognize theory as neither the master, nor [merely] the witness, but the accomplice of history."[20]

Further, such a bipolar vision of history can combine with the image of nature as having within it an agency countering the physical tendency to mere decay, and with a sense of human nature as having similar counter-capacities for rationality, generosity, and creativity. This will not be a Pollyanna dream of all sweetness and light. It will, insofar as it is genuinely bipolar, look without flinching at the evil in humanity, at the recalcitrant and cruel in nature, and at the senseless in history. It will also acknowledge, if it has a true binocular vision, that new possibilities for good as well as evil are offered in history in every age, and that human creative response to the lure of envisaged ideals is a potent ingredient in the shaping of every future, including our own.

THE FREEDOM TO HOPE

The conclusion to be drawn from all of this is not that everything is going to turn out well for our modern industrial civilization or for us, personally, but that we are free to maintain reasonable hope. Optimism must not be confused with genuine hope. Directly in proportion to its fatuousness, optimism often comes dangerously close to despair. Too often such despair is imbibed unconsciously in the myths we uncritically accept concerning nature, man, and history. By the time we start thinking at a more immediate level about alternative courses of action for ourselves and our society, we are trapped by assumptions that leave open no desirable directions.

The negative myths of nature, of humanity, and of history are not logically coercive. Where they claim the authority of science, they misrepresent the logic of empirical inquiry. Where they rest on intuition or mood or the temperament of an age, they are open to alternative intuition or changing times. And although they illuminate many data, they also ignore and overlook much else.

No ultimate imagery, indeed, can claim coercive authority over our minds and attitudes. In dealing with these matters we deal in uncertainty and risk. Whitehead's bipolar theory of history, humanity, and nature cannot — though more inclusive of relevant data — be conclusively proven true. We must plan our policies without the comfort of firm certitudes. But, once we are awakened to the freedom of our situation, there are considerations that should incline us toward cultivating (since we are logically free to do so) the myths of hope rather than those of despair.

First, the predictions that follow from the images of despair — even if they are conjoined with careful disclaimers of advocacy, as, for example, Heilbroner does — have a tendency to increase the likelihood of the very undesired outcome that is being predicted. Banks and civilizations function only on confidence. To predict disaster, even with compelling grounds, is to court it. To predict it without such grounds is merely perverse.

Likewise, on the opposite side of the coin, we know that sometimes the best way to encourage desired outcomes is to prepare for them and expect them. The British response to wartime rationing, though not perfect, was impressive in its demonstration of solidarity and fair play. That this was possible at all was due to the nearly universal expectation that almost everyone was abiding by the system. The mere act of prediction, therefore, can sometimes serve powerfully in advocacy, for better or for worse.

Wishing will not make it so, of course. There are dangers in some kinds of hope that must be clearly seen and countered. One danger is in hoping unrealistically, in "closing the other eye" to the problems and the evidence of what is unpleasant but probable. Well-meaning but naive hope can actually be counterproductive if precious time or resources are wasted foolishly. Hope needs to be grounded in fact, or it reduces to mere sentimentalism — a passive posture that is inherently unstable in the face of rebuffs. Sentimental or blind hope of this kind is perilously close, psychologically, to despair.

Another danger is hoping for the wrong things. Intelligent and rigorous hope must function within a clear assessment not only of what is reasonably possible but also what is worthy to be hoped for. We have assumed, throughout, that it is not realistic to hope for a future in our lifetimes, and probably beyond, that is free of material scarcity. If we discuss hope for the future, it must be within the acceptance of the physical limits that our traditional modern culture finds so distasteful. Many might say that in simply making that assumption we have abandoned all the hope that counts. If they think this, though, it may be because they still believe that the only things that count are the countable. Materialist, quantity-bound assumptions concerning worthy ends are still dominant and should be rejected. Hope is not properly to be measured by its estimates of future GNPs or dollars per capita. The more essential debate is between those who expect scarcity and anticipate what Heilbroner calls "the Hobbesian struggle" as "likely to arise in such a strait-jacketed economic society,"[21] and those who also expect scarcity but continue to argue and work for the real possibility of creative and humane responses to a world grown aware of its limits.

For all these reasons, then, the first order of business for thoughtful and concerned citizens of the modern world should not be limited, as it might appear, to the level of detailed policy discussion but should be extended to the still more fundamental level of what ranges of policies are ultimately open. The latter is more important because it is more basic; it is more needed because it is less often discussed.

10.

What's Holding Us Back?

If we try to think liberating thoughts about the history of science and technology and their relations to religion and social policy, we need at once to deal with a paradox: what I shall call the paradox of blame. The two contrary positions comprising this paradox are widely familiar, as I shall indicate in a moment, but I have not yet seen any serious attempt to put them together and resolve the paradox of blame as such.

THE PARADOX OF BLAME

First, what is this paradox of blame? It is simply the tension that rises from the fact that two of the leading accounts of the history of science and technology and the relation of this history to religion and values—the accounts by Lynn White, Jr., and by Lewis Mumford, respectively—place the blame for our current ecological and spiritual troubles squarely in different and seemingly incompatible places. White sees the "Historical Roots of Our Ecological Crisis," in his famous *Science* article,[1] as resting firmly in the biblical religious tradition; he blames our exploitation of the earth on the spiritual readiness of Christendom to "subdue the earth" all too thoroughly. Mumford, contrariwise, in his *Pentagon of Power*, points an indignant finger at modern science; he blames our technological rape of nature on the soulless consequences of the "crime of Galileo." One blames religion, the other science. How can two such seminal accounts of the history of our current cultural predicament be so disparate? Let us look at the individual positions more closely; they both have much that is important to say.

White's historical argument, to begin with, holds that the exploitative posture of Westerners toward nature becomes clearly visible in medieval Christian culture. The technology of plowing, for example, shows a new attitude toward the earth early in Christendom's development.

By the latter part of the seventh century after Christ . . . following obscure beginnings, certain northern peasants were using an entirely new kind of plow, equipped with a vertical knife to cut the line of the furrow, a horizontal share to slice under the sod, and a mold-board to turn it over. The friction of this plow with the soil was so great that it normally required not two but eight oxen. It attacked the land with such violence that cross-plowing was not needed, and fields tended to be shaped in long strips.[2]

The moral of this change is quickly drawn: "Formerly man had been part of nature; now he was the exploiter of nature." And the deepest root of this reversal was in the mind or soul: "What people do about their ecology depends on what they think about themselves in relation to things around them." What medieval people thought about themselves, White continues, was due to Christianity. "The victory of Christianity over paganism was the greatest psychic revolution in the history of our culture." And the attitude-shaping content of Christianity was profoundly anti-ecological from the creation myth onwards: Man named all the animals, thus establishing dominance over them. God planned all of this explicitly for humanity's benefit and rule: no item in the physical creation had any purpose save to serve humanity's purpose. And, although the human body is made of clay, the human is not simply part of nature but made in God's image. Thus, White concludes: "Especially in its Western form, Christianity is the most anthropocentric religion the world has seen." A "huge burden of guilt"[3] must be borne by Christianity for what has happened to the earth at the hands of Western technology.

Mumford, in contrast, emphasizes the reality of values in opposition to the "value-free" and ultimately value-denying ideology of modern science. The real clash between Galileo and the Church, he maintains, as we saw in chapter 1, was over the "disqualification" of the world: i.e., the banishment from responsible human thinking (science) of all concern for qualities beyond the meaningless "primary qualities" of matter in motion, those features of things open to mathematical representation and objective test.[4]

Beyond simple theory, Mumford continues, very painful practical consequences flowed from the feelinglessness of the scientific attitude toward what it studies and dominates. The European surge into the rest of the world, exploring Asia and Africa and the New World, sprang from the same imperatives of curiosity and greed, and manifested the same inhumane attitudes. Just as the scientist lusts after the secrets of nature, in Francis Bacon's words,[5] to "command nature in action," even to the extent of wringing those secrets from her by the equivalent of torture ("that is to say, when by art and the hand of man she is forced out of her natural state, and squeezed and moulded . . . , seeing that the nature of things betrays itself more readily under the vexations of art than in its natural freedom"[6]), so also the age of the Conquistador showed a distorted face to the rest of the world: power-hungry, dominating physically as well as cognitively, unfeeling toward its subject-victims.

Thus we have the paradox of blame. Christianity as culprit *versus* science in the dock. What led the history of technology away from humane values? Was it science? Was it religion? Must we choose?

RESOLVING THE PARADOX

I think the paradox can be resolved. What is needed is a somewhat more discriminating look at both the scientific and the religious phenomena. Science, after all, is not a monolithic thing. Systematic attempts to describe and understand the regularities of nature had been in the field long before the days of Galileo, Bacon, and Descartes. There is little tendency today, at least among the newer generation of historians of science, to equate the name "science" with the specific stream of thinking and practice that rises from the seventeenth-century mechanists. That enormously important stream, on which Mumford lays his blame, is perhaps what can rightly be called "modern science," since it has largely shaped the attitudes, beliefs, and institutions of modernity; but modern science of that sort is not the only science that ever was or ever could be. Before its rise there were the Babylonian, the Greek, the Arabic, and the medieval sciences. Even well after the development of modern mechanistic science, nonmechanistic alternatives like the biology of Paracelsus[7] (with its technological applications in Paracelsian medicine) or the chemistry of Diderot,[8] continued to compete for the European consciousness.

Still, it was modern science, not any of its alternatives, that Mumford rebuked. How is his indictment compatible with the charges laid against Christianity by Lynn White? One answer, suggested by White himself, is that "modern Western science was cast in a matrix of Christian theology."[9] Making a sharp distinction between the contemplative Greek (or Eastern) branch of Christianity and the active Latin (or Western) branch, White concludes that "The implications of Christianity for the conquest of nature would emerge more easily in the Western atmosphere."[10] Not only were Western Christians more inclined toward "doing," but also in Europe the very face of nature was seen differently: not as a set of aesthetic or spiritual symbols but as the result of God's own "doing." By the thirteenth century — long before Galileo — natural theology ceased to be the decoding of the physical symbols of God's communication with humanity and was instead becoming the effort to understand God's mind by discovering how God's creation operates. The rainbow was no longer simply a symbol of hope first sent to Noah after the Deluge: ". . . a Robert Grosseteste, Friar Roger Bacon, and Theoderic of Freiburg produced startlingly sophisticated work on the optics of the rainbow, but they did it as a venture in religious understanding."[11] Alfred North Whitehead, too, credits Christianity with providing a necessary condition for the rise of science in the medieval West. Any sort of science, as a systematic attempt to describe and understand the regularities of nature, must rest on a "belief that every detailed occurrence can be correlated with its antecedents in a perfectly definite manner, exemplifying general principles."[12]

Western science is one of the offspring of Christianity, then, epistemologically and attitudinally. Epistemologically, Christian theology assured researchers that there would be some point to their labors: that nature was regular and knowable, worth looking beyond the superficial chaos of appearances to the orderliness below, and worth penetrating with the intellect into what Bacon called "the heart and marrow of things."[13] Attitudinally, likewise, Western Christianity assured its adherents that nature was for our human penetration, both cognitively — as Adam had named the animals — and practically. God had commanded humans to subdue the earth. Thus technology could be linked to growing knowledge, for the great glory of God, and the conquest of nature that led to our own times could be sanctified.

One more thought should give us pause, however, before we accept this resolution of the paradox of blame too quickly. If there are various streams within science, as we have seen, so also Christianity is complex. It was Western Christianity, not Eastern, that gave rise to Western science. Western Christian theology may have been a necessary condition for the birth of Western science in general, but it is evidently not necessary that Christianity manifest the aggressiveness of European thinking, nor is aggressive Latin Christianity sufficient to account for the mechanistic, reductionistic, value-neglectful species of science that eventually shaped the mind of modern civilization. The histories of Western science, theology, technology, and values are deeply intertwined, but it would be simplistic to conclude that any one of these can take the whole burden of guilt for what has happened.

Therefore if the paradox of blame is made up of claims that seek to convince us that "Christianity (as such) is guilty," or "science (as such) is guilty," we may resolve it in one of two ways: First, we may consider these two alternatives to be logical *contraries* and deny them both without contradiction. Christianity *as such*, after all, is in itself neither aggressive nor exploitative: White himself points to Eastern or Franciscan forms that offer attitudinal alternatives. And science *as such*, similarly, is neither to be equated with its modern mechanistic stream nor, even in its modern form, to be held fully responsible for how it was born or for the cultural uses to which Western peoples have decided to put its results.

Second, and conversely, we may wish to affirm that both sides of our paradox are true. Christianity as such is implicated in the anthropocentrizing of the world under human dominion; it gave birth, license, and encouragement to science and technology.[14] The Church and the Conquistadors were hand in glove. And modern science, released from its Christian matrix, has reduced our consciousness of the world of nature. However we decide to resolve the paradox of blame, the visible and spiritual fruits of modern technology retain their fascination both as triumph and as tragedy.

11.

Demythologizing Technolatry

Every culture has its arts and crafts, its methods of doing things. Generally through human history these have been handed down by tradition through apprenticing practices by which crafts of often admirable sophistication can be attained and preserved. As I argued in part 1 of this book, modern scientific technology operates quite differently: Instead of tradition there is deliberate application of explicit natural law; instead of apprenticeship there is research and development.

This shift toward self-conscious, deliberate, highly rationalized ways of doing things is so pervasive in modern culture that the phenomenon deserves a name of its own and has been given one by Jacques Ellul in his now classic study *The Technological Society*.[1] Ellul calls our characteristically modern way of doing things *technique* and distinguishes it from the methodologies of other cultures by emphasizing the *mode of consciousness* out of which it arises and within which it operates. Ellul acknowledges that methods — ways of doing things — abound, but the field of technique (technical operation) is much more restrictive.

> Two factors enter into the extensive field of technical operation: consciousness and judgment. This double intervention produces what I call the technical phenomenon. What characterizes this double intervention? Essentially, it takes what was previously tentative, unconscious, and spontaneous and brings it into the realm of clear, voluntary, and reasoned concepts.[2]

Ellul's usage has the advantage of broadening the meaning of modern technology beyond its usual designation of hardware. The physical machine remains an important example of technique, since machines, to be machines, must be consciously designed and deliberately put to work. The machine, indeed, is our very paradigm of the clearly reasoned way of doing something.[3] It is made in the basic image of technique. But quite evidently the physical machine cannot exhaust the concept. Wherever calculative intelligence intervenes to design a methodology, there is technique. Technique is present in the carefully thought out organization charts of our great corporations; it is present in the scientific methods of breeding and animal husbandry used in our great agricultural industries; it is present in the minutely considered lesson plans and behavioral objectives employed in our most advanced schoolrooms. The "machine," therefore, need not be made of metal; it may be social or biological or even psychological. Its compelling attractions, in any case, are those that undergird technical skill.

THE WORSHIP OF TECHNIQUE

As I have suggested throughout this book, technique in this broad sense has become a potent (but frequently unrecognized) religious phenomenon in the modern world. As the conventional religions of our society succumb, by fundamentalist irrelevancy or by cultural surrender, to the implacable currents of scientific-industrial society, the worship of technique may in fact be becoming the dominant religious reality of our culture. In any event it will repay us to return in fuller detail to my argument of chapter 4, where I expressed serious doubts about "technolatry."

The vision of technique, functioning as a focus of ultimate religious veneration, is protean and hazardous to represent. Like "God" and "the Kingdom of Heaven" or the like, it is better communicated through the evocative imagery that gives it definiteness than through the lumpish efforts of literal prose. I commend the literature of science fiction[4] and the heady writings of Buckminster Fuller[5] to those who seek such imagery firsthand.

Beyond imagery, nevertheless, the worship of technique carries with it certain doctrines that arise out of its imagery; the doctrines, in turn, provoke and reinforce the sense of the sacred that may flow from devoted attention to the images of technique. I shall not repeat my earlier review of the doctrinal side of technolatry, but at a minimum I should note that technique, as a rational organization of method, presupposes the general metaphysical proposition that the world works always and everywhere by regularities open in principle to human discovery and lawful control. In its ideal form, the image of the machine supports a *deterministic* vision of the universe: reliable, predictable, intelligible. No unforeseen randomness, balkiness, or ambiguity is permitted in the image of perfect technique. The world of technique is in principle a soluble, a controllable, world.[6]

It is too painfully evident that such a world is not much like our own messy world of daily life[7]—not yet. Like any major religion, technolatry must face and deal with its own "problem of evil." Theodicy, in this case, involves a second major doctrine, this one concerning the nature of history and society. Technique, on this second major doctrine, is inevitably *progressive*. Problems exist, but discoveries will come in time to overcome them all; technical intelligence will not be denied its triumph. Not only so, but the momentum of technique has its own autonomous dynamic.[8] If individual A fails to solve the technical challenge, then individual B, somehow, somewhere, will succeed.

Moreover, for technolatry there is no domain in principle to which the clarifying virtues of technique are not appropriate. The economic and military are exemplar areas for advanced technique, but these are obvious areas for hardware — that is, for technique understood conventionally as technology. Even more pressing requirements for technique exist, so the believer insists, in the political and social areas where rational design has lagged. "In trying to solve the terrifying problems that face us in the world today, we naturally turn to the things we do best," writes B. F. Skinner. "We play from strength, and our strength is science and technology. . . . But things grow steadily worse and it is disheartening to find that technology itself is increasingly at fault."[9] Therefore, Skinner concludes (in a breathtaking inference), "What we need is a technology of behavior."[10] To the devoted technolater every apparent evil brought on by technique is to be countered by yet greater faith in technique. "Though he slay me, yet will I trust in him" (Job 13:15 KJV) is a profound religious expression; such is faith's pledge to the sacred.

Doctrine, however, is only the cognitive concomitant of powerful religious experience. Does technique stir the numinous dimension of supreme valuation without which there is no genuine religion, only philosophy and ethics? I affirm that it can and does provoke for many within our culture the sense of sacred mystery best defined by Rudolf Otto in his classic study *The Idea of the Holy*.[11] The elements of religious experience, Otto showed, are defined by the *mysterium tremendum*.

The *mysterium* of religious awe is widely experienced in our culture, when it is experienced at all, thanks to the vast and potent products of scientific technology. I have frequently polled students on this question and have learned to expect that if they report any personal sense of overwhelming mystery, wonder, and creaturely smallness before some unfathomable Other, that Other will have as its characteristic type the thundering magnificence of a Saturn space rocket, the towering grandeur of a modern skyscraper, or the unimaginable violence of a nuclear explosion. It will, in other words, be some incarnation of technique. Even those who feel they understand the workings of some particular technical theophany, moreover, acknowledge the mystery of technique's progressive autonomy as a historical force, above the finite efforts of individual technicians and irreducible to them alone.

The *tremendum*, too, defined by Otto in terms of the tingle of enormous power and sensed dynamic potential, is no less evoked by the images of technique. Thus it is that the *mysterium tremendum* frightens and fascinates at the same time; technique, that is, makes its devotees tremble before it but keeps drawing them back into its awesome embrace.

The *mysterium tremendum* is the essential religious experience. It may be sparked in some societies by a smoking volcano or by images of mythic gods and beasts; it may be stirred in other circumstances by mystic disciplines or by prophetic visions of the righteousness of God; in our society it may be evoked by the ideal of the machine, omnipresent, perfectly designed, infinitely efficient, totally triumphant.

I should not leave the false impression that I suppose great numbers to be constantly in the ecstatic grip of religious fervor, prostrated before some ideal vision of technique. On the contrary, just as there are few ecstatic Christians, even among the many sincere Christian believers left in our modern world, so the sincere devotees of technique in the main hold their faith deeply but untumultuously[12] — except, perhaps, at public celebrations such as the Indianapolis 500 car races, air shows, space shuttle launches, and other rituals of this kind.

Tumultuous or not, many of the important values that shape our society, our neighbors, and perhaps ourselves, are those which, drawn out to their fullest degree, are the values of technolatry. We are fascinated by devices (of any kind) to get things done (no matter what). The main reason for the popularity of the James Bond films, I suppose, is the fascination we have for the ingenious methods of killing (and of avoiding being killed) that we are treated to in the imagery before us. We endlessly hang upon technique in all domains: in sports, in sex, in business, in politics, in crime, in war. The spirit of technolatry, though usually not heroically manifested, is certainly ubiquitous, and without doubt our society's devotion to technique has borne much fruit: It is time we looked at the quality of these fruits, then, since for any spiritual condition it is true that "by their fruits ye shall know them" (Matt. 7:20 KJV).

THE INADEQUACY OF TECHNIQUE ALONE

I hope I may be excused from dwelling on the marvels that have been wrought by unstinting devotion to technique. We all know the catalogue by heart. Medical technique keeps more of us alive longer than ever before. Agricultural technique gives us more food than the world has ever known. Road-building technique festoons the earth with mighty ribbons of reinforced concrete in an effort to keep ahead of the technique of automobile builders. Aerodynamic technique moves us faster and further. Broadcasting technique fills our minds and shapes our leisure. Sports technique among the professionals has never been so keen. Political technique maintains the system without serious challenge, though with the satisfying entertainment values of apparent conflict and change. Sexual technique multiplies carefully infertile orgasms across the liberated land.

But each marvel, as I list it, brings to any informed mind the sober reminder of an equal and opposite problem. There is a gloomy side even to modern medical technique, not only in the underdeveloped regions of the world where our exported techniques have been directly responsible for the misery of increasingly hopeless growth in population,[13] but also among ourselves where (as Ivan Illich points out) ruinous costs, human indignity, medically caused disease, and degeneration plague our geriatrogenic society.[14] Likewise, scientific agribusiness reaps huge returns, but at a high price in violence toward the land, which may not indefinitely be able to bear the insults of pesticidal, fungicidal, herbicidal, artificially fertilized monocultural technique.[15] I decline even to mention—we know them all—the dark sides of unlimited road building, of automobile manufacture, of supersonic transport, of videoculture, of sports spectatoritis, of cynical political huckstering, or of empty sexual athleticism. There is something wrong at the root: specifically, with unlimited admiration for technique itself. Technolatry, though widespread as a functioning faith in our society, is an inadequate religious stance.

Unlimited adoration of technique is not appropriate, not merely because of particular problems that are currently too obvious, but for more basic reasons that may be summarized in three principles: (1) technique is not *sufficient* for qualitative excellence in any domain of human interest; (2) technique is not even *necessary*, on the whole and beyond an inevitable minimum, for such excellence; and (3) technique carried to excess is *dangerous* in characteristic ways. Let me illustrate these three principles briefly in a familiar nonscientific context and then apply them more generally to our society.

Consider the place of technique in the fine arts. There can be no gainsaying the fact that artistic technique is greatly valued in our culture, and with much reason. There is much more that one can do, in any field of art, if one has developed a high degree of technique. Technical excellence in music, painting, poetry, or the dance is the legitimate goal of much hard work in studios and practice rooms wherever the arts are taken seriously. But the principle remains that even the finest technique is not and cannot be the sufficient condition for artistic excellence. This fact has long been recognized. Indeed, one of the earlier uses of the word *technique* in the English language, in *Groves Dictionary of Music* (1884), makes this point quite emphatically: "A player may be perfect in technique, and yet have neither soul nor intelligence."[16]

We all know from personal experience, do we not, that this bleak reminder is correct? Even though we may be unable to define clearly what it is that we find lacking—"musicality," "interpretive sense," "soul," or *je ne sais quoi*—we know that "playing like a clock" will not substitute for "making real music." Just because it defies precision of measurement and articulation, "soul" is outside the reach of technique which, we remember, is by definition a matter of clarity, comprehensibility, and order in the way of doing things. If "soul" cannot be quantified and dissected it cannot be replicated or even recognized by the logic or the language of technique. If some readers are bothered by my undefined use of the word *soul,* I ask them to examine the source of this discomfort: Is it due to a tacit supposition that the only significant subjects for thought must be open to precise measurement and clear definition? And on what does this supposition rest? One possibility is that it rests on an unacknowledged faith commitment that insists on overriding even vivid personal intuitions of the indefinable, but musically vital, quality of "soul." If so, then I ask that a spirit of open empiricism be cultivated, since dogmatic closure here against the data of experience begs precisely the question at issue. Another possibility to consider is that there are those who have never noticed the differences between "soul" and perfect technique. If so, I hasten on, helpless, to discuss the next principle.

My first principle denies the *sufficiency* of technique for artistic excellence; my second rejects technique's *necessity*, beyond an obvious threshold, as well. In this domain it is difficult to know where this minimum level must be maintained for genuine quality. We must not forget that technique does not mean merely the same things as "method" or "manner," or "style." Clearly, nothing at all can be done in *no* manner or with *no* method. But technique, we recall, comes from the "double intervention" of clarity and calculation against the merely traditional or the spontaneous. To insist on the universal necessity of technique for high artistic quality would be to propose that all primitive or traditional art, whether dances by Bantu tribesmen or paintings by Grandma Moses, be excluded from claims to excellence. Current connoisseurship in the arts would give short shrift to such a sweeping proposal, and in this case I must agree with the connoisseurs. I particularly admire African and Eskimo sculpture. Great skill (as well as "soul") goes into all such excellence, of course, but very little if any technique proper, since these skills and methods are highly traditional and in many cases are far from maximally efficient. Likewise, since "technical" and "spontaneous" are antonyms, the possibility of artistic excellence in improvisation — in jazz or in theater, in the dance or at the harpsichord — shows still further that ubiquitous technique is not a necessary condition for high achievement.

I do wish immediately to make a significant qualification of this second principle, since otherwise I am sure to be misunderstood. Sheer spontaneity, without any order, clarity, limits, or logic, is not at all likely to result in artistic or any other kind of excellence. I repeat my initial comment: Developed technique in the arts is rightly valued for the liberating power that permits us to do much more — even spontaneously — with it than without it. Similarly, the physical instruments of artistic performance, the harpsichords and the saxophones, as well as the skills of the performers, are obviously grounded in sophisticated technique. Thus I wish to affirm that technique *is* needed at *some* level, but I insist that it is neither possible to locate that level with precision nor appropriate to draw it so high as to diminish our appreciation for the traditional or the spontaneous, even sometimes for the unschooled. The musty inefficiencies of tradition and the murky depths of spontaneity (or genius) are equally abhorrent to the clarities of technique, but not the less valuable for all that.

My third principle points up the *dangers* of excessive adulation of technique. In the area of art those dangers show themselves in three significant ways. First, public technolatry in this area of life tends to lead to discouragement and specialization. If Isaac Stern is admired mainly for his incredible technique, and if it is quite clear that only a life dedicated to endless practice (even given the rare talent required) will permit one to rise to such technical heights, then why pick up the fiddle oneself? Better, surely, to turn on the compact disk player and let the technique of high fidelity sound systems carry the professional specialist's awesome technique to one's passive ears. In this way art, music, dance, poetry, drama—even quality conversation—become spectator inactivities in a culture hypnotized by admiration of unattainable expertise.

A second danger runs close on the heels of the first. Without engagement, creativity, and wrestling with the "soul" of art, even the level of appreciation declines. When admiration is focused too exclusively and too passively on the production of technical effects, the perceived value of what *Groves Dictionary* called "soul" and "intelligence" erodes away; connoisseurship itself atrophies from little use.

Finally, and most seriously of all, perhaps, the technolatrous society, in its latter stages, must spread its values even into the professionalized artistic community itself. Fancy technique becomes the exclusive preoccupation. "Intelligence" and "soul" are discounted while fads and fashions flash by at an ever accelerating rate, with attention feverishly focused on the "how" rather than the "what," on refinements of technical manner rather than on qualities of artistic matter. Thus the worship of technique leads to the destruction or trivialization of the arts.

THE WEAKNESS OF TECHNOLATRY

Turning now to the modern world of high-craft technique, the gist of my argument will be that the same three principles—even the same general sorts of dangers—militate against the adulation of technique as ultimate end. Technique there must be, on these principles, but healthy technique must be freshly integrated into a higher devotion to the art of civilized life.

Will anyone claim that advanced technology is a *sufficient* condition for excellence in human life? If so, let such a person look around at the anguish and anomie that continue to be evident even in (especially in?) the most highly developed corners of our modern North. That saturation by sophisticated technology is no guarantee of contentment is becoming a platitude of our times. Sweden, as one of the most uniformly advanced nations in the world, is an instructive example. Quite aside from the often-cited (and sometimes abused) alcohol and suicide statistics, I think of the life work of

Ingmar Bergman, cinematic seer of our age, exploring again and again the emptiness of a land without poverty and without God, returning constantly to the search for human substance, for meaning, for . . . "soul." As in the case of music, the *je ne sais quoi* we miss evades precise definition by the logic of technique. Our modern malaise, infecting even those who are most comfortably cocooned by modern gadgetry, is a standing rebuttal to naive hopes that technological achievements, singlehandedly, might be sufficient to assure the full human life.

What, though, of the application of my second principle, implying that, beyond an inevitable threshold, technique is not even a *necessary* condition for the good life? Is high technology actually dispensable? With one major qualification, I argue that this is indeed so. First, ignoring qualifications, it is certainly the case that good and full lives have historically been led without dependence upon what we today think of as technology. It would be insufferable provincialism on our part to maintain the opposite. Engineering technique such as we are discussing is an extremely recent craft launched on the long stream of human history. Anyone whose excellence of life we admire prior to the past few generations, at the most, stands as a refutation of the claim that modern engineering technology is in principle a prerequisite for quality in human existence. Even in practice today there are those who seek renewed quality in their lives by deliberately turning away from technological society, into the woods or onto the distant islands, in the conviction that life led by tradition or lit by spontaneity will offer more than life ordered by the clarities and efficiencies of technique. As in the case of art, primitivism and improvisation in lifestyle may generate admirable qualities[17] and, however distasteful to the technolatrous consciousness, these alternatives show that high technology, though pervasive, is not in fact as necessary for quality in life as its evangelists may preach.

I must introduce my important qualification at this point. Just as in the case of art, I cannot conceive of pure spontaneity or mere tradition bringing about the *best*. High technology is not necessary in principle for the good life; the technological imperative, that is, cannot be mistaken for a categorical one. But since one can do so much more — since one is set free into much grander ranges of creative possibility — with appropriate technique at one's command than without it, then it is clearly a necessary ingredient at some level in aiming at the art of the best in civilized life. That level is not quantifiable nor precisely definable, despite the yearnings of technical intellect. It is a matter of judgment (something that the technical intellect has been carefully trained to mistrust) rather than of measurement. But this level of necessity is not only discernible, it is rapidly rising. If I may put the matter in a quasimathematical form, the level of the necessity of fresh, postmodern technique is directly proportional to the size of world population and inversely proportional to the reserves of natural resources. As population increases and resources dwindle, we are less and less in a position to look upon advanced technology as an optional matter. But since the well-meant introduction of technology, as we have known it hitherto, has been largely responsible for the demographic dislocations that have filled our world with unprecedented numbers of persons, and since the availability of that same technology has been almost wholly responsible for the unprecedented looting of the earth's treasure, it is obvious that significant changes in the quality of our techniques are needed if we are not to lock ourselves into an ever-tightening graveyard spiral (as pilots call such vicious circles) that will doom all our dreams of a better future.

I have anticipated in various ways the burden of my third principle: that technique carried to excess is dangerous. This is no secret and requires little more comment, perhaps, except to note some of the analogues between the dangers of technolatry in the arts and more generally in society. Then, in the light of all these observations, we will be in a position to press for certain changes in attitude and practice that will emerge as needed antidotes in our troubled society.

Fascination by unrestrained technique has led, as we are all aware, to the technologies of large-scale economic centralization. Our admiration of technolatry's cardinal virtue, efficiency, has produced a society dominated by institutions justified by ultimate appeal to efficiencies of scale, no matter how remote they have become from human interests or creative concerns. The literature of the global North has been rife for two decades or more with discussion of our sensed loss of control, within the "corporate state,"[18] of the economic and political machinery that feeds and clothes, entertains and medicates, transports and taxes, houses and buries us. "The System" is distinct from us, the powerless little people who dutifully conform our tastes to what is economic to produce for mass markets. Even the remote managers, like human cogs, feel swept along by the System they merely serve. Hypnotized by technique, which insinuates its values through multimedia propaganda, then confirms its success by spy and information retrieval, the members of society increasingly experience the passivity of specialization and discouragement before the monolith of unattainable, seemingly omnipotent technical virtuosity. If the psychological analysis of Erich Fromm is right, it is this passivity that lies at the root of modern hopelessness and social pathology.[19] Spectatoritis, not merely in the domains of sport or of the arts, but planted in the soul of society by gigantic and remote technique, is the death of creativity and confidence.

In the second place, analogous to the loss of personal connoisseurship in the arts, the sense of passive alienation from the System leads to a dangerous loss of personal responsibility in society. Every technician is merely doing his or her job, taking orders, keeping the machinery running. The crucial intuitions of right and wrong are dulled. Within the social machine that is the giant bureaucracy of corporate society—public or private makes no difference—no part need feel personally responsible, even involved. This may have been the most important moral lesson of the Watergate and Iran-Contra scandals, through which Americans saw with

shattering vividness what their well-bred and educated young social technicians were capable of doing automatically, without compunction or reflection at the time, when the efficient functioning of their intricately designed
political machine required it.

Our sense of helplessness before the seemingly autonomous system as
it continues to accelerate must not be allowed to sap our courage to define,
and press for, new direction. Old scandals recede. There are new abuses
to uncover and oppose. This will mean the nurturing of new consciousness
in ourselves as we, personally, awaken all too fitfully and dimly to our
situation; it will mean cultivating intuitions of humanity, of qualitative
dimensions in experience, of "soul," or of "the things that matter in life."
It will mean rejecting deeply ingrained assumptions. It will mean thinking,
and courageously urging others to think, some hitherto unthinkable
thoughts; it will mean sometimes trusting holistic judgment above calculations of demonstrable short-term utility; it will mean reorganizing our lives
and our careers according to the precepts of a deeper spiritual wisdom than
the too easily marketable doctrines of technolatry.

PART 4

TOWARD MULTI-MYTHIC ORGANICISM

12.

Probing for a Postmodern Consciousness

All three chapters in part 4 will be aimed at stimulating some needed thought about possible spiritual successors to technolatry for a desirable postmodern world. This topic could become a bog. Therefore I shall impose two limits on my speculations.

The first limit reflects the political slogan: "You can't beat somebody with nobody." As Thomas Kuhn notes, regarding revolutionary shifts in the history of scientific thought, "crises of confidence" in fundamental paradigms never by themselves result in radical change until "an alternative candidate is available to take its place."[1] The same principle is true, I suggest, with regard to the even deeper mythic paradigms of consciousness that concern us here. Modern consciousness and its attendant technolatry are currently suffering strong shocks from without and crumbling of confidence from within. But the transition to postmodernity will not happen without some alternative "candidate," as Kuhn puts it, standing ready. If so, it will be prudent to remain alert to what is actually available today. Perhaps, just as scientific consciousness gestated in the matrix of Christian world-images before the modern world was born, so somewhere in the world around us now we may find a precursor of the dominant consciousness of the postmodern world that is on its way.

My second self-limitation is based on the conviction that peoples of the global North generally are not likely to adopt modes of consciousness that are not already rooted deeply within the Western tradition. Not all the modern world is Western, of course; the Japanese, for example, may have different postmodern alternatives available to them than do Germans or Americans. The industrially powerful but spiritually battered North would do well to listen attentively to traditions from the long-neglected South. But since these short chapters can make no pretense of comprehensiveness, I have chosen to focus on the Western heritage that I and most of my readers know best.

Are there, then, within that heritage, actual candidates for consciousness that might let us hope for a better postmodern world? Whatever they are,

if they are to improve upon the flaws we have noted in modern consciousness, they will need to give promise of grounding social attitudes far more
intimately attuned to nature's needs than our present form of consciousness
has done. They will need to promise to leave behind the controlling, progressive, prideful postures of technolatrous conquest and exploitation. They
will doubtless also be based on a world-image far different from that of
objective consciousness. What might some of these candidates be?

RETURN OF MAGIC

There is an underculture, or as Theodore Roszak named it in the 1960s,
a counterculture,[2] ready to claim the role of successor to the modern culture
when it passes out of history's limelight. The original counterculture itself
lost prominence in the succeeding decades of triumphal conservatism, but
underground streams fed by this movement survive, surfacing in its most
vulgar form in the tabloid press and in more refined ways in "New Age"
thinking. What is especially noteworthy about this alternative culture is its
characteristic belief in the occult, the magical, the mystical, and the strange.
I propose to look first at this return to magical consciousness in our search
for a mythic matrix for a livable postmodern world.

In the first place, the resurgence is an interesting social phenomenon.
Occultism seems to be a permanent feature of Western civilization, rising
from time to time into prominence as it did in the early 1970s. That rise,
despite all the triumphs of objective modern consciousness, was as startling
as it was significant. Who could have predicted it? Certainly not I, at least,
despite much contact with bright and "with-it" young people in my classes
during the late 1950s and early 1960s. In those years we were wrestling, in
philosophy and religion, with the possibility of *any* responsible belief that
did not have the direct sanction of science. Objective consciousness, as it
had been since the seventeenth century, was on the offensive against credulity of all sorts, including the suspected credulity even of distinguished
theological scholars. It was avant garde to be critical; scientific skepticism
still had a youthful feel. Only the old and stodgy had a timidly kind word
for the possibility of the supernatural of any sort, however abstract and
sanitized. No one ever expressed interest in or sympathy for astrology—
much less witchcraft and magic. Such blatant superstition was never even
considered in my circles, though I knew that some credulous people must
be requiring the newspapers to keep printing those silly horoscopes.

How things changed! One of the vivid moments of truth about the change
hit me in—of all places—Los Alamos, New Mexico, at the beginning of the
1970s. Los Alamos is a most unusual town, sometimes called "Atom City,
U.S.A.," because of its significant scientific and technical contributions.
Built by the U.S. government and populated with top-quality physicists and
engineers, the city is still practically all made up of scientists or science

support workers. I expected (and found, among the adults) a bastion of objective consciousness, a veritable Vatican City of modernity. Imagine my astonishment, then, to be introduced at the Los Alamos High School, where I was serving as a consultant in humanities, and immediately to be plunged into serious and prolonged discussion with a large group of students on witchcraft! As a philosopher of religion, I was someone they felt they could talk to about their interests and concerns. Almost all the students professed to believe in magic. It was merely distinguishing black from white magic that disturbed them. One young woman professed herself a witch and others soberly agreed.

Moving back and forth between that youth world and the parental world of cyclotrons and lasers (the superintendent of schools met me in his laboratory in his white coat and gave me a fascinating tour of *his* magic) was an unforgettable experience for me. Witches in Los Alamos! Afterward, as I flew my Cessna over the rugged New Mexican terrain and watched the sparsely settled Indian country slide beneath me, I felt the gap again, between my airborne technological cocoon and the lands of rain dance and shamanistic flight. Did Don Juan teach Castañeda to fly without all this technology? Are there "separate realities" to learn from the Yaqui way of knowledge?[3]

Since then the craze for the occult has receded. It became faddish and, as one might expect in the modern world, commercialized. But the blossoming again of occult fascination even in late modern times was a portentous reminder of a very real "candidate" not far off center stage.

For modern objective consciousness all this is strictly nondata. It simply cannot be data; it fails to fit with what can be contained in the objective world-image; there must be something wrong with allegations and reports citing such things. Acupuncture, for example, has no basis in physiological theory nor in modern scientific medicine. No nervous system parallels the points on the body where those little needles are inserted and twirled; no known or imaginable bodily mechanism could kill pain or cure illness through such treatment. It *must* be fakery; its practice is rooted in ancient Chinese lore about spiritual points of power, and all that. How could it be anything but flimflam abetted by foolishness? And yet—James Reston, internationally known columnist, reported that it worked on him when he suddenly needed emergency surgery in China. And yet—one of my former students, someone I would trust with my life to tell the truth, experienced cure in China immediately after treatment with little gold needles. And yet—Americans watched during the Nixon visit to China while their television sets showed surgery and childbirth aided by acupuncture; one woman was even interviewed during surgery with no anesthetic but the rotating needles. I personally have enjoyed nine years of respite (at this writing) from arthritis pains and stiffness after only seven weekly acupuncture treatments from a young German doctor. But still most of us refuse to believe it. How can this be data? Don't bother to think about it; there's got to be something wrong somewhere!

Mental telepathy is just as bad. Objective consciousness refuses to acknowledge the data as data. There is no way ESP could happen in the objective world picture. No possible mechanism could account for what is claimed by researchers.[4] I recall an evening-long debate some years ago between H. H. Price, the distinguished Oxford philosopher who was then president of the British Society for Psychical Research, and a professor in the psychology department at a university where I then taught. We were in the psychologist's living room, and metaphorically this was appropriate since he never once left his familiar mental furniture, despite the wealth of reports of investigated incidents he was offered by Professor Price. The proferred data were nondata to the psychologist. Once admitted they would not be able to fit the scientistic image of the world. Therefore they could not be admitted.

I encountered the same reaction, from a computer specialist this time, concerning *The Secret Life of Plants*.[5] What a scornful rejection of any possibility that mere plants without nervous systems could feel or be aware or respond to emotional conditions in their surroundings! Ludicrous! A scandalous manipulation of the evidence! Had my critical friend read the book? What's the point? There's no use wasting time over such nonsense.

In this way, and many others like it, the world-picture of objective consciousness had closed the doors of perception against the deeply inexplicable, which is what the occult basically means. Not the merely puzzling, which objective consciousness allows and even revels in, but the deeply — threateningly — inexplicable is what is not admitted to consciousness, often literally not seen. Many experiments in perception, such as those classic ones by J. S. Bruner and Leo Postman,[6] have shown that it is difficult and disconcerting, at best, to see what is incongruous with one's categories of normal expectation. The objective world-picture which we reviewed earlier provides for objective modern consciousness just those basic categories of normal expectation. And to the extent that expectation channels perception, the world-picture of modern consciousness has acted as blinders on experience, keeping the gaze from wandering disturbingly far either to left or right of the well-worn path.

One positive implication of the persistent undercurrent of interest in the occult, therefore, is the assistance it has given in expanding possibilities of experience itself. It has constituted a creative disturbance, at the very least, to the complacency of modern consciousness. From the point of view of genuine science (though not that of scientism), these results should be regarded as valuable, since openness and humility before the data are two of objective consciousness's primary values. From a scientific point of view, this new openness to possible data will give researchers for the first time a chance to take the data seriously enough to *test* which of these data are reliable. From a philosophical point of view, one still less wedded to the scientistic world-picture, this implication of recent developments is even more cheerfully to be welcomed.

But before modern consciousness lowers its guard in the face of this first implication, we had better note a second one. Even the act of taking seriously the *possibility* of data surrounding the occult reflects a significant change in consciousness itself. It shows a major erosion in the confidence of modern mentality and a transition toward something unmistakably postmodern.

Consider the implications, for example, of taking astrology seriously — even to the extent of searching for data. A friend of mine in Philadelphia publishes a book largely devoted to methods of astrological birth control.[7] I have asked him to send me data that would compare astrological methods with other, characteristically modern, methods of limiting families and determining the sexes of children. But what am I asking? I am guilty of urging him to combine two utterly incompatible world-images.

Astrology has a long history, much longer than that of the modern world. It assumes a wholly different vision of the universe, best systematized by Ptolemy who wrote in his *Almagest* (c. 150 C.E.) not only the authoritative astronomical text that lasted until Copernicus and Galileo, but also the definitive astrological work of the ancient and medieval world. Ptolemy's image of things shows earth and humanity at the center of things, with the fateful stars and planets surrounding the human sphere with their mysterious influences. The universe as a whole is unified by meanings being emanated, being discovered, working themselves out. Humanity is terribly small and weak, but terribly important, too, in the scheme of things. Everything fits; everything matters. Great events are foretold in the stars; small children inherit their characters from the heavenly conjunctions under which they are born.

The Renaissance was another time of astrological resurgence. Renaissance humanism is usually thought of as a movement of liberation, and, indeed, astrology was not typically seen by the Renaissance as imposing impersonal fate on humankind but, quite the reverse, as a symbol of the humanization of the universe. The early scientist, Roger Bacon, was often cited in the Renaissance for his proastrological views. As Eugenio Garin, the historian of science, says of Bacon: "In his view all relations were ultimately personal relations rather than numbers and measures and causes."[8]

But what a radically different, uncompromisable perspective modern consciousness requires! Either the stars are vastly distant nuclear furnaces formed at random and positioned by blind gravitational forces — in which case they can obviously have no significance for human events or human character — or they stand in some ultimate, meaningful relation to the lives of recently evolved two-legged creatures spinning about on the third planet of one of the stars near the edge of the Milky Way Galaxy. No, wait! That last alternative is obviously an impossible, mongrelized one. Astrology as a value-laden, humanizing image of the world fits the Ptolemaic astronomical picture, but if we are to take the modern astronomical vision for fact, the absurdities begin to mount. How would the fate foretold by a red giant star compare with a white dwarf? Are there astral meanings emanating from black holes, into which all else is falling? Does being born under a quasar make you queasy?

Compromise is beyond conceiving. Either the modern world-picture is wrong at its very core about what the stars are, how they originated, how they move and interact, and what our rather peripheral place is in the whole vast universe, or astrology is totally unfounded. There is no having it both ways. And we should note, to raise the stakes even higher, that if we reject modern astronomy we must abandon not only that one science but also physics and chemistry and the whole modern worldview. Are we still willing to keep an open mind about possible data? Are there to be no limits to credulity in postmodern consciousness?

One more example, before we further weigh the strengths and weaknesses of the magical consciousness, calls for brief notice. Consider the implications of being open to the data alleged by the authors of *The Secret Life of Plants*. My computer specialist friend had much provocation for his scorn. To take seriously these claims about the possible awareness by plants of our emotional states requires us to suspend judgment about such other "scandals" as telepathy (how else can plants know our moods, since they have no sense organs?) and even about the nature of life and mind. What is mind? The objective consciousness, as we saw in chapter 1, has always been skittish about the question. But typically, where recognized at all, it has been considered a phenomenon of highly developed nervous systems. If plants have minds but no nervous systems, what are the implications for *our* minds? If there are effective realities other than, but operating in, the physical universe, what will happen to our vision of reality? To take these matters seriously, then, requires a nearly total shift away from the familiar consciousness of modernity and—besides—would force us at the outset to reorder, in possibility at least, our view of the plant world surrounding us.

The obstacles to compromise with objective consciousness, though less blatant than in the case of astrology, are still very large. Besides the radical shift in world-picture that would be required, one's experimental methodology could not remain unchanged. As stressed in *The Secret Life of Plants,* these experiments cannot be approached in a cool, disinterested, impersonal way. The experimenter must acknowledge personal subjectivity and treat it as one essential ingredient in the total outcome. A domineering or unfeeling, controlling attitude will cause the plants to withdraw, "go dead," refuse to cooperate. They must be loved—or at least be given genuine approval—before they will give in return. But this threatens the root of objective consciousness. To give up impersonality of approach would not be to compromise in hopes of finding data, it would be to profane the sacred value, to treat with the devil of credulity, to enter apostasy.

"So be it, then!" say some. Perhaps. But let us not suppose that these are minor adjustments. These are changes requiring a complete recasting of the modern world-picture and a radical surrender of the modern devotion to objectivity. Let us now assess the occult consciousness, supposing that this may be a genuine candidate for the mythic matrix of the postmodern world.

ASSESSING MAGICAL CONSCIOUSNESS

One of the most striking points in favor of magical consciousness is surely the enriching effect it must have on personal experience. I was too restrained earlier when I remarked on the benefits of increased noticing — of taking the blinders off — from (even) the scientist's point of view. Then I spoke merely of having access to a wider range of potential data, and that is true as far as it goes, but how much more needs to be said! For magical consciousness the world comes alive — really alive, with an interior being and meaning and purposes all its own — for the first time. Theodore Roszak writes eloquently of the "eyes of fire" that will see more vividly and more truly. The shaman typifies Roszak's sense of what magic should mean to postmodern people. He writes:

> Magic, as the shaman practices it, is a matter of communing with the forces of nature as if they were mindful, intentional presences, as if they possessed a will that requires coaxing, argument, imprecation. When he conjures, divines, or casts spells, the shaman is addressing these presences as one addresses a person, playing the relationship by ear, watching out for the other's moods, passions, attitudes — but always respectful of the other's dignity. For the shaman, the world is a place alive with mighty, invisible personalities; these have their own purposes, which, like those of any person, are apt to be ultimately mysterious. The shaman is on intimate terms with the presences he addresses; he strives to find out their ways and move with the grain of them. He speaks of them as "you," not "it."[9]

Later he continues:

> The shaman, then, is one who knows that there is more to be seen of reality than the waking eye sees. Besides our eyes of flesh, there are eyes of fire that burn through the ordinariness of the world and perceive wonders and terrors beyond. In the superconsciousness of the shaman, nothing is simply a dead object, a stupid creature; rather, all the things of the earth are swayed by sacred meanings.[10]

Indeed, if Roszak can be followed, what a different way of "seeing the world" this would be! How much richer than the deracinated experience of modern consciousness, isolated by anthropocentric smugness from an alien universe! I tasted a small sample of the difference when, during my reading *The Secret Life of Plants,* I looked with new eyes at the faithful old philodendron on my office window sill. "Perhaps you are a sentient being, my good old green friend. Certainly you are not mere office décor, like the other familiar objects on the window sill. Long life to you, and happiness, too!"

A second strength of such consciousness, besides the intrinsic good of enriched daily experience, would be the restoration of what Jacques Monod has called the broken covenant between humans and nature. Monod, the molecular biologist, even considers the possibility that our human need for such a "covenant" may be genetic and inborn. He speculates:

> If it is true that the need for a complete explanation is innate, that its absence begets a profound ache within; if the only form of explanation capable of putting the soul at ease is that of a total history which discloses the meaning of man by assigning him a necessary place in nature's scheme; if to appear genuine, meaningful, soothing, the "explanation" must blend into the long animist tradition, then we understand why it took so many thousands of years for the kingdom of ideas to be invaded by the one according to which objective knowledge is the *only* authentic source of truth.[11]

And, I may add, then we understand the great appeal of the occult, which, as we saw in connection with Renaissance astrology, "rehumanizes" the universe. Humankind, for occult consciousness, is not alone in an alien universe. There are other intelligences, evil and good, that surround, enrich, and limit human life. The need for seeing and feeling the universe a *home* again, then, is a second recommendation of magical consciousness for postmodern civilization.

The third recommendation is practical. We have seen the possible consequences of objective consciousness in ravaging the earth in the absence of any ground for moral limit on human exploitation of a "disqualified" nature. Magical consciousness would call halt to what must eventually end anyway, by human restraint or by environmental collapse. It is practically most vital to have a vision of nature that will supply motives for restraint and harmony in place of modern attitudes of excess and conquest. Here are the words of a California shaman:

> The white people never cared for land or deer or bear. When we Indians kill meat, we eat it all up. When we dig roots, we make little holes. . . . We shake down acorns and pine-nuts. We don't chop down the trees, kill everything. The tree says, "Don't. I am sore. Don't hurt me." But they chop it down and cut it up. The spirit of the land hates them. . . . The Indians never hurt anything, but the white people

destroy all. They blast rocks and scatter them on the ground. The rock says, "Don't! You are hurting me." But the white people pay no attention. When the Indians use rocks, they take little round ones for their cooking. . . . How can the spirit of the earth like the white man? . . . Everywhere the white man has touched it, it is sore.[12]

I wish I could stop here, on this poignant note, concluding that the magical consciousness of the shaman would be adequate for our postmodern world. But the matter is more complicated.

First, it is obvious from the quotation that the shaman's consciousness is perfectly congruent with the simple lifestyles, and above all the simple craft traditions, of the Indians. The magical consciousness restrained the crafts developed by the Indians; in return the restrained, organic craft traditions supported the possibility of living with an I-thou attitude toward nature. This is very beautiful, but modern society is too complex, and there are too many people to expect that postmodern society will be able to live by shaking acorns from the trees and picking up small round stones for its fires. Short of catastrophic destruction (which, alas, is always a vivid possibility in any discussion of such matters), the postmodern world, as we have noted more than once before, will be in need of elaborate technological life-support systems to feed and house huge human populations. *Different* technologies from characteristically modern ones, of course, will be the order of the day. Sophisticated solar energy collectors and means of storage, probably, in place of obsolescent oil refineries or hazardous nuclear plants — and the like. Recycling technologies. Miniaturization. But the point remains that the postmodern world will require *post*modern technologies, not *pre*modern ones. And the magical consciousness, unable to compromise with the scientific worldview or method, seems a dubious candidate for running the machines and advancing the discoveries that a livable postmodern world will require for its inhabitants to stay alive. If a huge disaster strikes humanity, of course the occult consciousness may well be the mythic matrix of the postmodern survivors. But if our hope is to search for a form of consciousness adequate for a humane and livable future, given predictable populations, the eyes of fire alone seem not enough.

A second danger comes in the echo of a question I left hanging in connection with the uncompromisable gap between astrology and the scientific worldview; "Are there to be no limits to credulity in postmodern consciousness?" It is all very well to rejoice in the values of at-homeness in the universe, but what about the values of truth? It is beautiful to see purposes and meaning in all of nature, but what about integrity to evidence? Once such integrity is abandoned, must everything that is asserted be believed? What divides responsible belief from dangerous, deranged nonsense?

Here I confess again my respect for the austere virtues of genuine science. Resistance to authority, the discrimination between warranted and unwarranted assertions, the readiness to put treasured convictions (ideally, at any rate) on the scales of independent confirmation—these are the great virtues of modernity *and are still virtues*, despite their inherent limitations when worshiped as supreme or sole.

What is the alternative to retaining them, somehow, in any postmodern consciousness that would deserve respect? Roszak dismisses objective consciousness as "an arbitrary construct in which a given society in a given historical situation has invested its sense of meaningfulness and value. And so," he concludes, "like any mythology, it can be gotten round and called into questions by cultural movements which find meaning and values elsewhere."[13] But I doubt that it is easy to "get around" the cultural values of objectivity without running even graver risks.

These risks are not merely in personal integrity of belief, though this is important enough to give us second thoughts, but also in social terror. If postmodern consciousness has no defense against credulity, not only will we expect the grossest superstition to flourish in individual minds but also cruel public fanaticisms of all sorts: literal witch hunts again, voodoo torments, cruel tortures—of which even the admired Native Americans, we recall, were sometimes skilled practitioners.

This brings me to my third warning. What is there in magical consciousness to act as a barrier against abuses of the occult in familiar, exploitive ways? To see the "magic" in nature with our eyes of fire may, as we have noted, call forth moral reactions of restraint, which would be all to the good both of nature and of humankind. But the history of magic also— perhaps even more prominently—contains the history of manipulation, greed, and exploitation "by other means" and "through other laws" of compulsion. The black arts may not be so far, in the mood and motive of their origin, from the sciences as the recent apologists of magic have suggested. Historian of science Eugenio Garin sees them as very close, "for magic is a practical activity which aims at the transformation of nature by interfering with the laws of nature through technical knowledge of how they operate."[14] If so, the dreadful specter arises of a postmodern society combining the worst aspects of exploitative modern consciousness with the worst aspects of rampant credulity and superstition.

We may shudder at these thoughts. But our concern is not a new one. The biblical religions, both Judaism and Christianity, have traditionally warned against the seductive promises of magic. They never denied the possibility or reality of the occult, of course. The existence of witchcraft and divination is assumed in both the Old and New Testaments, and the church fathers wrote extensively about it. The biblical position on the occult was fiercely hostile: "Thou shalt not suffer a witch to live" was probably the rule even when Saul, disobeying his own law, stole away to consult the necromancy of the witch at Endor (1 Sam. 28). In the New Testament we find dramatic conflicts between the early apostles and magicians with whom, as miracle-workers, they were often confused. But the Christians insisted that their power was solely the power of the righteous God, operating "in the name of Jesus Christ"; while the powers invoked by the rivals were unrighteous, proudly independent of the sources of all being and goodness.

The ultimate *control by goodness* was the crucial point to the apostles and to the church fathers as well. Tertullian, for example, writes an interpretation of the three Wise Men — the "Magi" of Eastern magic, the Babylonian astrologers who followed the stars to Bethlehem — in which their gifts at the manger symbolize their giving up of magic arts and turning over all such power to the incarnate God. To reinforce their reforms, as Tertullian tells the story, they "went home by another way."[15]

Saint Augustine also discusses the occult, particularly astrology. For Augustine astrology was perfectly possible but wrong. Knowledge gained through the occult arts symbolizes forbidden knowledge, the outbreak of human pride. Power gained through magic symbolizes forbidden control, the clinging to security other than proper faith in God.

Such criticisms raise an interesting thought: What of Christianity itself as the matrix for the postmodern world? A change is on its way, like it or not, as we have seen. Christianity offers an actual alternative both to modern objective consciousness and to the occult. Christianity, indeed, has been engaged in battle with both over many centuries. Is Christianity merely a fossil, a denatured remnant of the premodern world? Or may there be enough life in this once-great form of consciousness to serve again as the matrix for another civilization?

13.

Christian Organicism?

Christianity has long waged its battle on two fronts important to our transitional world: against scientistic reductionism and against occult apostasy. Christianity is still a social force to be reckoned with, despite its long series of losses to modern consciousness and its nearly complete absorption into an "official" culture form. Might it be possible for Christianity to bridge our current transition and take on new life as the adequate religious matrix for the postmodern world?

In many ways this is an intriguing suggestion. Christianity has already proved its power not only to survive vast historical upheavals but also to create a civilization after the transition. The change from rural Palestine to imperial Rome shows Christianity's resilience under altered conditions; the change from fallen Rome to medieval Paris shows Christianity's power to mold new forms. Even the fact that Christianity as a religion has been able to survive the fall of its own distinctive civilization and continue as well as it has through the three centuries of the modern world is impressive. I am reminded of Arnold Toynbee's hypothesis, likening the rising and falling of successive civilizations to the chariot wheels of history, on which the great religions advance. Perhaps the fall of the modern and the rise of the postmodern world should be welcomed by Christians as yet another opportunity for renewed life. What does the Christian world-picture offer that might be helpful for postmodern consciousness?

CHRISTIANITY'S WORLD-PICTURE

A primary point to note is that the Christian world-picture is not in the first place a theory or a set of doctrines but rather a set of stories and images evocative of attitudes and provocative of theological interpretation. These interpretations have differed — sometimes widely — over the ages, and (as we shall see later in this chapter) may quite possibly differ ever more as historical circumstances change. Still, one great interpretive framework has dominated most of the history of Christian thought and feeling in the West: the framework of "being" derived from Greek philosophy through which the stories and images of the Christian world-picture have traditionally been seen. Especially since the thirteenth-century synthesis of biblical *mythos* with Aristotelian *logos* achieved by Saint Thomas Aquinas, there has been a Christian consciousness that deserves recognition as "mainstream." Other "streams" have existed and may yet come into prominence, but mainstream Christianity needs our notice first.

The principal feature of the mainstream Christian worldview, fashioned from biblical images perceived through Aristotelian categories, is that nature was created from nothing by the sovereign God, Lord of all being. Traditional Christian consciousness cannot overstress the sense that absolutely all ultimate power resides in God. God is dependent on nothing either for being or for acting. The world is dependent for everything on God. All the seeming powers of the world are in reality "delegated," as it were, from the Holy Center of all powers; all the world's reality is creaturely reality, contingent upon God's creative will and sustaining action. God's absoluteness is so great, some medieval doctrines held, that the divine cannot be considered relative in any way, not even to the degree of being related to the world. The world is related to God of course, but the logic of this relation is not reciprocal: God is not related to the world. Another medieval doctrine drew the consequences that God could not be supposed to know the world directly, since cognition is a kind of relation. But God cannot be thought ignorant of the world, either! Instead God knows the world (perfectly) through perfect self-knowledge as its source of being, but the creative power does not establish a relation or make God "relative" in any way.

I repeat these doctrines not merely to titillate with crumbs of medieval logic but rather to underscore the lengths to which traditional Christian thought once went to defend the fundamental value of God's absoluteness. This absoluteness is not in power alone. All ultimate worth, as well, resides in God. God's goodness is complete. The world adds nothing essential. The world minus God equals zero; God minus the world equals perfection. Indeed, the world's worth is entirely derived from God's calling it good. Like the world's reality, its worth is genuine so long as God wills it, but it is derivative worth. Creaturely worth is nothing in itself or apart from God. "Neo-orthodox" Protestant theologians like Karl Barth in this century have underlined this point by insisting that creatures may claim no independent value apart from God lest they "boast themselves against God."[1] Even God's love for the world, as Anders Nygren argued, is entirely unmotivated by being attracted to any value the world could boast. Such attracted love is *eros*: needy, hungering for values it does not have. But God hungers after nothing. Divine love is always *agapē*: full, other-oriented, impossible for fallen creatures to emulate but only to receive in faith.[2]

The other side of this mainstream worldview, however, is that the domain of nature has been entrusted to humanity by God's decree. The human race is also creature, of course, and therefore has merely creaturely (derivative) reality and worth. But humanity, uniquely among creatures, was made "in the image of God" and thus (however the "image" is interpreted) has a special status in the world. While still definitely under God's ultimate authority, humanity has been put in charge of the rest of the world of creatures. Adam and Eve are told to subdue the earth and fill it. Our species symbolizes its superiority by giving names to the lower orders. The world belongs to us by right, to use as needed. But we are finally responsible to God for our stewardship.

How does this classical viewpoint commend itself to the needs of post-modern humankind? On the same criteria we have been applying to other fundamental spiritual outlooks, what shall we say of mainstream Christianity?

There are very significant virtues. The human tendency to self-assertion is put under ultimate authority. The anthropocentric hubris of the modern world is limited by other values. These values center in God, finally. But nature, too, may benefit from Christian consciousness if God is pictured as valuing even "the least of these" (Matt. 25:45). Let me illustrate. It is sometimes almost pathetic to listen to well-meaning environmentalists try to justify, in narrowly anthropocentric modern-consciousness terms, why some endangered species should be protected even at some cost or inconvenience to human life. How can the western sheepherder be convinced that the endangered eagles that cost a portion of the profits should be legally defended against pursuit? Will life be that much poorer for future generations who have never seen them if Africa loses her leopards or Florida her alligators? The strained and roundabout arguments of anthropocentric modern consciousness are seldom very convincing — when the chips are really down. If the only appeal allowed by the fundamental religious frame of reference is to some *human* interest or long-term benefit or aesthetic need, then alas for the vanishing wetlands, the birds of prey, and the bearers of exotic furs or hides! To say that any diminution in nature diminishes each one of us is attractive sloganeering, but how many can honestly say they personally feel the pinch? There are few, I fear; too few to carry the day. And even for those who believe that such arguments to long-term human interests are valid and convincing,[3] all other things being equal, how many would weigh such indirect diminution of interests more heavily than some clear, immediate, "hard-headed" cost on the other side?

The Christian consciousness can answer these questions less awkwardly, more directly, than the purely anthropocentric modern ethic will allow. The Christian can reply simply that golden eagles should be valued because God created them a species and still cares about them. In a community of creatures, under God, no single set of values (all human) is entitled to carry the day. God's mysterious way in forming even "Leviathan" must be respected by the believer (Job 38-42).

In the same way, the sheer fact that we humans are pictured as under moral restraints grounded beyond our own wills or purposes may help postmodern society to accept needed social and economic restraints that must come, willy-nilly, before long. One of the most pressing issues facing modern Homo sapiens is the manner in which human pride and greed can be effectively prevented from continuing the mad press toward growth in all sectors — population, consumption, investment, pollution, depletion — that must lead to terrible rending of the modern world's social fabric. If Christianity, which once nurtured the relatively stable feudal society, can now sustain the steady-state postmodern world, it will have gone far toward offering worldly, as well as heavenly, salvation.

In addition to these virtues, the Christian vision would offer postmodern persons a richer content of experience than moderns have typically enjoyed. Return to Christianity would reestablish the meaningful covenant, broken by the rise of the objective consciousness, between humanity and the larger universe. The world could be seen and felt again as home for qualities and meanings long since driven out by the austere vision of traditional scientism. And all this could be gained, in contrast to the occult consciousness, with greater moral guidance than the sense of magic alone can provide. The self-limiting or self-critical element we found missing in occultism is present in traditional Christianity's humbling vision of the all-righteous creator God.

All this is well worth praising, but mainstream Christianity leaves several vital points to be desired, despite these great strengths. I shall recount three weaknesses in mainstream Christianity and then ask whether they are essential to Christianity itself or whether, somehow, a non-Aristotelian, postmodern Christianity, better than mainstream Christianity at just these points — but still Christianity — can be conceived.

First, I find it a significant weakness in mainstream Christianity that all values in nature are merely extrinsic and derivative. Humankind stands accountable, true, but only to God, not to the vulnerable earth. God's absolute monopoly of first-order being and worth leaves the world around us with only surrogate status. This status alone, if protected by a keen awareness of God's stern interest in all creatures — God's "keeping them covered," as it were, by unfaltering concern — *might,* as I have said, afford protection to nature and enforce restraint against excesses of human exploitation and abuse. I regret, however, to point out that such restraint has not been a noteworthy effect of mainstream Christianity in the past. True, some important traditions within Christianity have dealt tenderly with nature: gentle Saint Francis looked on all creatures as his siblings and Saint Benedict founded an order that would treat farmwork as a form of prayerful service. But in the mainstream of Christianity, as we saw the historian Lynn White has effectively argued,[4] the Genesis 1 commandment from God to our species that we "multiply" and "subdue" the earth has had quite the opposite from a reverent effect: It has tended to sanctify instead limitless exploitation and uncontrolled population growth. God's command seems to whip us on in our desire to possess and control and use. Far from "keeping them covered," God seems in the biblical image to be sanctifying, with ultimate moral authority, the ravaging of nonhuman creatures. W. Lee Humphreys, scholar of biblical Hebrew, reinforces this point by noting that the Hebrew word *kābash* translated "subdue" in the Genesis story, is also associated with contexts—like "trampling down" the grapes in a winepress, like "vanquishing" one's enemies, like using a "footstool"—that suggest a harsh line against nature. There is even an overtone of rape in the word, since it is the term used when the wicked Haman was thought by the returning King Ahasuerus to have "forced" Queen Esther (Esther 7:8).[5] I doubt therefore that mainstream Christian consciousness, leaving nature entirely dependent on God's concern for its protection against human abuse, is adequate for the needs of the postmodern world. God, in instructing us to "subdue" and use, seems not concerned enough, in this picture, with the need for human restraint. In the days of ancient Hebrew life, of course, the need for such restraint was not so visible as it is today. The world was hardly at all exploited, and human beings were few. But the God who instructs us to "vanquish," "trample down," "force" nature is not the God whose advice a desirable consciousness could take uncritically. Likewise the God who urges populations to multiply can hardly be worshiped by a society grown familiar with the fatal consequences of exponential curves.

Second, I wonder whether the value implications of the mainstream Christian interpretation of God will be able to draw instinctive favorable response in postmodern men and women. The traditional view reflects the ancient oriental attitude toward absolute potentates—carried to infinity. The king can do no wrong; his will alone is sovereign; before it even the mighty, who serve solely at his pleasure, tremble and abase themselves. The very essence of the state resides in him. His slightest wish is instantly obeyed, and those who displease him are subjected to prolonged and hopeless torture. So likewise is God to the world, in the traditional picture—the divine absoluteness even requires a new logic of relations. But can, or should, postmodern men and women "go home again" to such values? The modern world has experienced much since the days of the Pharaohs. There are still absolute masters, of course, but centuries of moral investment have gone into widespread intuitions that there may be another, better way in which personal dignity may be preserved even in relationship with legitimate ruling power, and in which rulers interact with and are limited by the intrinsic rights and interests of the governed. Should we expect postmodern men and women to abandon these hard-won intuitions? If adequate postmodern, not premodern, forms of consciousness are what we are in search of, the world-pictures involved must focus and reinforce at least the best of modern sensibilities. In this the mainstream Christian interpretation of God is seriously defective.

Third, and finally, I must in philosophical conscience return once more to the problem of credulity. The question is not only whether mainstream Christianity can sustain an ecologically sound society, not only whether Christianity so interpreted can support fundamental moral intuitions, but also — and not least — whether traditional Christianity can be believed without opening the floodgates fatally wide. In asking this question I am not assuming that modern science is the final authority on what is responsibly believable. But we saw earlier that warranted belief on some kind of standard is needed to sort out the wheat from the cognitive chaff. Mainstream Christianity has not traditionally been enthusiastic about the offering of warrants for independent judgment, thus subjecting its value-laden assertions to tests of responsible belief. Even philosophically acute thinkers like Saint Thomas Aquinas acknowledged the fundamental role of authority. Within the boundaries of authority energetic argumentation could and did take place, but always within the "theological circle." Ought postmodern consciousness to be expected to "turn itself in" to arbitrary authority (any authority is arbitrary that refuses to stand accountable for its claims by offering reasons, not anathemas, to its challengers) after feeling the genuine force of duty represented by modern responsibility of belief? I think not. In this respect traditional Christianity fails to cohere with the best in modern methods of thought.

Thus I conclude that the mainstream version of the Christian world-picture is a dubious bridge to postmodernity. Whatever an adequate postmodern religious matrix will be like, it needs to be in touch with the best of modern values and of modern thinking if it is to bridge the gap constructively from this historical epoch to the next. This was once strikingly true of Christianity as it served as a link from Roman to medieval civilizations. Christianity managed to incorporate most of the highest of the classical values and was fortunate in having, in its ranks, intellectuals like Saint Augustine capable of using the best of classical philosophy as a vehicle for interpreting Christian imagery for the faithful and for the critic alike. Today our best values have undergone some change; our best cognitive vehicles have been further refined since Plato and Aristotle. Might it be that Christianity could rise to the historical challenge once again and develop a *non-traditional but still Christian* version qualified to carry the new day as once it carried the old?

ORGANISMIC THEORY, CHRISTIAN *MYTHOS*

I think we should be cautious in answering any such grandly speculative question, but I am not inclined to dismiss the possibility. Contemporary theologians are at work on a number of fronts. One front, for example, is the effort to articulate the Christian matrix of value-laden image and story in the terms or in a manner drawn from the philosophical approach of

Ludwig Wittgenstein. Another active front is the campaign to "demythologize" Christian imagery and interpret it in a way undergirded by the existential philosophy of Martin Heidegger. A third area of theological activity is attempting to understand the biblical *mythos* along the lines of Alfred North Whitehead's philosophy of organism, or process philosophy, as it is usually called. There are other movements as well, "political theologies," "liberation theologies," "theologies of hope," theologies based on theories of Marx, of Hegel, of Comte, or of avant garde psychology.

In all these cases the adopted or constructed theory acts as an interpretive conceptual framework (much as did the philosophy of Plato for Saint Augustine or the philosophy of Aristotle for Saint Thomas Aquinas)—this conceptual framework facilitating, clarifying, organizing serious attempts to think in terms of the great, definitive value-focusing imagery of the Christian tradition. The imagery, as I maintain, is primary for religious consciousness. But as I also have noted, the theory is important too. The theological theory not only expresses the value-imagery, as best its categories allow, but also it inevitably influences, by its way of organizing and categorizing, what the imagery is felt as signifying. That is (to put it another way) we turn to various theoretical frameworks, often philosophies, to help us think connectedly and in keeping with our primary religious images, which these theories are supposed to articulate, interpret, clarify, and relate to the rest of our beliefs. But as we become used to thinking our religious images in terms of one framework or another, the imagery itself is perceived differently. One framework will draw a certain aspect of the richly varied imagery into the foreground, casting other aspects into the shadowy background as "merely figurative"; another will select different aspects as central.

If we assume that the fundamental imagery of Christianity is what defines it for worship, not the theoretical frameworks that variously serve to articulate that imagery for thought, then Christianity may remain truly Christian in the essential religious sense while being very much transformed at the level of theory. We have seen this happen, at least once, when Saint Thomas scandalized the theological world in his day by adopting the philosophy of Aristotle for his vehicle in interpreting Christian faith. Hitherto Christianity had been set in a Platonic framework. Aristotle, Plato's pupil and severe critic, was perceived, when rediscovered, as an enemy of Christianity. But Saint Thomas showed that Aristotle was only the enemy of certain Platonic theoretical elements, not of Christian faith itself, which could be acceptably articulated in the new Aristotelian framework. His efforts were so successful in the thirteenth century that we tend to forget today how radical they then seemed to his contemporaries.

But today even deeper changes in theory are afoot. Both Plato and Aristotle agreed on certain theoretical fundamentals that were characteristic of classical Greek thinking but that are being challenged today. Both agreed, for a prime example, that *being*—true being—could not be changeable in any way. They agreed that being was more perfect than becoming, or than anything subject to change. They both had a place in their philosophies for a highest being, one which could not change in any way or even know change. For Plato this highest being was entirely impersonal, the Form of the Good; for Aristotle this being was eternally aloof Thought thinking only Itself.

These Greek philosophical convictions were of course imported into Christian theology when Christian intellectuals adopted the best theoretical framework available for the articulation of their faith. On the whole it seems entirely natural — even inevitable — after centuries of thinking in these terms. But there were costs incurred by so doing. The dynamic creator-sustainer of the biblical imagery had somehow to be thought in terms of classical Greek repugnance to change of any sort. As highest being, God could not any longer be thought to be making decisions, engaging in work (no matter how effortless), or interacting with the events of rebellious human history. As absolute, in the framework of Plato and Aristotle, God could not be thought (as distinct from felt) as related by concern for, knowledge of, or providential intention toward the world of finitude and becoming. Above all, God could never be thought on this framework to be frustrated, as the divine concern seems repeatedly to be in the primary religious imagery, or as momentarily angry, or as admitting a change of mind about anything. The many stories in which God is so pictured must move into the background, on this theoretical reading, as merely figurative expressions. Other passages stressing the otherness of God from changing worldly things — especially the mysterious announcement from the burning bush, "I AM WHO I AM" (Exod. 3:14), suggesting that God is Being Itself — move forward into prominence as expressing basic truth.

It all seems quite natural, and as we have seen at the start of this chapter it is basic to mainstream Christianity's way of thinking its essential value imagery. But what if the ancient Greek theoretical premise about the primacy of *being* is challenged by a contemporary philosophy that is impressed by the fundamental place of dynamic *becoming* in this universe made out of constant, vibrant energy? Matter, we have learned, is nothing but events of energy. And energy is "becoming" in identifiable form, or process. Given such a theoretical base, what would Christianity look like? It would have an untraditional theoretical understructure, certainly. But if the essential religious imagery of God and Christ and humanity and nature could be rethought without forcing, might not a Christian faith qualified for the postmodern world then arise?

I shall conclude this discussion with a sketch and assessment of this possibility. I do this mainly as an example of what hope there may be for flexible Christian responses to our historic needs in this transition time, but also partly because, of all the current theological reforms, this particular one, process theology, commends itself to me most strongly.

First, what are the general outlines of process theology? Its basic theoretical framework is drawn from the philosophy developed in this century by Alfred North Whitehead, a mathematician deeply interested in the startling developments of mathematical physics in this century. He begins with the un-Greek premise I suggested: that reality is inseparable from process, flux taking on form only to be transcended by more such events of process in the endless rhythm of this dynamic universe.

I cannot even begin to develop his viewpoint or his arguments here, which are fascinating but technical and expressed in a vocabulary all his own.[6] I shall just say, very simply, that in Whitehead's framework there is a significant place for God, who is required for theoretical reasons in the system. God is the everlasting entity needed in this system as the actual font of all pure possibilities, the cosmic framer of general real possibilities, the intimate lure in the universe toward heightened value, and the final repository of all worthy achievement. God's experience is of the world as its flux achieves and re-achieves definition in the ceaseless dialectic of becoming. God's love for the world is expressed in unending effort to enhance the quality of achieved definiteness, hence the intrinsic value, of every self-creating entity at every moment and in every place. God is directly felt by men and women in both of two major aspects: as the Abiding One ("Abide with me, fast falls the eventide" was one of Whitehead's favorite hymn citations), and as the Eros of the Universe, restlessly urging toward higher value.

More could be said, but it should already be clear that such a conceptual framework as Whitehead's must be interesting as making possible a fresh theoretical articulation of Christian imagery.[7] Any such articulation will necessarily conflict with the traditional one at crucial points, since the basic premise about being as static has been challenged, but this is to be expected when basic theoretical frameworks clash. This clash, however, should not be confused with an incompatibility between Whiteheadian philosophy and Christianity itself, unless the Whiteheadian framework is also shown unable to articulate satisfactorily the primary value-imagery of biblical faith. May it prove adequate, despite its initial unfamiliarity?

God, first, on the Whiteheadian scheme, cannot be thought to be unchanging in all respects. In one respect, as primordial font of all pure possibility, God is unchanging. But in respect to divine relationships to the world God is, like the rest of the universe, in process. God is even growing: moving everlastingly from perfection to still greater perfection. This is literally unthinkable from an Aristotelian framework, of course, but there is much biblical imagery that can be seen as supporting such a dynamic deity, intimately relating to events as they develop and responding creatively to them. Indeed, this seems the far more natural way of reading most of the stories of the Bible involving God. These images are dynamic—the voice from the whirlwind awing Job; the guide and military guardian of the Israelites leading out of Egypt and into the Promised Land; the urging, prodding, threatening, punishing, forgiving God who sends Christ at the fullness of time and receives the Son back after accepting the sacrifice of atonement. Surely such images are more naturally articulated by process theology than by the utterly static categories of Greek thought? Here, where there is a conflict, process theology would seem clearly superior to traditional Christian theoretical underpinnings for thought.

God, second, cannot on Whiteheadian grounds be thought to be absolute creator of the world and eternally independent of it. Instead God is to be conceived as an orderer and lure toward more valuable sorts of achieved order; God is coeverlasting with the world, and is as much dependent on the world as the world is dependent on God. Again this is shocking to many ingrained habits of thought, but a look at the Genesis imagery itself will show that the theological doctrine of *creatio ex nihilo* is not obviously there; it has had to be read into the understanding of the story. What the story itself shows, it may be argued, is an ordering God "starting out" with a disordered or chaotic world already at hand: "The earth was without form and void, and darkness was upon the face of the deep; and the Spirit of God was moving over the face of the waters" (Gen. 1:2). Again the Whiteheadian articulation seems at least as appropriate to the imagery of faith as its distinguished traditional predecessors.

There are other differences. The world, on process theology's interpretation, has genuine *value* of its own as well as *being* of its own. This might give a renewed force to the phrase: "And God saw that it was good" (Gen. 1:10). Finite goodness, that is, would no longer be a matter merely of God's arbitrary fiat but would be due to something intrinsic in things themselves. And if this is so, then humans and God, though far from equal, are in a distinct way cocreators of value. Our species has dignity, freedom, and rights of its own. God is our legitimate leader and guide into the good and into the better; God is never a sheer despot.

So much, then, for this minisketch of the outlines of process theology. Its virtues, measured against the needs of the postmodern world, are evident at once. On the practical side, it would provide postmodern consciousness a sense of organismic unity with nature and of the presence of intrinsic values in the world; it would offer a time-tested theoretical matrix for Christian imagery that could provide a sense of the meaningful place of human effort in a significant universe; it would reinforce ecological values and guide postmodern consciousness into the saving ways of restraint and wise holistic policies; and it would reflect the best of modern intuitions about human dignity, freedom, and the proper reciprocity between government and governed.

Its cognitive or intellectual virtues are similarly strong. It is carefully reasoned, showing respect for the legitimate modern sense of obligation to integrity of thought but without the devaluing, antiseptic abstractions that have flawed consciousness. And it is coherent with—no, rooted in—the major scientific results of the twentieth century: quantum mechanics, relativity theory, matter-energy convertibility, and the like. More than at the vital edge of science alone, it is coherent also with important developments in educational theory, with the widening appreciation of world religions, and with respected theories of art, history, and society. Christian process theology offers impressively strong credentials, therefore, both practically and intellectually, as candidate for the adequate religious matrix needed by the postmodern world. It would present a postmodern version of Christianity that might actually satisfy our most urgent requirements.

So we have found a happy ending—almost. But the conclusion is not quite so simply written as this discussion of process theology might suggest. There are still problems to be met and strategies for their solution to be suggested. One obvious problem is: Can process theology be *accepted* as Christian by Christians? If we are looking for religious answers to profound historical needs, a scholar's philosophy alone can hardly satisfy. Only if process *philosophy* becomes effective process *theology*—or, better still, becomes simply mainstream postmodern Christianity, "theology as such,"[8] as the great images are freshly understood—can large changes in social policy and common consciousness be hoped for. Philosophy, though it plays a vital role in the total economy of things, is an elite craft. We need power and mass appeal in addition to adequacy, in principle, for life and thought. The verdict on process theology, however, is still pending. It will be given in this larger sense not by philosophers like myself but by clergy, as they preach, and lay persons as they respond to the new ways of articulating the "old, old" story. The verdict will come, in other words, from the believing community, whose judgment on the appropriateness of the new way of thinking to the articulation of the images it reveres will be—and of right should be—normative.[9] What shall we do *in the meanwhile,* while the fateful process goes on?

Another problem is yet to be faced: Can process theology, or any other metaphysical position, be wholeheartedly *believed* under today's disconcerting transitional conditions? However well recommended as socially needed or as abstractly well-credentialed, Christianity's "burden of truth" remains heavy, as does any comprehensive religious worldview. Perhaps the times simply are not ripe for such all-comprehending claims to exclusive allegiance. Are there alternatives to huge, monolithic religious positions of this sort? If so, Christians and non-Christians alike need to think carefully about them. One such alternative will be the topic of the next chapter.

14.

Mystery and Multi-mythic Organicism

We are on a quest, in this book, for a vital and adequate response to the current transition from the modern to the postmodern world. We saw in chapter 11 the pressing need to go beyond the technolatrous objective *mythos* of modern consciousness that has served the modern world so well — and so badly — as its functioning religious matrix. In chapter 12 we noted the possible return of magical consciousness as an alternative deserving some respect but even more caution. Most recently we have considered Christianity as a viable candidate for shaping postmodern consciousness — not traditional mainstream Christianity, which we saw to suffer serious weaknesses in this role, but a postmodern rearticulation of the great archetypal images of biblical faith through an organismic, ecologically holistic, scientifically relevant process theology. The benefits of such a dynamic, postmodern version of Christianity, we saw, would be (1) a newly sensed unity with the natural environment, (2) a fresh realization of responsibility toward nature involving needed restraints on human exploitation, (3) a heightened appreciation of the virtues of scientific standards of warranted belief without the characteristic modern defects of alienative reductionism, and (4) a renewed lease on effective life for the ancient and powerful value-expressive and value-focusing imagery of the biblical heritage.

Before rejoicing in the successful conclusion of our quest, however, I raised two cautions that seem to me serious and in need of thoughtful attention. One of these cautions had to do with the question of whether process theology will ever be accepted by Christians as the appropriate theoretical articulation of their faith. Lacking such sensed religious appropriateness and left to itself as a technical system of concepts, Whiteheadian philosophy of organism is most unlikely to be a major force in shaping postmodern consciousness, but the verdict is still out and is likely to remain so for some time. What should be our strategy in the meantime — a period which may well last longer than our lives?

The second caution had to do with the even more general question of whether these times of turmoil and transition are suitable for any great religious synthesis. Even if process theology is quickly deemed *appropriate* by the Christian religious community, can we assume widespread conviction to follow, given the current situation? Assuming adequate metaphysical credentials, if they can be agreed upon, and assuming religious appropriateness, can we—Christians or non-Christians—accept this worldview (or any such) fully enough to expect that our lives will be changed, our consciousness altered, and our society saved? This, after all, is not a wholly voluntary matter. If there are serious grounds to doubt the probable effectiveness of any single religious metaphysical synthesis during the unstable transition time we face before us, then we had better develop a strategy for dealing realistically and constructively with our actual fragmented situation. Postmodern Christianity may be well-suited for a desirable postmodern world, but such a world does not exist. What does exist? How should we cope, not *sometime*, but *now?*

I submit that we are currently in a poor intellectual and valuational situation for the nourishment of great religious-metaphysical synthesis, and thus for the time being we shall have to develop other strategies of survival not dependent upon supposing that we see very clearly or very whole.

THE RETURN OF MYSTERY

Consider, first, our current intellectual situation. The sheer fact is that our best knowledge is so shot through with mystery that to call it knowledge may some day seem a little arrogant and quaint. I was given a pungent taste of this fact when, on the occasion of the five-hundredth anniversary of Copernicus' birth I was invited to participate in a conference, sponsored in Washington jointly by the Smithsonian Institution and the National Academy of Science, to celebrate both the memory of Copernicus and the advances of current cosmology. The outcome from the latter point of view was fascinating and more than a little funny. Distinguished scientist after distinguished scientist rose to present a paper on how much easier it was to (seem to) understand the universe in the days of Copernicus! They were not saying this in so many words, for the most part, but in total effect their presentations reinforced vividly how strange and deeply mysterious the known—or the thought-to-be-known—universe of current astronomy and cosmic physics must be recognized to be. It occurred to me that I was there hearing the authentic voice of postmodern science—of science no longer easily categorizable as "modern" in the familiar style of the last three hundred years. There was little of the attitude of controlling hubris, of reductive materialism, of confident progressivism at that historic conference. Instead I heard of mysterious entities, hidden energy sources, baffling results that force leading astronomers to wonder aloud whether their whole picture of things may be wrong in fundamental ways. Even our closest neighbor, the moon, is more of a mystery than ever. Our space explorations have given us vast new amounts of data and have ruled out certain theories of the solar system, but in some ways our puzzlement is even greater than it was before. Still more puzzling are the mysteries opened up by the discovery of "black holes" in space, the contents of which must forever remain unknown since no signal or information of any kind could in principle get out to us. Or the discovery of quasars, generating energy at theoretically impossible levels. Or bafflingly powerful X-ray emitters. Or inexplicably regular radio sources. So on and on. What seems most characteristic of postmodern astronomy—like all postmodern science is put well by William Pollard when he says:

> It should be evident from all this that when we speak of "mystery" in science we no longer mean unknown areas or puzzles which research in the future may be expected to clear up. We are not speaking of a mystery of anything unknown at all. Rather we are speaking of the mysteriously amazing character of the known. There is a true mystery of the known and our modern knowledge in science confronts us with that mystery very strongly.[1]

Certainly this intellectual situation is much more pervasive than astronomy or cosmology alone. Closer to home on earth, as intimately as within the atoms of our own bodies, the mysteries deepen in the elusive world of submicroscopic physics. The tendency of modern science, as we saw in earlier chapters, has been to analyze matter into its smallest particles, seeking the fundamental reality in the smallest fragment. Smaller and yet smaller particles have resulted from this determined drive downward, each "elementary" particle giving way to still more "elementary" ones as more and more accelerators are built to develop energies strong enough to smash the atom into still tinier bits. Nature seems all too cooperative! Each larger hammer splatters the atom still further, so far without limit, in principle, and without evoking any coherent theory. "Fundamental particle physics is a mess," one physicist friend complained to me succinctly. There are too many particles, now; there is no rhyme or reason to them all; the feeling is of Chinese boxes opening to show smaller boxes inside without limit.

Another friend, the late physicist Harold Schilling whose consciousness of his field was emphatically postmodern, suggested in conversation that the problem may be in the basic assumptions of modern physics, not in nature. Just before the Copernican revolution, he reminded me, the techniques of astronomy were refined to the point that each careful new observation required the postulation of a new epicycle to be added to account for the added phenomena. To the pre-Copernicans, each must have seemed like an important discovery, however frustratingly complex nature seemed to be. Perhaps, urged Schilling, we are asking an analogously wrong question of the atom by trying to split it into its supposedly fundamental particles. Perhaps "elementary particles" are theoretical fictions analogous to the epicycles of the pre-Copernicans. Perhaps we need a revolutionary new way of conceiving the atom not as built up out of tiny particles but as capable of manifesting particle-like behavior under certain conditions.

Later, at the above mentioned Copernicus Conference, I raised this question in conversation with the distinguished physicist Werner Heisenberg, father of the immensely significant "uncertainty principle" of fundamental physics. Heisenberg agreed immediately that the quest for particles was leading nowhere and was deeply misguided. I asked him whether he had some guess about what theoretical approach to the atom might point the way to needed revolutions in physics. His answer: Consider the atom in terms of "mathematical resonances," not tiny bits of anything.

William Pollard, another postmodern physicist and valued friend, prefers to think of the atom as made up of quarks, tripartite entities that can never exist except in combination—"one in three and three in one." Whether Trinitarian quarks or Pythagorean resonances or something else, the atom is a source of mystery today. Matter itself is far from understood; far less, then, is it capable of being the paradigm of explanation by which everything else can be understood. Pollard writes:

> The old materialism which reduced everything to simple masses in motion has been swept away. The contemporary materialist must visualize material reality in terms of matter and anti-matter waves in a kind of shadow world, and consider them to be made up of mass, charge, nuclearity, and other basic constituents according to various recipes. It is a strange and shadowy kind of materialism with none of the simple, substantial, and sturdy obviousness of the old established kind.[2]

In this context the recent triumph of molecular biology in discovering the basic code through which all life transmits genetic information becomes the occasion both of admiration and of wonder. The coded "tape" made up of sugars and phosphoric acid, called nucleic acid, is wound in two strands in the famous double helix form. The complementary strands of nucleic acid contain all the information required for producing the whole organism it encodes. The chemical "letters" comprising the code spell out "words" directing the manufacture of various proteins. The words together make up genetic "sentences" and "paragraphs" leading to the masterpieces of living organisms in all their complexity and variety. In this discovery there is the basis for the keenest admiration.

There is also stimulus for wonder at even deeper mysteries. Gunther Stent, a molecular biologist, points out that the code is the same across all the vast gaps that differentiate life-forms—from bacteria to plants and to animals including mammals. The same few letters, that is, spell out the unimaginable richness of all living things. This is wonderful in itself, but it is even more amazing that the code has remained so stable through all the evolutionary time—billions of years—that such universality requires. Stent speculates about this amazing stability but offers no final answers. He goes on to raise an even more baffling subject: "the general properties of the genetic code turn out to bear a curious resemblance," he writes, "to another symbolic system devised more than 3000 years ago for fathoming the nature of life, namely to the ancient *I Ching,* or 'Book of Changes'. . . ."[3] Stent proceeds to describe the hexagrams of the *I Ching,* notes their astonishing anticipation of binary mathematics, and then concludes:

> But however surprising may be the anticipation of binary digits by the *I Ching,* the congruence between it and the genetic code is nothing short of amazing. For if Yang (the male, or light, principle) is identified with the purine bases and Yin (the female, or dark, principle) with pyrimidine bases, so that Old Yang and Yin correspond to the complementary adenine (A) and thymine (T) pair and New Yang and Yin to the complementary guanine (G) and cytosine (C) pair, each of the 64 hexagrams comes to represent one of the nucleotide triplet codons. The "natural" order of the *I Ching* can now be seen to generate an array of nucleotide triplets in which many of the generic codon relations manifest in Crick's arrangement are shown. Perhaps students of the presently still mysterious origins of the genetic code might consult the extensive commentaries of the *I Ching* to obtain some clues to the solution of their problem.[4]

This may merely be a curiosity, and Stent's final remark may be ironic, but it shows how far from simple reductive arrogance even triumphant molecular biology has come. And still more mysteries abound. Not only do the origin and amazing stability of the genetic code evade our understanding but also an irreducible "plus" stands out. That plus is information and meaning. A related point is made by Barry Commoner. Noting that DNA and RNA molecules never appear spontaneously in nature apart from living organisms, Commoner concludes that DNA is not the secret of life, but, on the contrary, that "life is the secret of DNA!"[5] Although we have learned much about the ways and means of genetic structure, the mysteries of biology have not been eliminated; they have been driven deeper.

As we probe those depths our knowledge increases and so does our awareness of how much we do not understand. This is the key to all postmodern science. Schilling sums it up well:

> It is important to recognize that it is all of science we are talking about, not just physics. Today's literature about science abounds in references not only to the new physics but to the new chemistry, new biology, new psychology, new anthropology, and still others, implying that a new day has dawned for science in general.[6]

All this has been in illustration of our current intellectual situation. The mysteries of postmodern science are so pervasive that it seems an inappropriate historical moment to pin our hopes on a great cognitive synthesis. A metaphysical scheme, to be adequate, must relate to the best knowledge of the time. But what firm ground is to be found today? There is excitement and hope as well as bafflement in the air; I do not mean to paint a bleak picture, just a realistic one in which surprises are more likely than closure for the foreseeable future.

Similarly, I think that our current valuational situation is unpropitious for the emergence of a great religious consensus based on any single *mythos*. We find ourselves in a time of radical pluralism regarding the images by which men and women picture their world and their preferences within it. The value-drenched images of technolatry are still viable for many, perhaps most, in our modern world. But, as we have seen, the power of such a *mythos* is bound to wane as objective consciousness and the modern world itself encounter historical nemesis. There are signs already, as we have seen through the previous chapters, that wholly different mythic forms are ready to challenge the unquestioned hegemony of those rooted in modern science.

The challenges are themselves startlingly varied. Simply by juxtaposing chapters on magic and Christianity—themselves ancient rivals—I have tried to suggest something of this variety. For some people the historic images of cross and Christ and God remain potent, stirring to ways of life and perception and creative of distinctive community. For others these images are dead, as the surge of response to the "death of God" theologies of the 1960s illustrates. There seems no predicting or controlling this phenomenon of the "living" or "dying" of ultimate imagery. Whether myths live or die for given persons or communities is beyond voluntary control and is one of the mysteries we must be prepared to face and accept in our time.

Deeply different imagery, at any rate, is "living" today for many who may be united in the rejection of the scientistic *mythos* and technolatry. For some it may be the biblical world-picture that shapes and expresses their values; for others it may be the imagery of astrology, with mysterious emanations and influences binding the universe of human interests with the universe at large. For others, especially the young, the *mythos* of Native American culture is living and potent, depicting humankind in gentle animistic relations to the world around us, with shamanistic communication both possible and needed. Charles Reich found many followers for his imagery of a "greening" America in which Consciousness III would rise quietly to perform a greater revolution in our society than politics ever could.[7] Others entertain images of the marketing of what may be variously listed as "intermediate technology," "alternative technology," "village technology," "appropriate technology," "people's technology," "organic technology," "ecological technology," "biotechnics," or "soft technology" in place of the large-scale technolatrous corporate technologies of modern times.[8] Erich Fromm combines Marxist and Freudian imagery in his vision of a future society grounded in people-power and in pursuit of *biophilous* ("life-loving") values.[9] Victor Ferkiss offers us a picture of technological humankind living with a new naturalism or awareness of the dynamic dignity of the environment, a new holism or realization of how interconnected everything is, and a new immanentism or openness to finding the sacred not "up there" but close at hand in nature and society.[10] And Robert L. Heilbroner explicitly invokes the "magic" of mythic imagery, as we noted in chapter 8, urging us to rediscover patient Atlas as our spiritual focus in place of nervous and ultimately deadly Prometheus.[11]

These actual and proposed images illustrate some of the multiplicity of basic value-foci that we must expect to live with during this unsettled time of transition, at least. It makes the prospect of a single *mythos* for the bringing in of postmodern consciousness seem rather dim. But one feature in all this variety deserves notice: There does seem to be a gathering consensus, of sorts, if not in terms of the specific value-laden images themselves, at least in terms of certain fundamental values that are in distinct contrast to those typical of technolatrous modern consciousness.

These values include the readiness to accept limits and constraints on personal appetites and expectations. Whether these limits are imaged in terms of a concerned heavenly Person or an astral influence, a personified nature or the larger needs of society, is not the point here. Of main significance is that a basic value is placed on *self-control within a finite setting*.

These shared values also include the recognition of the integrity or the dignity of *the other as a perceived center of intrinsic significance*. What limits us is not blind, mechanical necessity, as the deterministic images of objective consciousness tend to depict. Instead, whether it be the needs of the people or the divine will, strangely perceptive plants or meaningful rhythms of organic balance, we are confronted with an Other to which we can relate and which we may respect as having interiority as legitimate and value-centering as our own, though very likely of a different sort. This readiness to value the semiautonomous Other makes possible the renegotiation of Jacques Monod's "lost compact" with the universe. The imagery depicting the sort of compact it may be tends to differ greatly, but the practical effect and the moral intent cohere.

If this is so, then despite the unlikelihood of a great cognitive synthesis or a single dominant *mythos* in our time, we are not without the basis for a creative response to our historic need. In the remainder of this chapter I shall sketch a spiritual strategy that I call Multi-mythic Organicism.

RELIGION "BETWEEN MODELS"

Multi-mythic Organicism is a religious posture for those, like me, who find this to be time "between models"—both cognitive and valuational— that might in more settled eras shape a single confident vision of the ultimate. It is a religious stance that affirms as legitimate and exciting the possibility of pluralism in mythic imagery within a context of undergirding fundamental values. It is not a religious response *without* organizing imagery but, rather, one with *many* value-focusing sets of myths welcome within it.

Such a religious posture would necessarily sacrifice the sometimes fanatical power that comes from wholehearted and single-minded involvement within a single grand myth. It would require a tolerance for ambiguity that, to some, would seem a far cry from the fervor that many associate with religious sincerity. But the other side of such tolerance is liberation: liberation from imprisonment in a single set of images that no longer seems quite large enough for life, and liberation from the parochialism of association and imagination that ties us to the *mythos* of a single community. Multi-mythic Organicism does not mourn over lost certitudes but rejoices in the new dimensions of possibility that come open to view.

These new spiritual possibilities, though plural, are not shapeless, of course. Some mythic forms simply do not meet Multi-mythic Organicism's criterion of appropriateness. The images of unlimited material "progress," for example, or the alienating world-pictures of scientism, or the exclusive preoccupation with the Promethean myth, would be resisted on behalf of fundamental organismic values that make this valuational posture take on, for all its mythic pluralism, a definite shape.

This shape reflects certain fundamental features of healthy organic life. At a minimum these would include, first, acknowledgment of the constant balance between growth and death *(anabolism* and *catabolism)* that maintains healthy organisms at proper scale and within finite limits. The miracle of homeostasis, in other words, becomes an object of deep valuation.

Likewise, second, a valued feature of healthy organic life must be the balance between local differentiation of function and holistic mutuality of connection. Even in unicellular organisms we find this balance between differentiation and connectedness; much more strikingly we find it exemplified in the higher, vastly more complex organisms wherein local semi-autonomy and the general good coexist harmoniously.

And, third, the balance between necessity and spontaneity will be a valued feature of healthy organic life. Living organisms neither are exempt from the general constraints of physical law nor are they mere flotsam on the causal tide of nature; they have the power of invention, of novel stratagems in response to novel challenge; they have some degree—more vividly manifested in the higher organisms—of creative self-determinism within the larger determinations of the natural order.

These three features: *homeostasis*, differentiated *holism*, and *creativity*, represent fundamental values for organicism. Drawn from the basic image of healthy life, they are capable of supporting definite attitudes even while remaining multi-mythically open to a variety of mythic exemplifications— Christian, Marxist, Astrological, Shamanistic, and the like—so long as these are suitably interpreted and lived. What might this mean?

First, Multi-mythic Organicism demands a sophisticated attitude toward our own belief systems. We need a revitalized sense of mystery in knowing. At best our cognitive constructs are only that: cognitive constructs. The better they are, the more they reveal the mysteries beyond.

I have dwelt enough already in this chapter on the need for a sense of mystery in the sciences. This, it seems to me, should be perceived as a healthy awareness, to be greeted without fear or despair. And it should be perceived as appropriate to all our cognitive constructs—philosophical, political, historical, religious—as well as scientific. Such a perception will lead to a new sense of limits in all our attempts at knowing, and a new readiness to accept those limits without rage and even with joy.

Our beliefs are finite dwelling places for our minds. We build them as carefully as we can, if we are wise, using the sturdiest materials we can find and then putting them together in the best way we are able. They generally serve us adequately, sustaining and defending us tolerably well. Built spaciously they can house our fellows in great number and can thereby make for civilized community. But it should not shock us that there are other such dwelling places besides ours, or that they will not last forever, or that there are vast domains still outside our highest arching vaults. Even a fine house need not be the only one—or the only type of one. Even a well-constructed house experiences the shocks of weather and the erosion of wear. This means that as we "live the transition" to the postmodern world, we should school ourselves to be alert to the main alternatives to our own familiar structures, and that we should discipline ourselves to recognize the need for repair, remodeling—or even sometimes moving. Admittedly finite dwelling places may, none the less, be better or worse, larger or smaller, than one another.

Ambiguity need not be destructive or paralyzing. It may be liberating and zestful if our attitudes are prepared for it and if our sense of human possibilities is kept wisely in touch with our sense of human finitude. Living the transition to the postmodern world challenges us to such attitudes toward our own beliefs.

Likewise, second, Multi-mythic Organicism requires a major change in our attitudes toward the natural environment. We need a revitalized sense of the mystery around us. In that sensitivity we shall regain our feeling for the semiautonomous "more" in nature that modern consciousness drove out: "more," that is, than we can fully comprehend in our finite theories of nature, and "more" than we can—or ought—to control for narrow human ends. Such a sense of mystery leads directly to the voluntary acceptance of organismic limits on our treatment of nature. It will require us to accept a broader time-frame for our policies regarding nature. The larger needs of "then" must be more heavily weighed in the balance with the parochial wants of "now." But, further, the very control-syndrome itself—the supposition that we have or should aspire to absolute autonomy unbalanced by holistic mutuality, whether in the short term or the long—will need to acknowledge its limits, not out of resignation but out of healthy affirmation of the human situation as properly one of organic partnership with, rather than sheer dominion over, the natural world around us.

For this attitude to be adopted with good will, another one is necessary, springing from the voluntary affirmation of homeostatic limits: namely, the acknowledgment of the virtues of thrift, simplicity, or bare sufficiency. As human numbers grow and the earth's resources shrink, the material share we can claim as fairly ours will necessarily diminish with the years ahead. The limits I speak of will be enforced by nature, whether we adopt them gracefully or not; my suggestion is that we seize the moral initiative.

Natural organic limits need not be demoralizing. They may spur us to a fuller sense of what besides material consumption constitutes fulfillment in human life. Rather than struggling vainly against the narrowing limits, only to taste the bitter fruit of defeat, we may prepare ourselves now, with dignity, to seek other creative satisfactions. Living the transition to the postmodern world challenges us to newly constructive attitudes toward nature.

Third, and still similarly, Multi-mythic Organicism requires that we cultivate distinctive attitudes toward our fellow humans. We need a revitalized sense of the mystery in human variety, creativity, and intrinsic worth. There is urgent need to upgrade our respect for the uniqueness, the privileged "insideness," the subjective stubbornness of human individuals. Each of us, is, in principle, hidden in the center of his or her consciousness from all others. We all see the world from our own point of view. There are structural similarities and holistic connections, of course, or there could be no language, no community, no distinctively human life. But it is also distinctively human to have a certain opaqueness all one's own—the mystery of "me," *my* being, *my* values, *my* birth, *my* death, *my* purposes, *my* creative spontaneity.

In this sense of mystery in dealing with fellow human beings, we shall find yet again the attitudinal basis for the voluntary acceptance of limits. One of our limits will be felt at the point where we have been accustomed to manipulating other persons. Whether in large numbers or singly, whether for benevolent motives or for selfish ones, the one-way manipulative, controlling attitude is wrong from the viewpoint of Multi-mythic Organicism. Technologies of behavior, however well intended, belong to the technolatrous frame of mind. They neglect the precious, mysterious, interior of the persons being controlled. What I earlier called the control-syndrome is what has brought modern humankind to its present parlous condition: We feel we must unilaterally control every aspect of nature to maximize our wealth; thus we must control our wealth to enjoy it; thus we must control our neighbor so that he or she will not steal from us; thus we must control the society to preserve our privileges; thus we must control world markets and resources so that our society will prosper; thus we must control a military establishment capable of controlling the covetous (or hostile, etc.) impulses of other societies who also have military establishments aimed at controlling our similar impulses; thus we must control the balance of terror . . . if we can! And so it goes, to competition, exploitation, and conflict. Unchecked by recognition of the mysterious dignity of others and the need for real mutuality, the control-syndrome leads to disaster. Self-limitation, in contrast, is always in the context of our subjective recognition of the dignity and freedom of our own selfhood. The dangers of living the transition require much more of the latter (voluntary limitation) and much less of the former (manipulation of others).

Equally, the healthy sense of mystery in other personal centers of experience and value will place limits on our expectation of mythological uniformity. The possibilities of pluralism will be accepted as natural and less threatening. The rich variety of religious options may be more cheerfully embraced. Given these attitudes, we may celebrate our differences rather than attack one other.

Self-limitation in dealing with other persons need not be demeaning. It may be evocative of new, creative social patterns based on mutual respect rather than mistrust, competition, conformity, and manipulation. Living the transition to the postmodern world challenges us to fresh, reconciling attitudes toward our fellows.

The organismic virtues of rich differentiation within the balanced limits of unity are what we fundamentally seek in our postmodern world. Richness and wholeness, variety and integrity, nurtured in sustainable mutual community, is what Multi-mythic Organicism is all about.

PART 5

ORGANICISM IN RELIGION

15.

Remything Judaism and Christianity

One of the ironies I have noticed in our present situation is that many people in the universities of the global North who have never had much personal use for institutional religion are now rediscovering the churches and synagogues with a vengeance. "Not for themselves," of course, but as engines of social change for the masses whose consciousness and ethical sensibilities need instant reform in the current ecological and historical crises that threaten us.

"GETTING RELIGION"

I have been struck at the numbers of my students in environmentally oriented courses who have hit upon this "solution" to society's ills. Granted, it usually does not come to mind at once. After becoming aware of the urgent need for a new multi-mythic, organic consciousness in our time, they first tend to think in terms of spreading the news through the mass communications media: a great blitz campaign over television and radio, magazines and newspapers, in support of a gentler, less frantically consuming, more organically restrained mode of life and thought. But then the thought usually strikes them that the modern exploitative, manipulative, materialist, unrestrained, growth-obsessed consciousness is nowhere more purely present than in our typical media. Modern consciousness at its most objectionable *is* their primary message. To expect these media to take the lead in ushering in a radically opposed postmodern consciousness, my students generally conclude, is ludicrous. Even if there were no moral qualms about the blatant mass manipulation of minds that would be involved (and there are plenty of such qualms), the commercial pressures that control the media would never permit such a commercially suicidal blitz campaign to occur. "Who would pay for it?" is the bottom-line comment on that suggestion.

Next my students often propose that education is the answer. The means, at least, would be compatible with the end (though in some school systems one might well wonder even about that). But this proposal has evident defects as well. Institutionalized education, unlike mass propaganda, is too slow a process to meet the urgent timetable on which an orderly transition may depend. Besides, education of the scope and depth required would remain an exercise for the élite. Ours is a historical challenge in which all are involved and in which great changes of value and perception must occur generally. The presence or absence of institutional educational credentials cannot be the distinguishing mark for healthful postmodern consciousness if our society as a whole is to navigate the transition successfully.

Thus institutional religion is rediscovered. Looked at from outside it seems to be the perfect instrument for needed value changes in society at large. The institutions are all in place; they do not have to be specially invented or paid for. They are supported and attended by a complete cross section of society; a mass audience is promised. They are not obviously controlled by commercial interests; they should be able to strike an independent note against the current powers that be. And, best of all, they already deal with values before a believing group ready to accept on faith what is preached and sung. Pictured as somewhere between the media of mass propaganda and elitist educational institutions, the churches and synagogues raise the flagging hopes of those in search of a needed engine of social change.

Since I have had intimate dealings with institutional religion all my life, my hopes (though real, as I shall show below) must be more moderate. Even the metaphor of the churches as "engine" for social change strikes me as brash. As an airplane pilot, I tend to think of engines as very important features indeed! They are generally out in front; they are as powerful as they are noisy; their pull makes all the difference. Perhaps the institutionalized religions were once potent enough to merit such a metaphor, but surely this is the case no longer. The real motivating forces, the active engines in our society are the other, often unrecognized religious realities of technolatry and objective consciousness, including their manifestations in economics and politics. The churches, more realistically, are just along for the ride.

Is this excessively harsh? I have tried to think of other more appropriate metaphors for institutional religion's place on the fuselage of modern society. If not the engine, then are the churches the rudder—at the tail end of things but still functional? Perhaps this is a better image, since in flight the rudder is really not supposed to steer (the ailerons do that) but simply to keep the turns coordinated. I had contemplated proposing the metaphor of the humble trim tab, but this seems unduly diminishing of the churches' role, not least since the setting of the trim tab is usually only noticed in straight-and-level flight. The rudder is a better image, especially since there are times, especially at dangerous moments, when it is vital to perform *un*-coordinated maneuvers; at such times the influence of a cross-controllable rudder is enormously important; in forcing itself stubbornly against the normal windflow, by creating drag and turbulence (even at the tail end), it may save the whole craft in a crosswind situation.

To extend this metaphor one more degree: Our modern society is on final approach to the postmodern world. The bumps are terrific and due to get worse. The shifting crosswinds are fierce and dangerous. The churches are not the engines speeding our craft along toward doom or happy landings, but they may have a crucial influence if only by disturbing the normal flow of the slipstream generated by our rush toward destiny. In the sections to follow I shall show some of the ways that Judaism and Christianity, our primary institutional religions, may play the stubborn rudder's role.

JEWISH ORGANICISM

A fuller discussion of Judaism would need to recognize the extent to which different strands and traditions exist side by side, with different emphases and interpretations. My brief treatment, which is meant merely to be suggestive of the values that Multi-mythic Organicism would commend and reinforce in the general Judaic *mythos,* will have to ignore this finer texture, though it is important for actual institutional Judaism. I hope that others will be stimulated to work out the details for specific application.

One of the ways in which Jewish consciousness has been most in contrast to the typical modern mind—one of the sources of the felt "differentness" that has often contributed to the sense of Jews as alien in the modern world—is the readiness to live under ritual restraints. In the previous chapter I identified one of the basic values of organicism as self-limitation: maintenance of balance, homeostasis. Cancers and bacterial cultures grow heedlessly until external limits force an end to such life; healthy organisms have inbuilt means of maintaining scale and due proportion. Any desirable postmodern consciousness will need to provide the basis for the voluntary acceptance of limits, and here Judaism's *observant attitude* may be of historic importance. Not all Jewish families are equally "observant," of course; not all varieties of Judaism require the same specific observances of their faithful. But deep in the fabric of Judaism itself remains the recognition that human beings live under authority; that not all things are permitted; and that to observe the Law of God is the faithful Jew's first duty. Life under the restraint of law, symbolized variously in daily acts of self-limitation, is at the center of historic Jewish consciousness.

There is no guarantee that an observant attitude in one part of life will bring about restraint in all parts, economic as well as ritualistic. The prophetic thunder within Judaism has rumbled again and again against the failure of ritual observance to follow through in ethical practice.

> "I hate, I despite your feasts,
>   and I take no delight in your solemn assemblies.

> Even though you offer me your burnt offerings and
> cereal offerings,
> I will not accept them,
> and the peace offerings of your fatted beasts
> I will not look upon.
> Take away from me the noise of your songs;
> to the melody of your harps I will not listen.
> But let justice roll down like waters,
> and righteousness like an ever-flowing stream.
> (Amos 5:21–24)

But the cultivation of an observant attitude toward life, though not all that is needed in an adequate postmodern consciousness, is an important advance over the distinctly unobservant attitudes of modernity. Jewish observant consciousness provides a basis for voluntary acceptance of limits, for restraints on the progressive hubris that has characterized our society's spiritual life, and for the homeostasis that we must learn to maintain if we are to live the transition to a new social order in dignity and health.

A second fundamental value of Multi-mythic Organicism is based on the holistic interconnectedness of healthy life. There is differentiation at all levels but always within a context of unity. Here Judaism deeply reinforces organismic consciousness both in its basic imagery regarding human beings and in its venerable attitudes toward the land and all the creatures living upon it.

Men and women are not shown in the Genesis myths (which Jews have tended to interpret somewhat differently from Christians who share the same stories) as radically different beings from the rest of nature. There is differentiation of function but no destruction of the holism in nature's web. The dust of the earth is the stuff of human form, and breath is the secret of life. The mind-body (or soul-body) problem that has plagued philosophy since the ancient Greeks is not a difficulty within classical Jewish thought, since the philosophically postulated different substances, mind-stuff and body-stuff, are not part of Judaic imagery. The problem of finding connections is outflanked at the start by a holistic vision in which the living human body is not a composite of two unlike realities but, rather, a unity of animate flesh.

Similarly, human intercourse with the land and all its creatures remains holistic though differentiated. One's land is not absolute property to do with as one pleases. The observant attitude requires restraints and a sense of mutuality for the sake of the poor, for the sake of the animals who live and work on the land, and for the sake of the land itself. Land, for example, is not supposed to be exploited to the maximum degree at the time of harvest. Deuteronomic law at one point justifies such restraint on the basis of concern for the poor and powerless:

When you reap your harvest in your field, and have forgotten a sheaf in the field, you shall not go back to get it; it shall be for the sojourner, the fatherless, and the widow; that the Lord your God may bless you in all the work of your hands. When you beat your olive trees, you shall not go over the boughs again; it shall be for the sojourner, the fatherless, and the widow. When you gather the grapes of your vineyard, you shall not glean it afterward; it shall be for the sojourner, the fatherless, and the widow. You shall remember that you were a slave in the land of Egypt; therefore I command you to do this" (Deut. 24:19–22).

Such consideration is not reserved for powerless human beings alone since the same sort of protection is extended in the same context to the beasts of the field. Ignoring all economic interest, which would argue against sharing one's harvest beyond minimum necessity with the working animals, Deuteronomic law commands: "You shall not muzzle an ox when it treads out the grain" (Deut. 25:4). Not muzzle the ox! He will be sure to help himself generously, with temptation placed so near. Yes, but the holistic sense of mutual connection to the animals with whom we live and work demands that we woo rather than rape. There is differentiation between the farmer and his oxen, but the proper organic relation involves mutuality, not mere exploitation.

Even the cropland itself is not mere property, to be used to the maximum without regard or restraint. The rights of Sabbath rest are extended also to the fields by the Levitical commandment:

Six years you shall sow your field, and six years you shall prune your vineyard, and gather in its fruits; but in the seventh year there shall be a sabbath of solemn rest for the land, a sabbath to the Lord; you shall not sow your field or prune your vineyard. What grows of itself in your harvest you shall not reap, and the grapes of your undressed vine you shall not gather; it shall be a year of solemn rest for the land (Levi. 25:3–5).

Nor is Sabbath rest the only consideration due the sustaining land on which humankind gratefully dwells. Leviticus imposes a requirement that, if observed, would forbid the permanent commercialization of our natural heritage. After seven Sabbaths of rest for the land, or forty-nine years, comes the Jubilee year in which not only persons who have fallen into slavery but also land that has been bought and sold are to be given their freedom again.

And you shall hallow the fiftieth year, and proclaim liberty throughout the land to all its inhabitants; it shall be a jubilee for you, when each of you shall return to his property and each of you shall return to his family. . . . The land shall not be sold in perpetuity, for the land is mine; for you are strangers and sojourners with me (Levi. 25:10, 23).

The land is not to be reduced to mere "real estate," then, in this paradigm of holistic consciousness toward nature. Neither people nor pastures are to be sold into permanent slavery. Jewish thought at this point has touched a profound theme of organicism and offers an important element in a viable postmodern consciousness.

Finally, Multi-mythic Organicism values what I called the intrinsic dignity of creative self-determinism in healthy organisms. People have purposes. They have an inwardness, a for-itself status that deserves respect. Domination of the poor by the rich, or of the unfortunate by the high and mighty, is morally repulsive. Jewish thought is keenly aware of the need for restraint against what I earlier called the "control syndrome," which so easily slips into callous manipulation and injustice. The larger prophetic tradition, which is deep and central to Judaism, demands economic justice within a framework of holistic respect for nature and obedience to God.

Domination itself is morally indivisible. As Deuteronomy and Leviticus suggest, domination of every last sheaf in one's field is related to domination over the friendless sojourner or the defenseless widow; domination of the draft animals on the land is related to domination over the earth itself. The Jewish prophetic tradition extends this concept pointedly, and modern Judaism is in a position to recognize the extent to which the tools and institutions of the modern world have permitted us of the modern world to dominate, unjustly and unequally, the resources of the planet. The keen social conscience of an Amos linked to a similar awareness of current events today will quickly uncover the extent to which privilege and greed are perpetuated by the techniques and structures of our modern society itself, the extent to which judgment is merited upon the dominating societies of the earth, and the ways in which redemptive social policies might painfully but urgently be put into effect. These insights are among the most appropriate for the times of transition that are upon us. The resources of the Jewish prophetic tradition in providing moral clarification for our turbulent age are much needed.

Needed also is the prophetic vision of the new world that longs to arise. Such visions of the ideal inspire and lure even as the prophetic ethical lash drives and pushes. Beyond domination and injustice lies the messianic promise of a society, under God, in harmony with itself and with the universe. Perhaps the best example of such a vision was authored by Isaiah:

> The wolf shall dwell with the lamb,
>   and the leopard shall lie down with the kid,
> and the calf and the lion and the fatling together,
>   and a little child shall lead them.
> The cow and the bear shall feed;

their young shall lie down together;
and the lion shall eat straw like the ox.
The sucking child shall play over the hole of the asp,
and the weaned child shall put his hand on the
adder's den.
They shall not hurt or destroy
in all my holy mountain;
for the earth shall be full of the knowledge of the
Lord
as the waters cover the sea (Isa. 11:6–9).

Here is a beautiful dream of a magical world quite unlike our own. It is a dream of integrity and wholeness, in contrast to the dualism between ruler and ruled, man and nature, world and God. It is a dream of harmony, in contrast to the ruthless pursuit of profit, domination, and control. And it is a dream of justice, in contrast to the inequalities and torments of our world. It is a dream well worth the dreaming. It summarizes the contributions to postmodern consciousness that may be hoped for from Judaism. In this dream we see how gladly we could welcome the Judaizing of modern consciousness for the humanizing of the world. It is a dream that forces itself out against the slipstream from our current path; in this way the *mythos* of Judaism may help us make our needed turn.

CHRISTIAN ORGANICISM

Christianity, too, offers grounds for hope as an instrument of constructive consciousness change. Even short of the extensive theological reforms that I discussed in chapter 13, Christianity in the churches as they exist today provides the leverage points, if they will be used, for significant assistance in changing the mind of the modern world. As in my treatment of Judaism, specific variations growing out of the multiplicity of traditions, denominations, and sects will need to be ignored; I shall simply focus on central traits that from the perspective of Multi-mythic Organicism are clearly to be appreciated. The following is not intended as a balanced appraisal of Christianity, but as a few suggestions—for those outside as well as inside the churches—about how historic Christianity may be perceived as a resource for living the transition to the postmodern world.

The need for learning to live with limits, which we have noted as one of the primary requirements of our time, is deeply embedded in historic Christianity. Homeostasis is nothing alien to a religion founded on reverence for the humble Carpenter from rural Palestine. The roots of Christian faith are deep in the lower classes of the Hellenistic world, where poverty and slavery were no strangers. There has been an antimaterialist note in Christianity from the beginning:

And he said to them, "Take heed, and beware of all covetousness; for a man's life does not consist in the abundance of his possessions." And he told them a parable, saying, "The land of a rich man brought forth plentifully; and he thought to himself, 'What shall I do, for I have nowhere to store my crops?' And he said, 'I will do this: I will pull down my barns, and build larger ones; and there I will store all my grain and my goods. And I will say to my soul, Soul, you have ample good laid up for many years; take your ease, eat, drink, be merry.' But God said to him, 'Fool! This night your soul is required of you; and the things you have prepared, whose will they be?' So is he who lays up treasure for himself, and is not rich toward God" (Luke 12:15–21).

Despite the sumptuousness of some churches in some periods of Christendom, Christian faith has never abandoned—in principle—its antimaterialist heritage. The vows of poverty taken by many clergy are reminders that material simplicity is an honorable estate. This is not a popular theme in modern churches, nor is it widely practiced, but it should not be forgotten, since it is deeply embedded in the Christian *mythos* and is potentially a recoverable resource for demanding times. Christianity need not be embarrassed, at least, by the need for a whole society to limit its material consumption and expectations: It has something constructive to say to the situation.

Another urgent point of self-limitation, as we have seen, is with regard to population. Christianity has by no means played a constructive role, worldwide, in the controversies over contraception. Despite all the polemics, however, it has never been the Christian position that people should breed mindlessly, like rabbits. Even the staunchest opponent of artificial birth control, Pope Paul VI, recognizes the "licitness" of avoiding pregnancies under many circumstances; his wrath is directed against the technical hubris and "illicit" means by which these licit ends may be sought. I have no intention of defending the papal stand on birth control, which has posed a grave problem of conscience for many within the Roman Catholic church, but it should be recognized that all Christians—including even the Pope—acknowledge the appropriately voluntary nature of human reproduction. Sexuality has always been perceived as a matter of choice, not fate. Jesus, as far as we know, did not marry or have offspring. Saint Paul, likewise, recommended the celibate life for those strong enough to take it. The vows of chastity taken by many clergy over many ages are reminders that Christianity puts human reproduction in a larger context of moral control. In my view it is not enough, given the threat to civilization itself posed by the exponential curves of human population growth, to rely on unaided "chastity" as the sole licit means of exercising that moral control. "New occasions teach new duties," as the famous hymn proclaims. But within an appropriate understanding of the moral requirements of our time,

Christianity's fundamentally voluntarist attitude toward sexuality and reproduction is a resource for living with the constraints that will be necessary to accept in the postmodern world.

Besides recognizing the value of constraints, Multi-mythic Organicism urges the need for holism, we recall, in relations among human beings and between humanity and nature. In the context of this need it is interesting to note the abundance of organic figures of speech that are employed in central places in the New Testament depicting the proper relationships for Christians with Christ and with one another. In one of the great climactic passages in the Gospel of John, Jesus adopts an organic metaphor:

> I am the true vine, and my Father is the vinedresser. Every branch of mine that bears no fruit, he takes away, and every branch that does bear fruit he prunes, that it may bear more fruit. You are already made clean by the word which I have spoken to you. Abide in me, and I in you. As the branch cannot bear fruit by itself, unless it abides in the vine, neither can you, unless you abide in me. I am the vine, you are the branches. He who abides in me, and I in him, he it is that bears much fruit, for apart from me you can do nothing (John 15:1–5).

The image of mutual "abiding" through organic holism is echoed by Saint Paul on more than one occasion. Writing to the Romans, he compares the young Christian community to an organism that has local diversification within an overall unity.

> For as in one body we have many members, and all the members do not have the same function, so we, though many, are one body in Christ, and individually members one of another. Having gifts that differ according to the grace given to us, let us use them: if prophecy, in proportion to our faith; if service, in our serving; he who teaches, in his teaching; he who exhorts, in his exhortation; he who contributes, in liberality; he who gives aid, with zeal; he who does acts of mercy, with cheerfulness (Rom. 12:4–8).

And in rebuking the Christians at Corinth for petty jealousies that ought not to exist within a community of organic mutuality, Saint Paul goes into yet greater detail.

> For just as the body is one and has many members, and all the members of the body, though many, are one body, so it is with Christ. For by one Spirit we were all baptized into one body—Jews or Greeks, slaves or free—and all were made to drink of one Spirit.
> For the body does not consist of one member but of many. If the foot should say, "Because I am not a hand, I do not belong to the

body," that would not make it any less a part of the body. And if the ear should say, "Because I am not an eye, I do not belong to the body," that would not make it any less a part of the body. If the whole body were an eye, where would be the hearing? If the whole body were an ear, where would be the sense of smell? But as it is, God arranged the organs in the body, each one of them, as he chose. If all were a single organ, where would the body be? As it is, there are many parts, yet one body. The eye cannot say to the hand, "I have no need of you." . . . If one member suffers, all suffer together; if one member is honored, all rejoice together (1 Cor. 12:12–21, 26).

These metaphors are important for Christianity, because they are the images underlying the Christian ideal of community. It is clearly the ideal of differentiation and mutuality, fellowship hospitable to variety, richness held together in wholeness. It is a worthy ideal of human relationships for a more holistic postmodern world.

In the New Testament there is less explicit attention paid to the relations between humanity and the rest of nature. But the imagery we find takes for granted an intimacy that is fully in keeping with the holistic values of Multi-mythic Organicism. Jesus takes nature as the manifest model of God's concern for all his creatures, reminds his disciples that we are all enveloped in the same concern just as we are all fellow creatures, and urges that human behavior be more natural, less anxious and alienatingly defensive about our material needs. God knows that we have such needs; after all, we are creatures and cared for along with all the other creatures. Not all creatures need to be credited with equal importance in God's eyes— there is, after all, differentiation within unity—but even the "least" have some importance, and human importance takes its place on that continuous scale.

And he said to his disciples, "Therefore I tell you, do not be anxious about your life, what you shall eat, nor about your body, what you shall put on. For life is more than food, and the body more than clothing. Consider the ravens: they neither sow nor reap, they have neither storehouse nor barn, and yet God feeds them. Of how much more value are you than the birds! And which of you by being anxious can add a cubit to his span of life? If then you are not able to do as small a thing as that, why are you anxious about the rest? Consider the lilies, how they grow; they neither toil nor spin; yet I tell you, even Solomon in all his glory was not arrayed like one of these. But if God so clothes the grass which is alive in the field today and tomorrow is thrown into the oven, how much more will he clothe you, O men of little faith! (Luke 12:22–28).

In this posture of relaxed acceptance of nature and the continuity of the human place in it, we note a Christian theme that could assist our civilization in finding a healthier relationship to the environment.

The third great value insisted on by Multi-mythic Organicism is respect for the intrinsic value of the other, as a center of potential creativity and purpose. Christianity offers support for such a value at two levels: both in terms of its condemnation of the distortion of moral relationships, and in terms of its characteristic ethic of love.

Judgment for sin is one of the crucial themes within Christian faith. Sin is a state of estrangement from God brought about by breaking relationships through pride or self-centeredness of other sorts. In a great Christian image drawn by Saint Paul, nature and humanity both are seen as suffering from this state of estrangement. In Adam's disobedience to God, the estrangement began; with the basic relationship broken, all others are distorted as well, including relationships toward nature. Our abuse of the natural order, on this Christian vision, is part of our sinful condition. Disregard for the other, in every domain, stems from this defective condition and will be met with just punishment.

It is true, certainly, that modern civilization has manifested disregard for the other, both human and environmental; we have, in Christian language, sinned against humanity and nature. One of the churches' contributions, unpleasant though it may be to hear, could be to help us face up to the seriousness of our estrangement and prepare ourselves spiritually for the pains of penitential restitution. Judgment is a hard word to hear, and in late modern times (especially in the "better" churches) the theme of judgment has been more softly spoken than have words of blessed assurance. But the days of transition are bound to be stormy and hard. Modern civilization has sinned against our fellows, our future, and the earth; the sin is returning, whether we like it or not, in heavy judgment. Modern humanity owes a great debt to nature, and this debt will somehow be repaid. The paying will be a time of anguish. But Christianity can, if it will, interpret the moral appropriateness of this judgment and help to shape constructive spiritual attitudes toward the pain to come—attitudes of humility, repentance, and a greater awareness both of our basic spiritual flaws and of the proper acts of contrition and repayment.

The other characteristic way in which Christianity supports the valuing of the other is more gentle, but in some ways equally difficult to hear. The central demand of Christian faith is for love—whether we *like* it or not! The paradox of *agapē,* or Christian concern, is that it is commanded. Love is usually thought of as a paradigm of something that operates by inclination alone, but Christian *agapē* is intended to rule and shape inclination, not the reverse. In this we see that *agapē* is different from the usual sort of love, *eros,* that begins with a need or desire within the self and attempts (as Plato shows in the *Symposium)* to attach the attractive beloved to the yearning self. On the contrary, *agapē* is focused on the other's well-being even if the other is not at all attractive. *Agapē* grounds an intentional consciousness in which the "intent" is turned wholly toward the object of concern. *Agapē* is a giving love, whether there is anything to be gotten back or not. It is the sort of gift that God is, when, without anything to gain, the drama of the Incarnation is set into being.

> For God so loved the world that he gave his only Son, that whoever believes in him should not perish but have eternal life. For God sent the Son into the world, not to condemn the world, but that the world might be saved through him (John 3:16–17).

If Christianity is true to its own center, *agapē,* it will teach its followers how to look for and respect, in thought and deed, the precious otherness that the world supplies. At a minimum this will apply to the otherness of persons — all persons, near or far, friend or foe — toward whom concerned respect will be forthcoming. Maximally, perhaps, Christian *agapē* will extend its range from the human and divine into the realm of nature, too. Some Christians have shown the way. Saint Francis, with his fraternal attitudes toward all fellow creatures, and Albert Schweitzer, with his "reverence for life," are two notable examples of lovers who do not stop with loving people alone.

In these ways, then, Christianity may be seen as a potential resource for the spiritual needs of the postmodern world. The churches, if they will, may give significant assistance to the birth and nurture of a more desirable postmodern world. There is hope that Christianity may yet play the needed role of stubborn rudder in our passage through the turbulence of these transitional times.

HOW REALISTIC OUR HOPE?

But will institutional religion actually stiffen itself against the primary windstream of our culture to perform this important role? I feel keenly the hypothetical qualifications one always needs to add toward the end of these discussions: *"If* Christianity is true to its own center . . . ," or "The churches, *if* they will. . . ."

No one can answer this question with assurance. In the old language: "Only God knows." But it is possible to distinguish some of the conditions under which these hopes might be met.

First, if Judaism and Christianity are to make a major difference to the course of our civilization, the multiplicity of institutions that are the actual vehicles of those faiths will need to learn how better to coordinate themselves. There is need for a deeper ecumenicity than ever before: not only within the various organized religions, and not only among them, but also among all mythic traditions that share in supporting the life-bringing values needed for the postmodern world. This need is not merely a reflection of the principles of Multi-mythic Organicism; it is a requirement of practical effectiveness.

In the third quarter of the twentieth century, some real progress was made toward effective ecumenicity. The World Council of Churches, mainly Protestant, was and is a phenomenon of real importance. At the doctrinal level there is little movement toward unity; I have participated in the elaborate waltzes of theological courtesy and conflict and have felt the frustrations that come from dealing at this level with those who are locked single-mindedly and unambiguously into hard-line interpretations of monovalent myths. But at other levels, where the commissions of the World Council operate closer to the domain of applied values, the benefits of differentiation within increasing unity are beginning to be realized. Readers of this book will take special interest in the activities of the Commission on Church and Society, with headquarters in Geneva, Switzerland. Among the activities of this agency of the World Council of Churches is the sponsoring of a series of ecumenical conferences and the publication of a number of papers dealing with Christian social thought in future perspective. Similar movements and activities have taken place under Roman Catholic sponsorship since the Second Vatican Council opened that church wider to current breezes; and intra-Jewish cooperative activities, especially with emphasis on social issues, have continued.

Such movement toward religious coordination, though real, is only the beginning of what is needed for our time of transition. The postmodern world cannot afford the starchy exclusivism that still remains the rule within the various institutional traditions. Myths increasingly need to be recognized as myths, and theoretical constructs as theoretical constructs, without anxiety or felt diminution of their importance. The primary values underlying great myths and constructs need more explicit clarification and reassertion within the context of creative pluralism. Pluralism of image, powered by firm commitment to underlying life-bringing values, needs to extend beyond the boundaries of Protestantism or Roman Catholicism or Judaism into every religious expression fit for the organic needs of the postmodern world.

At this point there is an obvious need for Christians and Jews to enter a discussion of Multi-mythic Organicism and Hinduism, Buddhism, Taoism, Jainism, Islam, and other major religious traditions of the world. The great religions of the world may have much in common, seen from the organismic perspective, and in the long run they will need to be drawn into a fruitful differentiated unity that sees beyond contrasting mythic styles.

Ecumenism pushed to such a degree will not be easy for the leaders of the institutions that have grown strong on separation. Some religious institutions seem to justify their very existence on the basis of their differences from other institutions, rather than on the basis of their common contributions to the upholding of ultimate values. Therefore it will require unprecedented humility on the part of the leadership, unprecedented flexibility on the part of the laity, and unprecedented good will on the part of all concerned to bring about the concerted effort that will be needed for effective change in the consciousness and the course of our civilization.

Is such unprecedented response likely to be made? The discussion of the first need leads us to notice a second, even more basic, need: the purification and inspiration of the institutional religions themselves. Who are the people on whom our hope for religious assistance rests? Are they somehow different from the rest of us? Have they a special leverage that the rest of us lack?

As to who the people are who make up the religious institutions around us, we know the answer: They are by and large simply the ordinary people of our culture. They are indeed, as my students see, a cross section of the population, for better or for worse. Consequently, the churches and synagogues are mainly in the hands of adherents to the average values of the modern world. We see this illustrated in every direction: in the insistence of one congregation on installing a new air-conditioning plant for its sanctuary, despite known danger to the ozone layer and desperate alternative human claims; in the pride taken by another parish in the canny investment of its building fund in growth securities; in the controversies — perhaps leading to firing or transfer — over clergy who have the tactlessness to preach the painful prophetic word in its contemporary relevance or to dwell too vividly on the disturbing demands of *agapē*. The "pillars of society" who support the churches and synagogues tend to be firmly based in the modern world. It is no exaggeration to conclude that the institutions of religion have been largely captured by modern consciousness.

But is there, nevertheless, some special leverage that the churches and synagogues may possess? If the "salt of the earth" are mainly savorless, is there still some catalyst that may return them to spicy sharpness? The answer may rest in the latent power of mythic imagery to reclaim response. At least adherents of organized religion regularly expose themselves to the once-potent archetypes of value and meaning that define their respective faiths. If the myths come alive with power for the transformation of consciousness, there is hope for renewal within the traditional faiths. That is, in the language of theistic mythology, if God wills to revive people and through them to redeem the world, this can surely happen, despite all obstacles. Still employing this language, we may say: it is the irresistible and mysterious power of God that holds the final answer to the problems of re-savoring the salt and renewing human consciousness for abundant life in the postmodern world.

In sum, then, our need is for a miracle. If the institutional religions of our world are to offer us much ground for hope, something will have to happen within them that we can neither predict nor control. This does not mean that we should abandon hope; on the contrary, the power of the great biblical images to renew response has been proven in the past, time and again. We have no ground for the despairing supposition that this power has been exhausted for all the future. Even moribund myths have a strange capacity for resurrection. But we also have no ground for the (basically technolatrous) dream of manipulating the consciousness of the coming age through the leverage of institutional religion. "Thy Kingdom come!" may be breathed as a prayer; it must not be interpreted as an imperative ordering up spiritual reforms on demand. Our age is surely in need of a miracle. God only knows if we shall receive one through present earthly followers.

16.

Toward Postmodern Faith

I conclude this book with a reflection on the role of Christian philosophers, whose inquiries may have unusual practical importance, since – as I have argued – faith is one of the powerful ingredients in the dynamics of history. Christianity in some eras has been a stabilizing force; in others it has been revolutionary. How it will influence the turbulent few years that remain in this century is hard to predict, but in some part what Christian faith shall be for the future – and consequently what our earth's future shall be – cannot help but be shaped by the kind of leadership we of this generation give in seeking understanding.

I propose therefore that we explore a bit more fully the inner structures of Christian belief with special attention to how these structures relate to ongoing changes in experience.

PRESSURES FROM EXPERIENCE ON FAITH

To discuss the pressure of changing experience upon Christian faith requires a clear sense of the differences and interactions between what I have called religious world models (RWMs) (chapter 6) and theological doctrines (or theories). Images, the stuff from which RWMs are formed, carry the primary weight of religious passion, though doctrines grown venerable by long association can also stir the passions as we all know. Still, it is the vivid image – the story, the mental picture, the myth – that touches directly on our centers of value. It is the "old, old story" that believers beg to hear. The poem, the oratorio, the vignette in stained glass are the forms that nourish communities of common loyalties. Theories, in contrast, often polarize and fragment. Historically it is from strife over theory that come councils and creeds and anathemas.

We need theory, of course. As thinking beings we are unable not to theorize to some extent. To use language at all is to be indebted to some theory of classification, at least, and perhaps also to theories of temporality and action, substance and quality. In view of this, it is best to recognize that the distinction between value-laden model and theological theory is ideal only. Perhaps we never encounter a completely pure (theory-independent) example of an "organizing image," though it is the task of the poet-visionary to evoke as best he or she can the concrete vividness of the intuited image by wooing and sometimes violating the generalities of speech, as it is the aim of the artist to use the conventions of universals in color and line to point to the specific.

Nonetheless, even without pure cases, we can recognize the difference between a learned discourse over the merits of the doctrine of the impassibility of God and the story of Gethsemane. It is equally possible to distinguish between the relatively abstract level of the doctrine of double predestination and the Parable of the Prodigal Son. Both levels are part of the complete religious phenomenon, because religious persons (and some more than others) need to think through the implications of the religious images that focus and express their fundamental intuitions into the sacred. The intuitions and the images, however, are primary in the religious phenomenon. Only in the context of worship does theological thinking-through take its rise.

For those pursuing the theological task of thinking-through, the natural tendency is to use whatever tools of theorizing may be at hand. In this way theological thinking resembles, borrows from, and becomes fruitfully entangled in the general questions of the day. Since this is one of the principal ways in which changing experience has its impact on religious belief, it deserves deeper scrutiny.

In the first place, it is notorious that mere sensory observations are logically unable to verify or falsify key Christian beliefs in any easy or straightforward way. For a determined resister, no observations whatever will be allowed to disprove faith. No degree of suffering or travail can contradict, for example, the image of a benevolent God who permits pain for our own good, who allowed God's own Son to suffer redemptively, and who in mysterious providence will bring all things together for the best. And yet it is clear that empirical scientific experience has in fact had a great influence on mainline Christianity in recent centuries. Almost no one considers it religiously vital to defend the pre-Copernican cosmology of biblical imagery. And despite the noisy campaigns of the "creationists," some of the most effective opposition to laws mandating teaching of the biblical creation story as an alternative to scientific evolution comes from established Christian leadership. How is this selective responsiveness — "no," to some experiences, "yes," to others — to be understood?

The answer resides in the buffering function of theological theorizing, which articulates the value-laden images of faith in a theoretical scheme which, in turn, allows some image-elements to be understood as figurative while other elements are taken as modeling essential theoretical structures. That *everything* in the image is to be taken as literal is of course also a possible theoretical claim, but one that is relatively recent and—even among Fundamentalists—relatively rare. Until some such theoretical artic-ulation occurs, nothing is "figurative," since nothing can be taken as map-ping anything literal. Once the model is mapped onto a theory, however, the normal empirical pressures and theoretical needs come into play.

Thus the old issue of falsifiability was wrongly put as though an obser-vation (e.g., of the suffering of an innocent child) could link logically to, and count directly against, a deep religious faith in the adequacy of the love of God as depicted in the stories and images of the Bible. This sup-position was a confusion. The painful illness of a child would in fact count against the theoretical generalization that a good God would act to prevent pain under all such circumstances; but against this theoretical claim (which has rarely, if ever, been made in the history of actual Christian thinking) theological theory has developed a mass of modifying ancillary theory.

Typical of such theory, for example, would often be subsidiary theories about an afterlife, and, as a necessary condition, theories about the human person, the nature of consciousness, the "soul," and the like. This, then, becomes the point where empirical pressures from rival scientific theory are logically relevant. Can brain physiology adequately account for all the phenomena of consciousness? Are mechanistic and reductionistic models of thinking about to show the mind as epiphenomenal and the "soul" there-fore a redundancy? Can self-awareness and personhood be synthesized by the hardware available to artificial intelligence? How much empirical back-ing is there for alleged out-of-the-body states of consciousness? "Back from the grave" experiences? All these questions—involving an amalgam of sci-entific theory and observation as they do—relate indirectly to the earlier falsification question by significantly influencing the viability of any theo-retical defense of the benevolence of God based on the prospect of an afterlife. These issues are far from settled, of course, and therefore these are surely areas to watch carefully for developments that will have profound implications for the sort of theoretical articulation of religious models that may be responsibly possible in the future.

We have taken it as established, since chapter 2, that responsible thought has long since reached closure on the cosmological questions that were live issues in the day of Galileo. The articulation of religious imagery, therefore, has long since ceased to map the biblical cosmological picture as modeling any essential structures for theological theory. The "creationist" debate is more interesting, however, since the current tactic is to point out areas of uncertainty or unresolved perplexity within scientific evolutionary thought and to use specific scientific issues as though they were a license to coun-terattack against the scientific legitimacy of the field of modern biology as a whole. Such extremes are clearly unwarranted, but even for more mod-erate thinkers there is much work to do. Theologians and Christian phi-losophers are still in need of working out how to map the biblical image of the natural order onto adequate theory that will do justice both to the vast body of scientific data and also to the religious intuition that humanity has a profoundly significant role and responsibility within the natural order. This is an area of unusual interest, not only to theological specialists, but also, in this case, to citizens concerned for the quality of public science education and to all of us who are eager to find ways to draw back from our culture's spiritual alienation from nature.

The first key way in which experience has its impact upon Christian faith, then, is through the impact of theological theory—itself in dialogue with the general issues of the world of experience and secular thought—upon the religiously vital images of the worshiping community. This impact is primarily expressed by theory's ability to bring some features of religious imagery prominently forward as modeling essential structures, and in letting other features, though not abandoned, recede as unmappable. Available theories change, of course, as do the recognized empirical-theoretical constraints, from era to era, as we are forcefully reminded by the historians of science. Unlike scientific change, religious change is partly disguised by the massive conservatism of the community toward its value-laden imagery, which continues to be venerated despite profound shifts, brought by theory, which both (a) interprets how literally it is to be thought and (b) influences faith by emphasizing those features that are to be stressed in meditation and prayer.

The second key source of change also results in reform through reemphasis, but in this case the pressure of experience is not mediated through theory but rather is applied directly at the level of value-laden imagery because of shifting value intuitions themselves. Too often, when philosophers speak of the relation between Christianity and "experience," we focus so heavily upon the sorts of sense experience constituting "evidence" in the empirical sciences that we omit aesthetic, moral, and even religious experience from our notice. All these latter sorts of value experience, however, play an important role in the dynamics of change.

There is such a thing as a characteristic value expression—the "style" or "personality"—of an era, as one can tell from looking at the architectural monuments of a civilization and from reading its drama, its poetry, and its sacred books. The symmetries and finite balances of the architecture of classical Greece, for example, express consensus on the meaning of beauty no less clearly than the appeals for moderation and "hitting the mark" in Greek ethical writing reveal a similar consensus on the moral good. The leaping asymmetries of medieval cathedrals, in contrast, together with the immoderate ideals of hermits, flagellants, and saints, show different shared intuitions of the holy, the beautiful, and the right.

This general phenomenon is reflected, not surprisingly, in the great value-laden images of the Bible. The value overtones of Hebrew experience with kings, for example, become ingredients in the images of the biblical God. Experiences of kings were not all positive, of course, but the sense of awe, of legitimate even if arbitrary power, of splendid majesty, of fear before the throne—all these elements could be taken for granted for many centuries in formative, value-orienting intuitions as to how a deity should appropriately be imaged.

This consensus no longer finds immediate acknowledgment among worshipers who have inherited the legacy of the age of democratic revolutions. It is not that God must be leveled to become a good democrat; but royalist images, once effective in portraying the divine awesomeness, no longer elicit the responses that once could have been taken for granted. God the Boundless Artist, God the Perfect Companion, God the Good Shepherd, God the Still Small Voice, God the Nurturing Mother, are images that may come forward for many today as more worthy of worship than God the Emperor, seated remotely on the throne.

Similar changes in widely shared contemporary intuitions concerning warfare and the application of torture have made a noteworthy difference, likewise, in the stress put upon biblical images of Armageddon and eternal hell. Some among us still are apparently able to relish the visions of pain and destruction that appear in scripture, to be sure. But a clearly discernible tendency against dwelling upon those aspects of Christian stories is found in the practice of mainstream believers today. Our value intuitions are selective. Attitudes toward war and the systematic infliction of pain have significantly shifted from what they were in the days when Assyrian crowds gathered cheerfully in Nineveh to watch men, women, and children prisoners of war slowly flayed alive or torn to pieces or die a hundred other agonizing deaths for public amusement. Sense experiences, one assumes, are little different now, from biblical or Roman times, but persons in a civilization where typical value intuitions are offended even by too much pummeling in the prize-fight ring cannot be expected to respond in all ways like persons living in a culture for which the bloody delights of the Colosseum were normal fare.

In consequence, significant religious change is pressed by alterations in an epoch's sensibilities of value as well as of fact. These two dimensions of experience must not be too sharply separated, of course, since what is taken to be *so* is regarded always with some valuational tone, and what is taken to be *valuable* is seen always as connected with what is so. Still, it is clarifying of the dynamics of religious change to distinguish the pressures of experience that are mediated through the theories of believing thinkers from those that are immediately felt in the emphases—and in the reverent neglect—by which believers portray to themselves their sacred stories.

It will be interesting to see whether changing cultural consciousness about sex roles and stereotypes, to take one more example, significantly influences how the New Testament is read on the Fatherhood of God. No historical question is clear a priori. We really cannot predict how value intuitions of gender-related matters will alter in the next century; nor can we forecast how selective appreciation of Christian imagery may develop. We do know that in former times Christians have created ways to express value intuitions of femininity despite heavy textual stress on the masculine. We also can anticipate that Christian images of ideal family life will have a reciprocal bearing on how our culture resolves its attitudes toward feminism.

The logical point this illustrates is that a reciprocal relationship must finally be acknowledged between religion and experience. Factual information about what is the case, learned from sociologists, psychologists, and anthropologists, interacts with value concerns nourished by people in a culture that has already been partly shaped in its values by a mixture of biblical images: some of a definitely subordinate "women's place" and some of spiritual egalitarianism. The resulting conflict of values is felt in the context of a need for enlarged and improved theological theory on the part of the thinkers of the religious community. That theory, in turn, gains its value impact from the aspects of sacred imagery that will be drawn forward into prominence as modeling essential realities. And, ultimately, the experience of the family and the work place is different for Christians when these are seen and felt as domains of value with a dignity expressive of divine purpose.

PRESSURES FROM FAITH ON THE FUTURE

Faith is shaped by experience, slowly but inevitably; it has been the thesis of this book that experience is likewise shaped by faith. We experience the universe about us, social and physical, differently because of the metaphors and models that focus and guide our perceptions. But we are not locked forever into religious or scientific preconceptions. The universe about us— valuational and sensory—presses back upon our metaphors and models. In this mutual pressure is found the ultimate dialogue that moves the history of thought and changes the face of civilizations.

If my analysis of the interactions of religious faith with changing experience is at all near the mark, then it is of prime importance for us to ponder some basic experiences that our civilization, along with the rest of the world, will be sharing. It will be in the light of such experiences that our own philosophical labors can then be best assessed.

One major feature that seems very likely to be present in the experience of most humankind, even the presently wealthy nations of the global North not excepted, is of painful scarcities. The pressures of growing populations—and, more especially the pressures of growing industrialization with energy-intensive and resource-hungry technologies—on the earth's finite material supplies cannot fail to reach limits, some of which are now being felt and all of which will intensify over the next decades. The psychological temptation to denial of these realities is strong, especially in optimistic America, where many people prefer to believe leaders who preach that material growth can be resumed indefinitely and that economic plenty for all—the traditional American dream—is merely a matter of better federal budget management. But neither wishing nor witchcraft will remove the implacable facts of finitude. This is hard for us to hear, but the affluent life is over, even for the more fortunate nations; for the less fortunate there are no doubt tragic abysses of suffering yet unplumbed.

Under these circumstances, we should expect to experience struggles of all sorts: among individuals, among groups, among regions, and among nations. The possibilities of resource wars, one of the commonest sorts of conflict in human history, seem clearly on the rise. International terrorism, chemically, biologically, or even atomically armed, is no longer a far-fetched scenario.

Fired by panic over faltering material progress at home and desperate human need abroad, it seems likely that the next decades will experience a redoubling of efforts to exploit as much as possible from the earth to satisfy immediate cravings. Environmental safeguards, attitudes of restraint toward the delicate balances of the ecosphere, conservation measures aimed at preserving a heritage for unborn generations—these will be widely attacked as romantic impracticalities.

An ideology suited to support such an attack is available in reductionistic scientism, whose categories encourage attention to the smallest material particle and its properties as key to the understanding and controlling of the universe. With such a simplified key, however, both purpose and value must remain locked in mystery, and human beings must remain anomalies in a meaningless material realm from which they are alienated but which, by the same token, they are unhindered from exploiting. This ideology, long nourished by traditional modern sciences, has recently been under attack from more newly arrived sciences, especially holistic ecology; but it seems likely that the coming attitudinal climate will offer reductionistic modes of thought and feeling new opportunities for resurgence. It may even be that the science of ecology, itself, will become less holistic as efforts are made to bend it to the modern consensus.

So far this seems a bleak picture, but there will surely be resisters to these trends toward heedless materialism. The environmental concerns of the 1970s have now been largely embodied in law, and polls show that citizens of many nations, in great numbers, remain willing to sacrifice, if necessary, for the needs of a healthy natural order. Value intuitions themselves seem to have evolved significantly. The sciences will continue to debate among themselves. In conformity with all ages, our future will present a mixed situation. It will be a challenge for Christian philosophers, and an opportunity.

As we turn to the responsibilities of Christian philosophers, we should be clear about what is within our power, even ideally, and what is not. Since ought implies can, we need not feel responsible for the great movements of valuational change that press directly upon the images of faith. We cannot be mythic engineers.

The life and death—and, sometimes, the resurrections—of potent religious images provide the context for our work. What is or is not a "living option" is not wholly up to us. Still, there are many contexts, and what is not "living" for one community at a given time may be "living" for another at that time—or for the first at a different time. We must beware of the prophets who declare this flatly to be a "post-Christian age" as though the "age" were uniform. In the communities constituted by many university faculties, it may be that Christian symbols have lost the power to move; but even there it is important to distinguish between conscious rejection of certain theological theories by those whose minds belong to a "world come of age," and a more serious depth-indifference to Christian images. Many Christian philosophers are no less "of age" at the point of theory but still find themselves responding to the poetry of faith, to the great hymns, to the grandeur of the liturgical year, to the ethical heights demanded, and to the depths of personal communion provided in fellowship with other worshipers. Our age, secular though it has become in many ways, has still not entirely lost the ability to be moved by the images of the Infant in the manger and the Friend on the cross.

Unlike theologians, who work within a specialized context of a particular faithful community, Christian philosophers work in the broader world of thought and feeling, a world indeed "come of age" technologically and scientifically, but still a world for which the values proclaimed in the Gospels ring a response. Thus, though we are not mythic engineers, we should be aware of the shifts in value intuitions going on in our age and should be alert to the relevance of these movements to those values implicit in the Christian images. In particular, Christian philosophers need to be alert to the areas where value-conflicts may exist within the Christian stories themselves, as with ambivalent attitudes toward women, which we noticed before, or with the much-discussed internal value struggle in our images between attitudes of exploitation toward nature and attitudes of responsible restraint. When critics, with some justice, denounce the rapacious implications of the Genesis commandment to "subdue the earth," it is important that Christian thinkers who share the values of these critics point to balancing images and stories that support values of holism and equilibrium in our human transactions with the earth. If religious sanction has been given to environmentally harmful policies in the past—because of the earlier noticed phenomenon of selective attention—it is appropriate, and even vital, to withdraw such apparent sanction from the future, in which temptations to potentially catastrophic exploitation may be anticipated.

Such activities, though vital, are not what Christian philosophers as such are mainly challenged to do in the foreseeable future. Our proper domain of activity is not primarily at the point where value-experience impinges directly on the images of faith but, rather, where theory is rethought and the images of faith are thereby indirectly rearticulated and remapped for a new age.

One great area for Christian philosophers, therefore, will be coming to terms with science for a postmodern world. Science, of course, is not a monolithic entity. There are many sciences, and they are not entirely coherent among themselves. But the methods and results of the sciences represent the most careful and systematic coming to terms with delimited domains of experience available at any given time. Christian philosophers need to be in continual dialogue with their colleague scientists, consequently, if theological theory is to remain fully responsible to the most authoritative articulation of experience available.

I have maintained throughout this book that the authority of the sciences is not absolute, however, and the dialogue with philosophers needs—in the interest of the sciences as well as of philosophy—to be genuinely two-way. Christian philosophers, like all philosophers, are obliged to be, as Whitehead states, critics of abstractions. Scientific abstractions, since the beginning of modern science in the anti-purposive reactions of Galileo against the teleologies of Aristotelian physics, have concentrated on the "objective" aspects of experience; these abstractions, likewise, since the early adoption of Cartesian methodologies of reduction and enumeration, have stressed specialization and the separation of the knower from the subject known. The abstractions of modern science, that is, have excluded from the start experiences and approaches that in the long run human beings generally, and Christian philosophers particularly, are unable to discount or ignore. It shows no lack of respect for the sciences, then, to listen with critical ears when claims are made—on the basis of theories and practices that distort or flatten human experiences—that may overspill the domain delimited by a given scientific field.

Aware of this situation, in which some sciences themselves have been hindered by the limitations of their own abstractions, Christian philosophers will be responding to one of the prime needs of the future when they wrestle with the theoretical and methodological needs of a postmodern science, grounded in more adequate abstractions and more holistic practices. Not only will we, as philosophers, be helping in the human enterprise of understanding more completely the natural order in which we live, but also will we, as Christians, be contributing to a broadened matrix within which theological theory can responsibly articulate the traditional images of faith.

If we speculate a moment on what it could mean for Christian thinking if holistic ecology becomes the bellwether postmodern science, replacing reductionistic hypermodern physics as the paradigm for respected intellectual practice, we see that the "inclusionist" images of humankind and nature would be mapped onto our theories rather than the "exclusionist" images of humankind over against, or not fully a part of, nature. Biblical images of exploitation and domination could recede, seen as metaphors for a time suited, perhaps, to another historical situation. Epistemologically, philosophical and theological thinking could become more contextual and less inclined to remain at the level of analysis alone—of meanings or of texts—although analysis would remain an essential tool in the service of full understanding. Metaphysically, philosophical and theological thinking could again look to the concrete, purposive organism and its interactions in populations and systems, as paradigmatic of significant reality including by transcending the human. Axiologically, philosophical and theological thinking could recognize intrinsic value in sentient, interest-seeking organisms and see in healthy life itself the pervasive values of creativity, homeostasis, and holism.

Such organismic thinking, grounded in a postmodern science that Christian philosophers would at last not be obliged to fight at fundamental levels, would have far-reaching implications for the Christian imagery that modeled it. The value-laden features of the Christian *mythos* that would become prominent would tend against the ethic of exploitation in any aspect of life. Raping the earth, raping women, raping the oppressed of our society and of the world are not, after all, so easily separable. Environmental theology, feminist theology, and liberation theology are all responses to perceptions of something deeply wrong in our seeing and feeling as well as our acting. This wrongness springs from the root of our civilization's modern ideology: aggressively reductive scientism entrenched in political and economic structures as well as in thought and attitude. Postmodern organicism, if it could replace that alienating modern ideology, could ally itself with the redemptive powers of Christian myth to work toward removing the wrongness.

Assuming Christian *mythos* modeling such a theory, the response to scarcity in our future by a freshly rearticulated Christian faith, for example, can be anticipated to involve three key elements. First, postmodern organismic Christianity will take a strong initiative toward meeting scarcities by stressing and celebrating human *creativity*, in the image of the divine creativity, as capacity for doing more with less. Ecologically sensitive, postdomination Christianity need not be reactively antitechnological. Oppressive technologies, of course, like all oppressions, need to be resisted, but gentler, appropriate technologies are not beyond the reach of the fertile human imagination. One of life's proper responses to shortage is to create adequate supplies in responsible ways. Christian imagery, not only reflecting on the original creative God but also on Christ's multiplying the loaves and fishes or bringing wine from water, will amply model this truth for a world that may need encouragement to avoid the self-defeat of despair.

But, second, creativity cannot be celebrated without *limit*, on pain of runaway growth. Organismic theory will point to the internal homeostasis that controls excesses within healthy life, and biblical images will vividly model patterns of restraint—"When you gather the grapes of your vineyard, you shall not glean it afterward; it shall be for the sojourner, the fatherless, and the widow" (Deut. 24:21)—and punishments for excess—"Fool! This night your soul is required of you; and the things you have prepared, whose will they be?" (Luke 12:20).

Homeostatic controls on runaway creativity are made possible, third, thanks to intricate feedback systems within organisms operating as complex wholes. Such *holism* in organismic theory can be modeled well in Christian images, such as Christ's metaphor of the vine and the branches or Saint Paul's extended figure of the organic interrelatedness of all the functions of the church and, by implication, of normative human society. Postmodern social organization, if just distribution of scarce goods is to be sought, will not be based on the reductive, atomistic social models of the modern era. A Christian organismic conception of "indwelling" among differentiated but mutually responsive parts will lay the basis for fair play and the dignity of widely shared participatory engagement.

The globe we now inhabit is deeply in need of more such sharing. The future will surely not diminish the importance of holism on a world scale. Survival itself may be at stake. One more task for Christian philosophers, then, will be the careful examination of the theoretical bases for a larger ecumenism that may be able to lay the foundation in attitude and value for a just and mutual world order.

To what extent is a wise postmodern organicism capable of being modeled by the traditional imagery of other world religions? To that extent still deeper springs of human motivation may be able to be constructively redirected to policies of creativity, homeostasis, and holism in defense both of the natural environment and of unique personal values. To that extent it could be enriching to the diversity of the human spiritual phenomenon, without being dangerous to the coherence of human physical community, that there may be irreducible differences among the great religions of the world.

Some theologians might have a difficult time with these conceptions, but Christian philosophers who appreciate the logical differences between models and theories may find such final multi-mythic pluralism in keeping with their faith as well as in line with their reason. "In my Father's house are many mansions" (John 14:2 KJV). A diversity of models capable of characterizing a single underlying theory is nothing logically extraordinary in other contexts. Where it touches on religious models, of course, there are intense values at stake — that is what makes such models "religious" in the first place. But a multi-mythic personalistic organicism that can draw the world to a more stable, just, and fuller future is an ideal that Christians and Muslims, Hindus and Buddhists, might well, after due consideration, all come (justly) to claim as their own.

It would, of course, be grandiose foolishness for anyone to suppose that Christian philosophers can accomplish all these great ends by themselves. Especially the last, ecumenical, enterprise needs to be worked on by philosophers of many faiths — and of no traditional faith, except in the values of personhood and the wisdom of life itself — if it is to be accomplished. These ends, which lie at the frontiers of postmodern epistemology, axiology, and metaphysics, are philosophically of the highest interest; they are clearly in keeping with Christian compassion; and they are urgent.

Notes

1. INTRODUCTION

1. Dennis Meadows, et al., *The Limits to Growth* (New York: Universe Books, 1972), p. 29.

2. For a thoughtful (and dramatic) exploration of this problem from a Christian viewpoint, see Susan Power Bratton, *Six Billion and More: Human Population Regulation & Christian Ethics* (Louisville, Ky.: Westminster/John Knox Press, 1992).

3. See Garrett Hardin, "The Case Against Helping the Poor," *Psychology Today* (September 1974), pp. 38ff.

4. See, for example, H. S. D. Cole, et al., eds., *Models of Doom: A Critique of the Limits to Growth* (New York: Universe Books, 1973).

5. For greater detail and defense, see my *Basic Modern Philosophy of Religion* (New York: Charles Scribner's Sons, 1967), parts 1 and 3.

6. Ibid., chapter 3.

7. R. M. MacIver, *The Web of Government* (New York: Macmillan, 1947), p. 4.

8. Alfred North Whitehead, *Science and the Modern World* (New York: Free Press, 1967), p. 5.

9. Ibid., p. 12.

10. Ibid., chapter 3.

11. Ibid.

12. Cited in Jacob Bronowski, *Science and Human Values* (New York: Harper & Row, 1965), p. 66.

13. Since writing this I have been assured by Professor Priscilla Laws that good scientific work has indeed been done in this personal style, including the work of Rutherford at the turn of the century.

14. Israel Scheffler, *Science and Subjectivity* (Indianapolis: Bobbs-Merrill, 1967), p. 4.

15. Ibid., p. 1.

16. Ibid., p. 5.

17. Ibid.

18. Bronowski, *Science and Human Values*, pp. 66–71.

19. Scheffler, *Science and Subjectivity*, p. 2.

20. Whitehead, *Science and the Modern World*, p. 54.

21. Lewis Mumford, "The Pentagon of Power," *Horizon* 12, no. 4 (1970), p. 10.

22. Cited in E. J. Dijksterhuis, *The Mechanization of the World Picture* (London: Oxford University Press, 1961), p. 362.

23. See David L. Hull, *Philosophy of Biological Science* (Englewood Cliffs, N.J.: Prentice-Hall, 1974), for detailed arguments against the presumptions of reduction.

24. Michael Polanyi, *Personal Knowledge* (New York: Harper & Row, 1962), pp. 347–358.

25. Barry Commoner, *The Closing Circle: Nature, Man, and Technology* (New York: Bantam Books, 1972), p. 73.

26. Ibid., p. 191.

27. Jacques Monod, *Chance and Necessity: An Essay on the Natural Philosophy of Modern Biology* (New York: Vintage Books, 1972), p. 21.

28. Ibid., p. 170.

2. HELLFIRE AND LIGHTNING RODS

1. See chapter 11, below.

2. James Gustafson, *Ethics from a Theocentric Perspective*, vol. 1, *Theology and Ethics* (Chicago: University of Chicago Press, 1981).

3. See chapter 4, below.

4. Lynn White, Jr., "The Historical Roots of Our Ecologic Crisis," *Science* 155 (March 10, 1967).

5. Alfred North Whitehead, *Science and the Modern World* (New York: Macmillan, 1925), ch. 1.

6. Thomas S. Kuhn, *The Structure of Scientific Revolutions*, 2nd ed. (Chicago: University of Chicago Press, 1970), "Postscript—1969," p. 184.

7. See Paul Churchland, *Matter and Consciousness*, 2nd ed. (Cambridge, Mass.: MIT Press, 1988).

8. B. F. Skinner, *Beyond Freedom and Dignity* (New York: Alfred A. Knopf, 1971).

9. *The Subversive Science*: *Essays Toward an Ecology of Man*, eds. Paul Shepard and Daniel McKinlay (Boston: Houghton Mifflin, 1969).

4. TECHNOLOGICAL FAITH AND CHRISTIAN DOUBT

1. Harvey Cox, *The Secular City: Secularization and Urbanization in Theological Perspective*, rev. ed. (New York: Macmillan, 1965, 1966).

2. W. Norris Clarke, "Technology and Man: A Christian Vision," in *The Technological Order*, ed. Carl F. Stover (Detroit, Mich.: Wayne State University Press, 1963). Quoted from the revised version reprinted in Carl Mitcham and Robert Mackey, *Philosophy and Technology*, p. 250.

3. Ibid., p. 252.

4. Cox, *The Secular City*, p. 20.

5. Clarke, "Technology and Man," p. 251.

6. Jacques Ellul, "Technique and the Opening Chapters of Genesis," in *Theology and Technology: Essays in Christian Analysis and Exegesis*, eds. Carl Mitcham and Jim Grote (Lanham, Md.: University Press of America, 1984), p. 129.

7. Ibid., p. 125.

8. Ibid.

9. Egbert Schuurman, "A Christian Philosophical Perspective on Technology," in Mitcham and Grote, *Theology and Technology*, p. 111.

10. See, however, my *Philosophy of Technology* (Englewood Cliffs, N.J.: Prentice-Hall, 1988), chapter 2.

11. See chapter 11, below, for a fuller treatment.

12. See chapter 2, above.

13. See Stanley Carpenter, "Redrawing the Bottom Line: The Optional Character of Technical Design Norms," *Technology in Society* 6 (1984), pp. 329–340.

5. EXPLANATION IN SCIENCE AND THEOLOGY

1. Carl G. Hempel and Paul Oppenheim, "Studies in the Logic of Explanation," reprinted in *The Structure of Scientific Thought*, ed. Edward H. Madden (Boston: Houghton Mifflin, 1960), p. 22.

2. Ibid., p. 28.

3. Ibid., p. 29.

4. Ibid.

5. Ibid., italics added.

6. See Abraham Kaplan, *The Conduct of Inquiry* (San Francisco: Chandler, 1964), especially chapter 1.

7. John Hospers, "What Is Explanation?" in *Essays in Conceptual Analysis*, ed. Antony Flew (New York: Macmillan, 1956), p. 105.

8. Hempel and Oppenheim, "Logic of Explanation," p. 22.

9. Ibid., p. 21.

10. Ibid., p. 20.

11. See Auguste Comte, *Introduction to Positive Philosophy*, ed. Frederick Ferré (Indianapolis: Bobbs-Merrill, 1969).

12. Henry Margenau, *The Nature of Physical Reality* (New York: McGraw-Hill, 1950), pp. 25–30.

13. Stephen Toulmin, *The Philosophy of Science* (New York: Harper & Row, 1960), pp. 53–54.

14. Hospers, "What Is Explanation?" p. 98.

15. Margenau, *The Nature of Physical Reality*, p. 29.

16. Ibid., p. 28.

17. Ibid., p. 29.

18. Stephen Toulmin, *Foresight and Understanding* (Bloomington: Indiana University Press, 1961), p. 28; Thomas S. Kuhn, *The Structure of Scientific Revolutions* (Chicago: University of Chicago Press, 1962).

19. Toulmin, *Foresight and Understanding*, pp. 41ff.

20. Ibid., p. 42.

21. Ibid.

22. Hospers, "What Is Explanation?" p. 107.

23. Ibid., p. 108.

24. Toulmin, *Foresight and Understanding*, pp. 42ff.

25. Cf. Sir Herbert Butterfield, *The Origins of Modern Science 1300-1800* (London: Bell, 1950), for an account that does not overlook the experimental elements contributing to Aristotle's overthrow but that at the same time makes vivid the *conceptual* revolution underlying the birth of modern science. For further examples, see Toulmin, *Foresight and Understanding*, especially chapters 3 and 4.

26. Hospers, "What Is Explanation?" p. 116.

27. Ibid.

28. See Stephen Toulmin, "Scientific Theories and Scientific Myths," in *Metaphysical Beliefs*, ed. A. MacIntyre (London: SCM Press, 1957). But note the evo-

lution of Toulmin's thought on these matters, as expressed in *The Return to Cosmology: Postmodern Science and the Theology of Nature* (Berkeley: University of California Press, 1982).

29. For a more detailed discussion of the appropriate tests that may be applied to models and theories of this latter kind, see my chapters in Kent Bendall and Frederick Ferré, *Exploring the Logic of Faith* (New York: Association Press, 1962).

30. Alfred North Whitehead, *Science and the Modern World* (New York: Macmillan, 1925); Mentor Books edition, p. 88.

31. Ibid.

32. Cf. Bendall and Ferré, *Exploring the Logic of Faith*.

33. Hospers, "What Is Explanation?" p. 95.

34. Ibid., p. 117.

6. ORGANIZING IMAGES AND SCIENTIFIC IDEALS

1. See my "Metaphor in Religious Discourse" in *Dictionary of the History of Ideas: Studies of Selected Pivotal Ideas*, ed. Philip P. Wiener (New York: Charles Scribner's Sons, 1973), vol. 3, pp. 201–208.

2. For an eloquent expansion of this theme, see Jacob Bronowski, *Science and Human Values*, rev. ed. (New York: Harper & Row, 1965).

3. For an extended discussion of the types, character, and functioning of models, see my "Mapping the Logic of Models in Science and Theology," *The Christian Scholar*, Vol. 46, no. 1, (Spring 1963), pp. 9–39. Also published in *Philosophy and Religion, Some Contemporary Perspectives*, ed. Jerry A. Gill (Minneapolis: Burgess, 1968); and in *New Essays in Religious Language*, ed. Dallas M. High (New York: Oxford University Press, 1969).

4. See my *Basic Modern Philosophy of Religion* (New York: Charles Scribner's Sons, 1967), especially chapters 2, 3, and 4.

5. Historian Lynn White, Jr., suggests a switch to the imagery of Saint Francis in his influential "The Historical Roots of Our Ecological Crisis," *Science* 155 (March 10, 1967), pp. 1203–1207. Theodore Roszak offers "the Old Gnosis" in *Where the Wasteland Ends: Politics and Transcendence in Postindustrial Society* (Garden City, N.Y.: Anchor Books, 1973). I discuss "polymythic organicism" in *Shaping the Future* (New York: Harper & Row, 1976). In the present book I have changed my terminology to "multimythic organicism" to avoid confusion with Freud's "polymorphous perversity"!

6. B. F. Skinner, in *Beyond Freedom and Dignity* (New York: Alfred A. Knopf, 1971) urges a science-generated RWM that offers clear answers to such questions in terms of human engineering.

7. My current effort is to address these issues in *Being and Value: Toward Postmodern Metaphysics* (Albany, N.Y.: State University of New York Press, forthcoming).

8. For an illuminating and authoritative account, see Roger W. Sperry, "The Great Cerebral Commissure," *Scientific American* 210 (1964). Also see Roger Sperry, "Hemisphere Deconnection and Unity in Conscious Awareness," *American Psychologist* 23 (1968), pp. 723–733.

9. Ferré, *Basic Modern Philosophy of Religion*, pp. 373–406.

10. See Marshall Walker, *The Nature of Scientific Thought* (Englewood Cliffs,

N.J.: Prentice-Hall, 1963), chapter 1, for a strong defense of the reduction of scientific "understanding" to empirical prediction.

11. This includes principles and also practices, methods, standard instrumentation, aims—all that goes into what T. S. Kuhn calls the "paradigm" for normal science. See his *The Structure of Scientific Revolution*, 2nd ed. (Chicago: University of Chicago Press, 1970), especially section 2. For our purposes the key principles and implicit or explicit imagery or beliefs of the scientific community at any given time (what Kuhn calls "metaphysical paradigms" and "values" in his postscript to this second edition) are of primary interest.

12. Stephen Toulmin, *Foresight and Understanding* (Bloomington: Indiana University Press, 1961).

13. Ibid., p. 39.

14. Ibid., p. 55.

15. See Plato's *Timaeus*, trans. F. M. Cornford (Indianapolis: Bobbs-Merrill, 1959) and T. S. Kuhn's discussion in *The Copernican Revolution: Planetary Astronomy in the Development of Western Thought* (New York: Vintage Books, 1957), pp. 28ff. Another good treatment is provided in Stephen Toulmin and June Goodfield, *The Fabric of the Heavens: The Development of Astronomy and Dynamics* (New York: Harper & Row, 1961), especially chapter 2.

16. Toulmin and Goodfield, *The Fabric of the Heavens*, especially chapter 9.

17. For an excellent discussion of the radical shift in the concept of space, and its loss of "place" in the Newtonian worldview, see Joseph J. Kockelmans, "Reflections on the Interaction between Science and Religion," in *The Challenge of Religion*, ed. Frederick Ferré, Joseph Kockelmans, and John E. Smith (New York: Seabury Press, 1982), pp. 296–316.

18. For some ground-breaking literature, see Mary Daly, *Beyond God the Father* (Boston: Beacon Press, 1973); Carol Ochs, *Behind the Sex of God* (Boston: Beacon Press, 1977); and Elizabeth Dodson Gray, *Patriarchy as a Conceptual Trap* (Wellesley, Mass.: Roundtable Press, 1982).

19. See the literature of limits—pro and con—represented in part by Jay W. Forrester, *World Dynamics* (Cambridge, Mass.: Wright-Allen Press, 1971); D. H. Meadows, et al., *The Limits to Growth* (New York: Universe Books, 1972); H. S. D. Cole, et al., *Models of Doom* (New York: Universe Books, 1973); E. F. Schumacher, *Small Is Beautiful* (New York: Harper & Row, 1973); M. Mesarovic and E. Pestel, *Mankind at the Turning Point* (New York: E. P. Dutton, 1974); William Ophuls, *Ecology and the Politics of Scarcity* (San Francisco: W. H. Freeman, 1977); Donella H. Meadows, et al., *Beyond the Limits: Confronting Global Collapse; Revisioning a Sustainable Future* (Post Mills, Vt.: Chelsea Green Publishing, 1992), and my own discussion in chapter 1 of this book.

20. Barry Commoner, *The Closing Circle* (New York: Bantam Books, 1971). See especially pp. 298–299.

7. RELIGIOUS WORLD MODELING AND POSTMODERN SCIENCE

1. Stephen Toulmin, *Foresight and Understanding: An Enquiry into the Aims of Science* (Bloomington: Indiana University Press, 1961), chapters 3 and 4.

2. See chapter 5, note 12, above.

3. Alfred N. Whitehead, *Science and the Modern World* (New York: Free Press, 1967), p. 54.

4. René Descartes, *Discourse on Method* (1637; Indianapolis: Bobbs-Merrill, 1960), part 5.

5. Jacques Monod, *Chance and Necessity: An Essay on the Natural Philosophy of Modern Biology*, trans. Austryn Wainhouse (New York: Vintage Books, 1972), pp. 172–173.

6. Theodore Roszak, *Where the Wasteland Ends* (Garden City, N.Y.: Doubleday, 1973), p. 203.

7. Theodore Roszak, *The Making of a Counter-Culture* (Garden City, N.Y.: Anchor Books, 1969), p. 215.

8. Frederick Ferré, *Basic Modern Philosophy of Religion* (New York: Charles Scribner's Sons, 1967), chapters 2 and 3.

9. Monod, *Chance and Necessity*, p. 164.

10. Harold K. Schilling, *The New Consciousness in Science and Religion* (Philadelphia: United Church Press, 1973).

11. Eugene P. Odum, *Ecology* (New York: Holt, Rinehart & Winston, 1963), p. 4.

12. See, for example, Theodore C. Foin, Jr., *Ecological Systems and the Environment* (Boston: Houghton Mifflin, 1976).

13. See, for example, Jack B. Bresler, ed., *The Environments of Man* (Reading, Mass.: Addison-Wesley, 1968).

14. Donald Worster, *Nature's Economy: The Roots of Ecology* (Garden City, N.Y.: Anchor Books, 1979), p. 332.

15. Ibid.

16. Ibid., p. 339.

8. LIMITS, MYTHS, AND MORALS

1. Robert L. Heilbroner, *An Inquiry into the Human Prospect* (New York: W. W. Norton, 1975), p. 143.

2. Ibid., pp. 143–144.

3. Thomas Kuhn, *The Structure of Scientific Revolutions*, 2nd ed. (Chicago: University of Chicago Press, 1970).

4. Dennis and Donella Meadows, et al., *The Limits to Growth* (New York: Universe Books, 1972). See also their *Beyond the Limits: Confronting Global Collapse; Revisioning a Sustainable Future* (Post Mills, Vt.: Chelsea Green Publishing, 1992).

9. MYTHS AND HOPE FOR GLOBAL SOCIETY

1. Bertrand Russell, "A Free Man's Worship" (1903) in *Mysticism and Logic* (London: Penguin Books, 1953), p. 51.

2. Alfred North Whitehead, *The Function of Reason* (Boston: Beacon Press, 1962), p. 25.

3. Ibid., pp. 25–26.

4. See Richard Rubenstein, *After Auschwitz* (Indianapolis: Bobbs-Merrill, 1966), pp. 41ff.

5. For a delightful illustration, see Ward Cannel and June Macklin, *The Human*

Nature Industry: How Human Nature Is Manufactured, Distributed, Advertised, and Consumed in the United States and Parts of Canada (Garden City, N.Y.: Anchor Books, 1973).

6. See, for example, Theodore Roszak's *The Making of a Counter-Culture* (Garden City, N.Y.: Anchor Books, 1969), especially chapters 7 and 8.

7. Colin M. Turnbull, *The Mountain People* (New York: Simon and Schuster, 1972).

8. Robert L. Heilbroner, *An Inquiry into the Human Prospect* (New York: W. W. Norton, 1974), p. 26; Garrett Hardin, "The Case Against Helping the Poor," *Psychology Today* (September 1974), pp. 38ff.

9. Mihajlo Mesarovic and Edward Pestel, *Mankind at the Turning Point* (New York: E. P. Dutton, 1974).

10. Viktor E. Frankl, *Man's Search for Meaning: An Introduction to Logotherapy* (original title: *From Death Camp to Existentialism*), part 1, trans. Ilse Lasch (New York: Washington Square Press, 1963).

11. See also Rubenstein's disturbing book, *The Cunning of History* (New York: Harper & Row, 1975).

12. Robert Coles (reviewing Turnbull's "The Mountain People") in *Natural History* (March 1973), p. 90.

13. Alfred North Whitehead, *Adventures of Ideas* (New York: Macmillan, 1933), p. 376.

14. See ibid., especially Part IV, Chapter XX, "Peace."

15. This category includes a wide range of historians, doubtless the majority, since most tellings of the stories of human experience tend to attribute some degree of causal control to human intentions and human will.

16. Heilbroner, *An Inquiry*, p. 132.

17. Whitehead, *Adventures of Ideas,* p. 23.

18. Ibid., p. 6.

19. Ibid., pp. 6–7.

20. Roberto Mangabeira Unger, *Knowledge and Politics* (New York: Free Press, 1975), p. 18.

21. Heilbroner, *An Inquiry*, p. 89.

10. WHAT'S HOLDING US BACK?

1. Lynn White, "Historical Roots of Our Ecological Crisis," in *Science* 155 (March 10, 1967), pp. 1203–1207.

2. "The Historical Roots of Our Ecological Crisis," reprinted in *The Environmental Handbook*, ed. Garrett de Bell (New York: Ballantine Books, 1970), p. 19.

3. Ibid., pp. 19–23.

4. Lewis Mumford, "The Pentagon of Power," *Horizon* 12, no. 4 (1970), p. 10.

5. Sir Francis Bacon, *The Great Instauration*, from *The New Organon*, ed. F. H. Anderson (Indianapolis: Bobbs-Merrill, 1960), p. 19.

6. Ibid., p. 25.

7. Allen G. Debus, *The Chemical Philosophy: Paracelsian Science and Medicine in the Sixteenth and Seventeenth Centuries* (New York: Science History Publication, 1977).

8. See Denis Diderot selections in *Les Philosophes: The Philosophers*, ed. Nor-

man L. Torrey (New York: Capricorn Books, 1960), pp. 198–232.

9. White, "Historical Roots," p. 23.

10. Ibid., p. 21.

11. Ibid., p. 22.

12. Alfred North Whitehead, *Science and the Modern World* (New York: Free Press, 1967), p. 12.

13. Bacon, *The Great Instauration*, p. 20.

14. See also Harvey Cox, *The Secular City: Secularization and Urbanization* (New York: Macmillan, 1965).

11. DEMYTHOLOGIZING TECHNOLATRY

1. Jacques Ellul, *The Technological Society*, trans. John Wilkinson (New York: Vintage Books, 1964).

2. Ibid., p. 21.

3. See for delightful discussions of this theme, Robert M. Pirsig, *Zen and the Art of Motorcycle Maintenance: An Inquiry into Values* (New York: William Morrow, 1974).

4. See, for example, the works of Arthur C. Clarke, including *The City and the Stars* (New York: Harcourt, Brace and World, 1953).

5. A good sample of stirring "mental mouthfuls and ventilated prose" can be found in R. Buckminster Fuller, *No More Secondhand God* (Garden City, N.Y.: Anchor Books, 1971).

6. In Clarke's *The City and the Stars*, he introduces the ingenious device of the character Khedron, the jester, whose function in the totally planned, "perfect" technological city, Diaspar, is to introduce a limited amount of instability through his (officially sanctioned) pranks. "Let us say that I introduce calculated amounts of disorder into the city," he says. Thus even randomness is programmed, in judicious amounts, into the Central Computer, as a prophylactic against the decadence of excessive stability—even chaos is subordinated to technical control.

7. For arguments opposing the doctrinaire determinist conception of our world, see my "Self-Determinism," *American Philosophical Quarterly* 10, no. 3 (July 1973), pp. 165–176.

8. Ellul, *The Technological Society*, p. xxviii.

9. B. F. Skinner, *Beyond Freedom and Dignity* (New York: Bantam Books, 1971), p. 1.

10. Ibid., p. 3.

11. Rudolf Otto, *The Idea of the Holy*, 2nd ed., trans. John W. Harvey (New York: Oxford University Press, 1950).

12. For a fuller discussion of the contrast between ideal and actual religion, see my *Basic Modern Philosophy of Religion* (New York: Charles Scribner's Sons, 1967), pp. 70ff.

13. See Ansley J. Coale, "The History of the Human Population," *Scientific American* 231, no. 3 (September 1974), pp. 41–51. See also Paul Demeny, "The Populations of the Underdeveloped Countries," ibid., pp. 149–159.

14. Ivan Illich, *Tools for Conviviality* (New York: Harper & Row, 1973), especially chapter 1.

15. Thomas W. Wilson, Jr., *World Food: The Political Dimension* (Washington,

D.C.: Aspen Institute, 1974), chapter 3. See also, Barry Commoner, *The Closing Circle*, (New York: Bantam Books, 1971), chapter 5.

16. Cited in *The Oxford English Dictionary* (New York: Oxford University Press, 1971).

17. This is the guiding principle behind the Outward Bound program, which has been reported on ecstatically by several of my students who have tried and survived its rigors. For a discussion from the viewpoint of American literature of the rhythms of withdrawal to primitive nature for sustenance, see Leo Marx, "Pastoral Ideals and City Troubles," *Western Man and Environmental Ethics: Attitudes toward Nature and Technology*, ed. Ian G. Barbour (Reading, Mass.: Addison-Wesley, 1973), pp. 93–115.

18. Charles A. Reich, in *The Greening of America* (New York: Random House, 1970), coined this term to designate the amalgam of "public" and "private" bigness in ruling of our lives. Herbert Marcuse offers a similar critique from a different temperamental and philosophical standpoint in *One-Dimensional Man* (Boston: Beacon Press, 1964). The literature beyond these is extensive.

19. Erich Fromm, *The Revolution of Hope: Toward a Humanized Technology* (New York: Bantam Books, 1968).

12. PROBING FOR A POSTMODERN CONSCIOUSNESS

1. Thomas S. Kuhn, *The Structure of Scientific Revolutions*, 2nd ed. (Chicago: University of Chicago Press, 1970), p. 77.

2. Theodore Roszak, *The Making of a Counter-Culture* (Garden City, N.Y.: Anchor Books, 1969).

3. Carlos Casteñeda, *A Separate Reality* (New York: Pocket Books, 1972). See also his *The Teachings of Don Juan: A Yaqui Way of Knowledge* (New York: Ballantine Books, 1968).

4. See, for a classic example, J. B. Rhine, *Parapsychology: Frontier Science of the Mind* (Springfield, Ill.: C. C. Thomas, 1972). See also his *Progress in Parapsychology* (Durham, N.C.: Parapsychology Press, 1971). For ongoing discussion of parapsychological research, see the ongoing *Journal of the American Society for Psychical Research*, ed. Rhea A. White.

5. Peter Tompkins and Christopher Bird, *The Secret Life of Plants* (New York: Harper & Row, 1974).

6. Cited, with interesting conclusions drawn, in Kuhn, *The Structure of Scientific Revolutions*, p. 63.

7. Art Rosenblum and Leah Jackson, *The Natural Birth Control Book* (Philadelphia: Aquarian Research Foundation, 1974).

8. Eugenio Garin, *Science and Civic Life in the Italian Renaissance*, trans. Peter Munz (Garden City, N.Y.: Doubleday, 1969), p. 162.

9. Roszak, *The Making of a Counter-Culture*, p. 244.

10. Ibid., p. 248.

11. Jacques Monod, *Chance and Necessity: An Essay on the Natural Philosophy of Modern Biology* (New York: Vintage Books, 1972), p. 169.

12. Cited in Lee, *Freedom and Culture*, in Roszak, *The Making of a Counter-Culture*, p. 245.

13. Roszak, *The Making of a Counter-Culture*, p. 215.

14. Garin, *Science and Civic Life*, p. 146.

15. Tertullian, *De Idolatria*; cited in Dijksterhuis, *The Mechanization of the World Picture* (London: Oxford University Press, 1961), p. 95.

13. CHRISTIAN ORGANICISM?

1. Karl Barth, *Church Dogmatics: A Selection* (New York: Harper & Row, 1969), passim.

2. Anders Nygren, *Agape and Eros* (New York: Harper & Row, 1969).

3. See, for a strong example of such an argument, George Vetz and Donald Lee Johnson, "Breaking the Web," *Environment* 16, no. 10 (December 1974), pp. 31–39.

4. Lynn White, Jr., "The Historical Roots of Our Ecological Crisis," *Science* 155 (March 10, 1967). See also the discussion of the "Paradox of Blame" in chapter 10, above.

5. W. Lee Humphreys, "Pitfalls and Promises of Biblical Texts as a Basis for a Theology of Nature," in *A New Ethic for a New Earth*, ed. Glenn C. Stone for the Faith-Man-Nature Group (New York: Friendship Press, 1971), pp. 99ff.

6. Whitehead's primary statement was in *Process and Reality: An Essay in Cosmology* (New York: Humanities Press, 1929). A useful aid in reading it is Donald W. Sherburne's *A Key to Whitehead's Process and Reality* (New York: Macmillan, 1966).

7. An important effort in this direction was made by John B. Cobb, Jr., in *A Christian Natural Theology: Based on the Thought of Alfred North Whitehead* (Philadelphia: Westminster Press, 1965).

8. See the concluding reflections of John B. Cobb, Jr., "New Directions," in *Liberating Life: Contemporary Approaches to Ecological Theology.* ed. Charles Birch, William Eakin, and Jay B. McDaniel (Maryknoll, N.Y.: Orbis Books, 1990), p. 263.

9. For amplification of this point, see my *Basic Modern Philosophy of Religion* (New York: Charles Scribner's Sons, 1967), pp. 380–386.

14. MYSTERY AND MULTI-MYTHIC ORGANICISM

1. William G. Pollard, *The Mystery of Matter* (United States Atomic Energy Commission, Office of Information Services, 1974), p. 54.

2. Ibid., p. 50.

3. Gunther S. Stent, *The Coming of the Golden Age: A View of the End of Progress* (Garden City, N.Y.: Natural History Press, 1969), p. 64.

4. Ibid., p. 65.

5. Barry Commoner, *Saturday Review* (October 1, 1966), p. 75.

6. Harold K. Schilling, *The New Consciousness in Science and Religion* (Philadelphia: United Church Press, 1973), p. 45.

7. Charles A. Reich, *The Greening of America* (New York: Random House, 1970).

8. See, for the classic example, E. F. Schumacher, *Small Is Beautiful: Economics as if People Mattered* (New York: Harper Torchbooks, 1973).

9. Erich Fromm, *The Revolution of Hope: Toward a Humanized Technology* (New York: Bantam Books, 1968).

10. Victor C. Ferkiss, *Technological Man: The Myth and the Reality* (New York: Braziller, 1969); *The Future of Technological Civilization* (New York: Braziller, 1974).

11. Robert L. Heilbroner, *An Inquiry into the Human Prospect* (New York: W. W. Norton, 1975).

Index of Subjects

absoluteness, 151
acupuncture, 141
acid rain, 42, 48
aesthetics, 77
Africa, 124
afterlife, 192
agapē, 55-56, 151, 185-186, 188
AIDS, 48
alchemy, 39, 91
anabolism, 168
analysis; forms of, 11
animism, 72
anthropocentrism, 22, 33. *See also* Galileo; Descartes
anthropology, 72, 165
anthropomorphism, 22
apostasy, 105, 144, 150
art, 124, 131, 132
artifacts, 39-41, 43-44, 46
artificial intelligence, 192
arts, 100, 127, 131-132, 134, 135, 149; fine arts, 131; occult, 149
Asia, 124
astrologers, 149
astrology, 91, 140, 143-144, 146, 147, 149, 166; Renaissance, 146
astronomy, 10, 80, 92, 144, 162-163; modern, 144; postmodern, 163
automobiles, 42, 53
axiology, 44, 200
barometer, 39
beauty, 13, 17, 41, 111, 193
behavior, 6-7, 11-13, 48, 61-63, 69, 109, 116, 129, 170, 184; human, 62; modification, 48
belief(s), 5, 6, 12, 14-15, 64, 76, 89, 94, 105, 106, 111-112, 120, 125, 140, 147, 148, 155, 161, 169, 190-191
biblical heritage, 161

biblical images, 157-158, 188, 191, 194-195, 198-199
bioeconomics, 95
biologist, 22, 66, 90, 99, 146, 164; molecular, 22, 146. *See also* Jacques Monod
biology, 19-20, 92, 125, 164-165, 192; modern, 192; molecular, 19-20, 92, 164-165; of Paracelsus, 125; sociobiology, 92
biosphere, 32, 43, 48, 85
Buddhism, 76, 107, 187
Canada, 85
cancer, 92, 99
catabolism, 168
catastrophe, 102, 119
Challenger, 48
chaos, 3, 126
chemistry, 19-21, 125, 144, 165; of Diderot, 125; molecular, 19-20, 144, 165
Chernobyl, 48
China, 141
Christian imagery, 155-156, 158-159
Christianity, 5, 6, 11, 15, 29, 33, 50, 53, 54-55, 75, 76, 83, 86, 91, 107, 120, 124-136, 148-149, 150-154, 156-157, 160, 161-162, 177, 181-186, 190-191, 193, 199; mainstream, 151-154, 157, 161; postmodern, 160, 161-162; postmodern organismic, 199; Western, 126
chlorofluorocarbons (CFSs), 31
climate changes, 32
circular motion, 66-67, 80-82
civilization, 2, 8, 11, 28, 30-32, 37, 40-41, 43, 47, 48, 54, 75-78, 84, 86, 87, 89, 91, 99, 101, 106, 109, 115, 118, 120-121, 126, 140, 146, 149, 150, 182,

medieval, 9, 15, 17, 40, 124-126, 143,
150, 151, 155, 193; cathedral, 18;
Christendom, 15; civilizations, 155;
doctrines, 151; guilds, 40; insistence
on rationality of God, 9; Paris, 150;
people, 15, 124; sciences, 125; society, 15; West, 126; world, 143
metaphor, 41, 43, 45, 46, 75, 78-79,
115, 176-177, 183, 200; Christian, 79
metaphors, 77, 184, 195, 198; mythic,
77
metaphysics, 200
Middle Ages, 90
mirror, 41
models, 46, 64-65, 67, 69-70, 74, 75-
76, 78, 83, 95, 167, 192, 195, 200;
metaphysical, 75
modern, 1-2, 4, 5, 7-8, 9, 11, 12, 13,
15-19, 21-23, 28, 29, 30, 31, 32, 36-
37, 38, 39, 41, 42, 43, 44, 52, 53, 54-
55, 69, 85, 86, 92, 94-96, 100, 114,
120, 122, 128, 129, 130, 132, 133,
134, 135, 139, 141, 143, 144, 146-147,
150, 152-154, 161, 166, 170, 176-177,
180-181, 185, 188, 196, 199, 200; age,
85; agribusiness, 32; attitudes, 95,
146; civilization, 31, 43; consensus,
196; era, 39, 86, 200; heritage, 23;
hopelessness, 135; humankind, 170;
idealogy, 199, ideals, 92; industrial
world, 44; life, 90; living, 2; malaise,
134; methods, 94; mind, 177; mood,
114; *mythos*, 21; North, 133; objective consciousness, 141; oil refinery,
18; people, 15; science, 36-37, 39,
41, 44; scientific medicine, 141; scientific thought, 42; skyscraper, 129;
society, 29, 31, 147, 176, 177; techniques, 94; technological society, 31,
42; technology, 30, 41; theology, 30;
thinkers, 19; times, 2, 100, 120, 141,
166, 185; tools, 37, 96; vision, 9;
world, 1-2, 4, 7-8, 11, 13, 15-18, 21-
22, 32, 38, 69, 85, 122, 128, 130-132,
139, 141, 143, 144, 150, 152-154, 161,
166, 177, 180-181, 188; world-picture, 144-145; worship, 31
modernity, 1, 2, 7, 10, 23, 36, 77, 125,
141, 144-148, 178

morality, 37
Motherhood, 84
Multi-mythic Organicism, 108, 167-171,
177-178, 180-181, 183-185, 187
mutuality, 85, 107, 116, 168-169, 171,
178-179, 183-184
mysterium tremendum, 129
mystery, 115, 162-164, 169-171, 196
myth, 6-7, 11, 15, 67, 77, 101, 105-106,
108, 111-116, 124, 168, 190, 199
mythos, 6-10, 18, 22, 44, 45, 151, 156,
161, 166-168, 177, 181-182, 199;
Christian, 10, 182; of Judaism, 181;
modern, 23; scientistic, 18-20
mythic matrix, 6-11, 105, 140, 145, 147
mythology, 148, 188; theistic, 188
myths, 104-108, 114-115, 118, 121, 166,
168, 178, 187, 189
Native Americans, 148
National Academy of Science, 162
natural order, 8, 9, 30, 33, 66, 80-82,
84, 86-87, 111-112, 168, 185, 192-
193, 196, 198
natural resources, 4, 50, 85, 134
natural selection, 10, 61
nature, 4, 8-9, 17-18, 21, 22, 23, 30,
33-34, 37, 42, 50-51, 60-63, 66, 68,
69, 73, 74, 76-77, 80-82, 84, 86, 87-
91, 94-95, 99, 106-107, 110-121,
123-126, 140, 146-148, 151-154, 157,
159, 163, 165, 167-170, 178, 180,
183-186, 193, 196, 198; human, 76-
77, 111, 115-117, 120; theology of, 60
Nazism, 5
neo-Platonism, 9
New Age thinking, 140. *See* culture,
counterculture
New World, 124
Noble Savage, 115
Northern nations. *See* global North
nuclear, 3, 31-32, 40, 42, 48, 84, 91,
129, 143, 147; capability, 3; destruction, 84; explosion, 129; furnaces,
143; nemesis, 32; plants, 42, 147;
power, 40, 91; technology, 48;
wastes, 48 winter, 31;
occultism, 140, 153
organicism, 85, 95, 107, 168, 177, 180,
199-200; postmodern, 200

Index of Names

DATE DUE

MY 26 '95			
SE 1 8 '98			

DEMCO NO. 38-298